PILGRIM OF PEACE

A Life of George M. Ll. Davies

i Merêd,
gyda diolch am dy gyfeillgarwch,
a'r cyfraniad i'r gwaith ac i fy mywyd

PILGRIM OF PEACE

A Life of George M. Ll. Davies

JEN LLYWELYN

First impression: 2016

© Copyright Jen Llywelyn and Y Lolfa Cyf., 2016

The contents of this book are subject to copyright, and may
not be reproduced by any means, mechanical or electronic,
without the prior, written consent of the publishers.

The publishers wish to acknowledge the support of
Cyngor Llyfrau Cymru

Photographs: Collection of the author unless otherwise stated

Cover photograph with permission
of the family of George M. Ll. Davies
Cover design: Y Lolfa

ISBN: 978 1 78461 240 5

Published and printed in Wales
on paper from well-maintained forests by
Y Lolfa Cyf., Talybont, Ceredigion SY24 5HE
website www.ylolfa.com
e-mail ylolfa@ylolfa.com
tel 01970 832 304
fax 832 782

"It is impossible to describe George Davies
without recourse to superlatives.
When he came into my office unannounced,
I could think of nothing that described the effect he had on me,
save some superlative like
'the sun in splendour'.
Of all the people in the Fellowship of Reconciliation,
George Davies was perhaps the most remarkable."

Rev. Richard Roberts, Blaenau Ffestiniog
first Secretary of the Fellowship of Reconciliation

Quoted in Gwynfor Evans,
Welsh Nation Builders

We remember a pacifist and a man of the people,
a man who was both cheerful and sad, funny and god-fearing,
otherworldy and practical.
He was described by his contemporaries as
'a perfect saint in a hellish world'.

Maldwyn Lewis
Heddwch, 1999–2000, Rhif 21

There can be no real pacifism
unless we have the courage and the conduct
of real peace-makers.

George M. Ll. Davies

Contents

Acknowledgements

Throughout this process, George's family and friends have given information and encouragement; the first chapter, 'Meeting George M. Ll. Davies', lists them in more detail. I have received great love, warmth, pictures, letters and family anecdotes. A cold grey biography this is not!

George's granddaughter Nancy White, in particular, has been with me all the way, with hugs and love.

Professor Paul O'Leary was my academic supervisor from 2001 to 2010, and I can't say enough how much I appreciate his knowledge, integrity, and friendship.

The staff of the National Library of Wales are always helpful and efficient. It's a great place to research and write.

The Gwynedd Archive holds papers relating to George's death and inquest. They have given me permission to use this material.

Since I began my research in 2000, the help and encouragement I have had from those in Wales and beyond has been very precious. I can't name you all – but thank you.

Diolch yn fawr i bawb yn y Lolfa am eu help a'u cefnogaeth trwy'r broses gyhoeddi.

Most of all, I am fortunate in my family's constant support – Judes and Tim; Alan, Marrianne and Bronwen; and particularly Jim, who read every word of the PhD thesis several times and has given invaluable help preparing this text. Love you all.

1

'Meeting' George M. Ll. Davies

GEORGE M. LL. Davies died when I was nine months old – but I know him well.

In 1999, as part of my first degree with the Open University, I undertook an Oral History project. I had heard that there were Conscientious Objectors in the First World War, but a chance remark from a Quaker I knew, Iorwerth John, led me to interview six Second World War 'Conshis'. I started with Iorwerth, who had a home in Cwmystwyth in Ceredigion.

Iorwerth told me about his war service as a social worker for the Quakers in Tiger Bay in Cardiff. While talking about his colleagues, he asked me if I'd heard the name George M. Ll. Davies. I hadn't. He went to his study and returned with a volume of the 1960s biography of George by E. H. Griffiths (in Welsh – quite beyond me at the time!), and showed me a photograph of George. A compelling face. I saw wisdom, humour, mischief, compassion, intelligence, sadness. George had been a huge inspiration to Iorwerth in the 1920s, when Iorwerth was a camper in the Welsh Schoolboys' Camps and George was the chaplain. Iorwerth became a 'Conshi' – but he said George never judged or condemned anyone who decided to join up; he would support them whatever decision they made.

I next saw Islwyn Lake, a Methodist minister living in Porthmadog. His story was fascinating to one who had not long moved to Wales – Islwyn had taken part in several protests in support of the Welsh language. I was surprised, thinking most ministers I'd known in England would have been dead against such political protests! Islwyn went to school in Goodwick, near Fishguard, and had been taught English by one D. J. Williams (well-known in Wales). And DJ had a great friend, and when he visited, Islwyn was invited to meet him ... George M. Ll. Davies! Meeting George influenced Islwyn's decision to become a CO in the Second World War.

My next interviewees were brothers, Erastus and Pearce Jones, brought up in the Liverpool Welsh community in the 1920s, and what they told me informed me about George M. Ll.'s youth. My fifth was Ifanwy Williams, who gave me the women's take on Conscientious Objection. I felt privileged to have met these lovely people.

I then went to see Gwynfor Evans, Plaid Cymru's first MP, in Carmarthenshire. He was nearing the end of his life, and physically frail, but his mind was very clear. He told me of his youth, and of getting into politics. Then he asked if I'd heard of George M. Ll....

Gwynfor and George had met in the 1930s, when Gwynfor was a law student and George was visiting a friend: 'attired in his long cloak, a man of princely appearance'. (The long cloak was typical George-apparel for many years; people remembered him striding around the Valleys with it flying out behind him.) Gwynfor told me many stories about George. For instance, Gwynfor, looking for his three-year-old son Guto, found George, with Guto on his lap, and the two of them laughing till tears ran down their faces! Gwynfor never did find out what was so funny!

The two men became close friends. Gwynfor told me how George had died. It made him sad to talk about it, and made me sad, too. Gwynfor told me that in all the years that he'd known George he'd never been given any clue about George's bouts of depression, and had expressed amazement at his 'unfailing and infectious buoyancy'. George was, it seems, from this evidence and stories from others, very good at hiding it – or, at hiding himself from others when he was depressed. Perhaps both. I felt very involved with George from this point on. I am not an absolutist pacifist, nor religious, and I don't agree with everything George said or wrote. Yet I liked what I'd heard about this man. I, too, live with depression, and I admire the way George lived with his 'elephant in the room'. There wasn't much effective treatment for mental illnesses: it appears George had a very early form of electric shock treatment in about 1914 (rather experimental at that time), and perhaps again in 1949 in Denbigh Hospital. A few of his friends knew George had depressed times, and were supportive, but Leslie, his wife, seems not to have coped well. (Living with a depressed person can be as difficult as being one.)

In 2000 I graduated from the OU. I needed to know more about George, and encouraged by Gwynfor and the other COs (including, by that time, Dr Meredydd Evans, a great fan of George), I applied to the then University of Wales in Aberystwyth, to attempt a PhD thesis. Dr (now Professor) Paul O'Leary was appointed as my supervisor – luckily for me! He explained that I would need to write not only about George Davies, but about the contexts of his life. So I set about reading, researching, and finding people to interview. Becoming fluent in Welsh has been essential to the research process.

I spoke to George's daughter Jane Hedd in Somerset, and his granddaughter Nancy White, who visited me from South Africa. I went to see George's niece Elin in Newport, Pembrokeshire, and her younger brother Gwion in Llanfairfechan – the younger two children of George's oldest brother, J. Glyn Davies.

Gwladys Japheth (née Roberts) had known George and his wife Leslie when they had lived in Llŷn during the First World War – I spoke with her in Llanuwchllyn. Her friend Meinir Burden, from Bala, told me stories of George's later years when he would visit her family at Pant y Neuadd, in Parc.

I met Peggy Gay in the Rhondda, and Barrie and Sheila Naylor, who had worked at Maes-yr-haf in the Rhondda with

George in the 1930s and 1940s. Dr Emyr Evans, who lived in Cheltenham, had long conversations with George at a weekend conference in Tretower in 1942. I talked with Gronwy Davies, a charge nurse at Denbigh Hospital in 1949, the last person to see George alive.

Many of these people are no longer with us. It was a privilege to talk with them. I learned so much – not just about George, but about his beloved Wales.

Many biographers report close encounters with their 'subjects'; I am not immune from this phenomenon. I have had vivid dreams about George, and – believe this or not, as you will – messages directly from him, about my research, and about the people involved in his life. He even, once, laughed at me (kindly!) from beyond the grave. I wish I'd been able to spend time with him when he was alive.

I was awarded a PhD in 2010. My Welsh has improved substantially since I started my research, and I have been able to translate some of George's own writings from the Welsh. He would have been delighted at this. The language was important to George – as to me – as part of the depth of Welsh life and culture. He championed Welsh throughout his life.

Almost every time George M. Ll. Davies is mentioned in Wales, he is described as 'saintly', or 'a saint'. I don't want to undermine that. He has my total respect, always. But getting to know him as I have, I know that this 'saint' was also a man, fully human, and in many ways flawed. I love him no less for that.

Jen Llywelyn
Trisant, 2016

2

The Liverpool
Welsh Community

IN 1885, LORD Mostyn called Liverpool 'the metropolis of Wales'. Some years earlier, John Bright, the Quaker campaigner and Liberal MP, referred to Liverpool as 'the capital of Wales'. Whether either man was right is arguable: the census of 1881 showed that 9 per cent of Liverpool's population of 552,500 were first-, second- or third-generation Welsh, living predominantly in Everton, Toxteth, Kirkwall, and West Derby, where their compatriots had built houses. But certainly, a significant Welsh middle class was burgeoning in Liverpool, whose influence reached far into the social, religious and economic life of the city.

George M. Ll. Davies was born into that affluent Liverpool Welsh middle class in 1880. The attitudes and values of this close-knit group, and the oppressiveness of the Welsh-built suburbs they lived in, were George Davies' foundation in life, and he never completely escaped their influence.

The first generation of Welsh migrants arrived in Liverpool in the 1600s. Many settled near the river, in an area that became known as 'Welsh Town'.[1] Trade in food and building materials, notably slate, increased between Liverpool and ports such as Beaumaris and Amlwch on Anglesey. Later, the roads between Liverpool and Anglesey were improved; the Menai Bridge was completed in 1827. The Holyhead-Chester railway (1848) and the line to Blaenau Ffestiniog (1879) were also crucial to the passage of workers and materials.

Stories of the growth of Liverpool came back to those in north Wales, and so many moved there to find work that one of the urgent needs was chapels; the first, Pall Mall Wesleyan Methodist chapel, opened in 1787. At the time, two-thirds of the Welsh incomers to Liverpool were from Anglesey. In March 1804, a Welsh Charity School opened on Russell Street; it was needed 'to educate, clothe and apprentice poor Welsh children born in Liverpool'.[2] In 1831, according to Welsh Charity figures, there were 8,000 Welsh people in Liverpool; by 1851, an estimated 20,000, and by 1881, 21,563 in Liverpool and 4,871 in Birkenhead. (Figures were similar for London: in 1871 the census recorded 17,575 Welsh-born inhabitants.)

Liverpool grew fast: 100,000 houses were constructed in the city in the nineteenth century. In 1830 the railway arrived. The Corporation concentrated its vision and investment on developing the port facilities and civic buildings, but only in 1842 did work begin on public health. In 1844, evidence given to the Royal Commission on Municipal Councils suggested that 40 per cent of the inhabitants of Liverpool lived in slums: 20,000 in cellars, 40,000 overcrowded. Some of the new housing areas were described as 'planned slums'. Work went on apace, however, and in 1847 the first Medical Officer of Health was appointed; the city had gas by 1847, and water by 1857. Manchester banned unhealthy back-to-back housing in 1844, but this was not prohibited in Liverpool until 1864.

The Welsh migrants established building businesses, employing their fellow-countrymen. Liverpool needed industrial buildings, which had large roofs and used huge quantities of slate and stone, and skilled workers who travelled from north Wales. Welsh people were also concentrated in timber yards, cotton warehouses, and shops. They sent home for brothers and cousins, who brought families and friends. Numerous clerks and domestic servants were required to service the new businesses and middle-class suburban houses;

again, Welsh migrants to Liverpool made the most of these opportunities to help their relations from the north of Wales.

The biggest contribution of the Welsh in-migrants was the construction of much of the housing in Liverpool. According to J. A. Picton, writing in 1903, the development of Everton in the nineteenth century was:

> ... almost entirely the work of Welsh builders, several of whom... have succeeded in amassing considerable property by their exertions. A large part of the population is from the principality. Placards in the Welsh language may be seen on the walls and Welsh newspapers in the shop windows. The sharp click and gutteral intonation of the Cambrian dialect [sic] may be heard from many a cottage door. On the whole they are an industrious, steady and sober race.[3]

The English builders tended to build shops in the towns and outskirts; the Welsh builders specialised in houses and terraced cottages, initially in Bootle, Parliament Fields, and Princes Road, Toxteth. They evolved a six-roomed house with a scullery, and built according to plans approved by the Health Committee of Liverpool Corporation. Some builders added cupboards and wardrobes; others put bay windows on both storeys, even in working-class houses.

When the English builders started copying the Welsh houses, the Welsh builders responded by putting bathrooms into their houses. After some years, the pioneer Welsh builders formed a group of building societies and housing companies – created, controlled and directed by Welshmen. In 1836 the North and South Wales Bank was founded, and this financed many Welsh builders, usually known to the Bank's officers because they were members of the same chapels.

Hundreds of the Welsh-built houses were the work of just one firm, that of Owen Elias, a Calvinistic Methodist from Llanbadrig, Anglesey, who arrived in the city in 1819, and died in 1880 (the year George M. Ll. Davies was born). Elias heard

17

tales of homeless labourers, so he built them houses, with rents of around 3/6 a week. He, like many Welsh builders, was a Temperance man, and imposed restrictions on licensing where he built his houses. He made his mark on Walton by naming roads with the initials of himself and his two sons William and (later) Alfred: Oxton, Winslow, Eton, Neston; Andrew, Nimrod, Dane; Wilburn, Ismay, Lind, Lowell, Index, Arnot; M is missing – perhaps demolished when the Junior School was built; then Askew, Linton, Frodsham, Ripon, Emery and Dyson.

Welsh people in the city, wanting either a first home or a progression up the social ladder, followed the builders when choosing the district they wanted to live in. Other big builders in Liverpool were Ellis Evans (Clynnog, Caernarfon) and Manoah Evans, who built in Toxteth and were both members of the imposing Princes Road chapel, known locally as 'the Welsh cathedral', where George M. Ll. Davies' family were members. The minister when George was a boy was John Williams of Brynsiencyn on Anglesey, of whom we will hear more later. The Welsh streets in Toxteth included Elwy Street and Madryn Street; they were to be demolished, but thanks to recent campaigns this threat now appears to have been lifted.

Owen Kendrick Jones built nine streets in Bootle with Welsh names: Aber, Anglesey, Bala, Conway, Denbigh, Flint, Holywell, Rhyl, Bangor. Most Welsh companies, builders or otherwise, would employ only Welsh-speakers; Henry Lewis of Anglesey went further, employing only Welsh-speaking people from Anglesey. The Welsh language, and even local dialects of Welsh, prospered in this English city because the Welsh builders stuck together.

J. Glyn Davies, later Professor of Celtic Studies at Liverpool University, and a well-known writer of Welsh sea-songs and songs for children (such as *Fflat Huw Puw* and *Llongau Caernarfon*), wrote and lectured about his upbringing in the Liverpool Welsh community. His frank, personal and passionate (even acerbic) book, *Nationalism as a Social Phenomenon*, discussed aspects of 'nationalism', then looked at the Welsh community in Liverpool, and finally at his upbringing in a Liverpool Welsh suburban home at the end of the nineteenth century. This book is particularly important to us, because J. Glyn Davies was George M. Ll. Davies' oldest brother – older by ten years.

Glyn pointed out that the Welsh-language adult Sunday schools (from 1810) had equipped the Welsh incomers with a substantial education. English people with that same level of culture were well-off, and lived in expensive suburbs. But the Welsh incomers were poor, and English people in similar poverty were, Glyn wrote, 'barbarous'. The Welsh migrants:

> ... had to live in the cheapest and lowest parts of Liverpool, surrounded by illiterate and rough neighbours. They could make no contact with English people of their own culture, who lived in expensive suburbs. The suburbs were the Promised Land.

Glyn mentioned 'illiterate and rough neighbours'. Possibly he meant the Irish contingent: in 1841, 290,000 Irish migrants had arrived in England and Wales; by 1861 there were 600,000. Government policy, the potato famine, and familial decisions tied to inheritance of land were the main reasons for them leaving Ireland. Irish immigrants were three times as likely as others (including the Welsh) to be in unskilled labour, and their households were larger – sometimes several families per dwelling.

The social stratification, then, is clear: Irish at the bottom, the Welsh in the middle, and the English at the top. And the most uncomfortable place is always the middle. For the new middle class, rising to the upper class was an impossibility; but falling from middle-class respectability was a terrifying thought. The Davies family had to face that fear in 1891, when George's father John Davies' business went bankrupt.

In her excellent PhD thesis about the middle classes in Pontypool, Bridgend and Penarth between 1850 and 1890,[4] Julie Light reports that historians of Wales have tended to

19

treat the middle classes as 'a rather shadowy group'. In Wales itself, the nineteenth-century middle class consisted largely of those in local/central government, the 'learned professions', and the 'commercial class'. In Liverpool, however, where the Davies family lived and worked, there was yet another version of 'middle class' – a strong and affluent Welsh middle class, in an English city. Members of the Welsh middle class in Wales – quarrying entrepreneurs such as John Jones Talysarn (George's maternal grandfather) – had created the prosperity of the Welsh middle class in Liverpool, such as merchants and large-scale building contractors.

Liverpool Welsh chapel congregations were anxious that their flock, of largely rural origin, should be looked after in this huge city, and kept together for safety and succour. To this end, they built over fifty chapels for themselves, some with school houses. There was a considerable element of snobbery – even in Non-conformist chapels, where a class system began to emerge. There were two 'Welsh' Anglican churches. Over the years several Welsh-language periodicals, journals and newspapers were established. There were Welsh-language literary societies, where many people had their first experiences of their literary heritage. Many of these were part of the social life of the chapels.

Gareth Miles[5] claims that some members of the Liverpool Welsh community came close to being 'the only strong, self-conscious bourgeoisie the Welsh nation ever had'. D. Ben Rees appears to agree, calling Gwen Davies, George's mother, an 'aristocrat'.

But in *The North Wales Quarryman*, R. Merfyn Jones refers to a Welsh 'aristocracy' in nineteenth-century Gwynedd, and explodes the myth that all the Welsh migrants to Liverpool had struggled up out of rural hovels. Liverpool's growth had brought prosperity to Welsh quarry owners and engineers. Merfyn Jones includes a photograph of John Jones' family in front of their large, newly-refurbished house in Dolwyddelan, the womenfolk, including young Gwen (later George and Glyn's mother), all in crinolines and looking very prosperous indeed! Throughout her life, Gwen Davies liked to spend a few weeks every year in Llandrindod Wells, where the 'well-to-do clans' met in the summer. Writing about John Jones Talysarn, known as 'the people's preacher', Merfyn Jones comments in *The Liverpool Welsh*... that our ignorance of the Welsh middle class makes it difficult 'for the Welsh historical imagination to bracket [John Jones'] name, and all the Calvinistic forcefulness it represents, with croquet and polite society in Llandrindod'.

Liverpool, originally just a port with a small jumble of houses around the docks, began to expand further inland. Like north Wales, its middle-class population began to enlarge alongside the city's affluence. Middle-class home owners desired domesticity, privacy – and separate rooms for their live-in servants. Merfyn Jones wrote that an essential factor of 'middle-class-ness' was having a domestic servant. Even after John Davies' bankruptcy, the family still had a servant, as the 1901 census shows: Elizabeth Roberts, aged thirty-six, from Llanystumdwy near Pwllheli, a 'general domestic'. Next door at No. 36, John Jones, a Timber Merchant from Denbigh, and his wife from Pwllheli, also had a 'general domestic' (from Earlestown in Lancashire). At No. 40, H. Harrison (HM Inspector of Schools) and his wife had both a 'housemaid domestic' (from Llwyngwril, Meirioneth), and a cook (from Shrewsbury). Presumably Mr Harrison earned enough to enable his household to have two servants.

The need for a servant in order to maintain status would explain Gwen Davies' high state of anxiety in September 1909, when Mary, her current domestic help, announced that she was leaving for America. Gwen wrote to Glyn, George's oldest brother, then at university in Aberystwyth, shrieking indignation at the maid wishing to leave before she had served her full term, and frantically asking him to 'find me a girl'.

Middle-class suburbs were planned to be separate both

from the suburban man's place of work, and from working-class homes, which were near enough to factories to walk to work in the mornings, and near enough to get home for dinner at midday. Higher-class suburbs were served by trams or perhaps railways, and had gardens, trees and parks. But the disadvantages of the new suburbs became evident, wrote F. M. L. Thompson, when particularly women began to feel isolated from the rest of the world by their all-round gardens: 'settings which fostered a pretentious preoccupation with outward appearances, a fussy attention to trifling details of genteel living, and absurd attempts to conjure rusticity out of minute garden plots.'[6]

It nevertheless remained the ultimate aim of the middle classes to have a neat and presentable fortress, where the women could entertain (and impress) friends and be genteel, and where the man could hide at the end of the day. The neatness of the front garden and the thickness of the curtains would proclaim to the world that the family was prospering: Oscar Wilde called it 'washing one's clean linen in public'. And if there were disadvantages to the suburban life, they had either to be tolerated or overcome. There was no going back.

3

Growing up in Liverpool

THE SECOND GENERATION of the Liverpool Welsh community was born into a certain affluence. Many of those who originally arrived as builders and clerks had moved into houses in more prestigious areas of the city, including the new suburbs:

> The clear separation of work and home, the insistence on social distancing, the treatment of the home as a feminine domain, the importance attached to domestic privacy, the exclusion of a vulgar prying multitude, can all be seen as parts of a code of individual responsibility, male economic domination and female domestic subordination, and family-nurtured morality which served to give the bourgeoisie a social identity and mark them off from the upper class and the lower orders.[1]

John Davies (1837–1909), father of George Davies and his three older brothers, was born into this middle-class Liverpool Welsh environment. He became a tea and coffee merchant, and was involved in many activities outside the home, while his wife Gwen spent her time at home reading, writing poetry, and overseeing her household.

John Davies' father had travelled in 1823 from Aberystwyth to London to work at Steens' tea merchant's warehouse. In 1834 he was sent by the firm to open an office in Liverpool, at the time the main tea port in England. After a few years he set up his own business, with Steens' co-operation, and organised the distribution of all their tea from Liverpool to London. He kept forty horses for the purpose.

Later, young John began to work in his father's business, and eventually became a pillar of the Liverpool Welsh society, and a municipal councillor. His wife Gwen, Glyn wrote, was 'socially ambitious, and imbued all her family with that spirit'. At least, she tried; all four sons questioned her values, and to a greater or lesser extent turned from them later in their lives. It is clear from her letters to her sons, and from theirs to one another, that Gwen Davies was a dreadful snob; she certainly enjoyed her status as the wife of John Davies, who was on the Liverpool Municipal Council and the Waterworks Committee, and an elder at Princes Road chapel. Like his wife, he valued his comparative social status: in 1884 Glyn was present with his father at the inaugural meeting of the Welsh National Society in Liverpool. A five-shilling subscription was proposed, but defeated 'on the grounds that such a [low] fee would let in joiners and warehousemen and other undesirables'. To Glyn's discomfort, it was his father who objected; clearly, John Davies did not see the proletariat as desirable members of the Welsh Nationalist Society.

However, John worked hard on the campaign to set up the first Welsh University in Aberystwyth in 1872, helped by his English Catholic friend John Maitland, the editor of the *Liverpool Mercury*, and was involved in bringing the National Eisteddfod to Liverpool in the same year, but Glyn wrote: 'It was the civic sense with a slight sentimental bias that set him working for Welsh causes, not nationalism.' The only part of Wales that John Davies ever expressed a fondness for was Llŷn, by which he meant Edern.

J. Glyn Davies was born in 1870. Two children before him, Arabella and Richard, died very young – Arabella (Amy) of diphtheria at two, and Richard even younger. Gwen Davies ('Mater', as her sons called her) seems never to have recovered from Amy's death. According to Gwion, Glyn's son, some kind of healing happened when Glyn's eldest daughter was named 'Gwen' for her grandmother, and became the apple of the older Gwen Davies' eye. The younger Gwen wrote, 'I knew no one again would ever think me as marvellous as [Nain] did.'

After Glyn came Frank and Stanley, and then, on 30 April 1880, George was born. He was named George Maitland Temple Davies, after John Maitland, and William Temple, the Archbishop of Canterbury (whom his mother admired). Later George himself replaced 'Temple' with 'Lloyd' after his mother's brother's family, the Lloyds of Llandinam.

Notwithstanding their parents' social pretensions, the impression given in Glyn's book is that the four Davies boys had a relatively happy upbringing. All four brothers were later loving and tender fathers, and indeed, uncles (all Glyn's children, especially Gwion, loved their Uncle George). This suggests they had had good fathering themselves. George certainly enjoyed holidays and jaunts with John Davies ('Pater'), particularly their times in Llŷn, a place the Davies boys loved as much as their father did. John Davies was far more fun than Gwen.

Glyn's son Gwion remembers George as a 'ray of sunshine', 'radiant and homely', with his warm, 'Wel wel wel – nice to see you'. Uncle George insisted that Gwion be sent to Aberdaron and Edern for holidays (to keep up his Welsh), and had a 'way of unravelling things' if Gwion was perplexed about life. But Gwion's great hero was Uncle Frank, George and Glyn's Merchant Navy brother – hence Gwion went to sea like Frank. Frank and Glyn made a lot of model boats, in great detail, much to young Gwion's joy, and he still had some of them at Llanfairfechan when in his 80s.

George Davies was born in 1880 at Peel Street in Toxteth, in a large house with no front garden, and steps to the front door directly off the pavement. They then moved round the corner to Belvidere Road, facing Princes Park (where Gwen Davies liked to take her constitutional). The houses there are a little further back from the road.

In 1891, the family moved to 38 Devonshire Road, a tall house with an impressive portico, and a short path to the steps. (There is a plaque on the house, stating that J. Glyn and George M. Ll. Davies lived there.) If Gwen Davies had been able to continue 'moving up', she and her family would, no doubt, have moved further along Devonshire Road, where the houses have long front gardens with trees and a U-shaped driveway for carriages.

But that same year everything changed for the apparently successful Davies family. When John Davies was fifty-four, his business went bankrupt. For the Davieses, F. M. L. Thompson's 'male economic domination' was shattered. Gwen Davies had to run the family in the face of her husband's retreat into shame. She succeeded in maintaining a 'family-nurtured morality' to a large extent, but the four sons paid their parents' bills for many years. John Davies' obituary in the *Liverpool Daily Post and Mercury* of 18 March 1909 says that he was 'formerly an active public man in this city', but had 'retired' in 1891, and 'has not taken any prominent part in municipal or other public affairs... He was a typical Welshman with a keen regard for everything pertaining to his country'.

Gwen Davies was anxious to keep up appearances. (Jerome K. Jerome had written not long before, 'Being poor is a mere trifle. It is being known to be poor that is the sting.') Her silk skirts swished as she swept defiantly to the family pew in the front of the chapel on Sunday mornings, even after the bankruptcy. Perhaps it was a relief to the Davies family to be able to retreat behind those thick suburban curtains and escape from that 'vulgar prying multitude'.

George Davies and his brothers reassessed many values at this time. George particularly, following the experience of the bankruptcy, seems to have adopted a lifelong policy of actively avoiding prosperity. This was also the start of his obsession with what he called 'the transitoriness of all things'. But the situation brought the family together, and transformed his father: in 1916 George wrote to his mother:

... position, influence, prosperity, ability, were as mere rubbish compared to the tenderness and love that bound us together during the dark days as we thought them. I feel nothing but gratitude now to our Father [God] for the seeming humiliation of those days. I also see dear old Pater's failings in a new light and realise that but for his disgrace in the eyes of men, he might never have learned the lesson of humbleness and simple affection that made him so beloved of all.

The bankruptcy was declared on Glyn's twenty-first birthday. The family was shunned by some 'friends', and by various members of the family. Gwen's brother, David Lloyd Jones, the Presbyterian minister in Llandinam, wrote judgemental letters to Gwen, which hurt her. John Davies wrote many replies reproving his brother-in-law for his un-Christian attitude, but he did not post them; he threw them in the fire the next morning, when he'd cooled down. One day, however, Glyn, always the most impulsive and irascible of the four brothers, found one, and decided to post it. John Davies was aghast. David Lloyd Jones did not write again.

The Davies' fellow chapel-goers turned out to be, by and large, unwilling to continue friendships with John and Gwen because of the stigma of bankruptcy. Gwen tried to keep her head high and sit with the boys in the same pew at the front of the chapel, until she was requested to move further back. John, however, felt so ashamed that he would creep in by another door and sit alone in the corner. But at least he was allowed to continue attending. Perhaps his problems were not caused by his own rashness, and were therefore looked on tolerantly.

It was a painful time for the Davieses. The historian Eric Hobsbawm wrote that in the nineteenth century 'the risks of incurring [bankruptcy] were extremely modest', and that 'the very horror of bankruptcy is itself a symptom of its comparative rarity'.[2] Poor John Davies was one of the unlucky few, then, and while his immediate family closed around him in support, his other 'family', that in Princes Road chapel, turned their backs on him.

George was angry for the rest of his life at the attitude of the chapel people. The Davieses were, however, very moved when a friend who was a member of the Catholic church in the city – rumoured to have been John Maitland, John Davies' old friend – bought a lot of their furniture when it was auctioned, and gave it back to them. Later, in a letter to his brother Stan, George wrote, 'That hard Liberal legal world dropped old Pater like a hot potato and all his warm humanity counted nothing to them'.

Peggy Gay, who met George in the 1930s in the Rhondda when they were both working at Maes-yr-haf, told me that as late as the 1930s and 1940s he spoke scornfully of 'fur-coated snobby chapel-goers'. And even in 1949, shortly before his death, George wrote, 'God created the countryside, man created the town, but the devil created the suburb. There is no good neighbourliness in a suburb.'

In 1874, the Liverpool Welsh Sunday School Union carried out its own census of chapel and church attendance. It was found that out of 26,840 Welsh people in Liverpool at the time, 62 per cent attended Welsh-speaking places of worship, 24 per cent English places of worship, and 11 per cent none. The chapels, therefore, were largely responsible for the survival of the Welsh language in Liverpool. Apart from services on Sundays, there were meetings during the week for socialising and education, as well as Bible studies and prayer meetings. (Pearce Jones, who was brought up in the still sizeable Liverpool Welsh community in the 1920s, told me, 'The chapel was our village.') In middle-class homes, English increasingly became the main language, reflecting the widely-held belief of the times that English was the language of progress; but still many homes were monoglot Welsh.

The dramatist and poet Saunders Lewis (1893–1985), a founder member of Plaid Cymru in 1925, was brought up in Wallasey, near Liverpool. He considered that out of around 100,000 Welsh-speakers, at least half were monoglot Welsh speakers. Girls from Anglesey and Caernarfonshire would go to Liverpool to work for his aunt as maids, and when they returned to Wales after a few years they still had very little English. He wrote, 'There was a monoglot Welsh-speaking community in Liverpool in my time, just as in a village somewhere in Anglesey. Thus it was not in English England that I was born at all, but in a completely Welsh and Welsh-speaking community.'³

The main difference, though, between Liverpool and 'a village somewhere in Anglesey' was that the secular and religious leaders in Wales at that time were cultured shopkeepers, artisans, and farmers, while the leaders of the Welsh community in Liverpool were merchants, financiers, and industrialists.

Most of the Liverpool Welsh suburban families spoke English at home. But Gwen Davies spoke Welsh to her children and servants – mostly, according to Glyn, because of her 'idolatry of her father'. Gwen wanted her children to be able to read her father's sermons and his biography. Glyn recalled that Gwen was asked by a friend (who had dropped Welsh) 'if she was not afraid of her children speaking English with a Welsh accent, but she ran the risk rather than let them grow up in ignorance of her father'. Glyn Davies wrote that he considered himself unusual, because when he started school he knew no English, but he soon picked it up from the other boys. Gwen Davies always spoke English with her husband John, and her sons spoke in English with one another and at school.

Glyn spoke Welsh and English, but read only the amount of Welsh necessary for memorising verses for Sunday school. He said that he, and other friends, could not follow 'pulpit Welsh' or read the Bible. They read in English. Nothing in Welsh (at the time) could compare with the *Boys' Own Paper* in English, or the adventure stories 'from *Robinson Crusoe* to Ballantyne'.

The suffocating life in Liverpool was broken by the annual summer holiday in Wales. Glyn Davies wrote sardonically that this was where his friends realised that Welsh was useful: 'a little bad Welsh would add to their prestige as little gentlemen who after all did not disdain Welsh, and whose little slips bespoke familiarity with well-placed English.'

All this must be seen in the context of the report known forever in Wales as 'Brad y Llyfrau Gleision' (the Treachery of the Blue Books). In 1847 the Westminster government had sent three monoglot-English inspectors to assess (among other things) the quality of education in Wales. Their inept and anti-Welsh report recommended that in order for people to prosper they should be speaking English: definitely not Welsh.

So using English rather than Welsh would demonstrate these boys' ambition to their peers, parents and subordinates.

The Davies brothers' attitude was somewhat different. They spent their holidays in Llŷn, and according to Glyn, this 'saved' the four boys' Welsh: 'Summer holidays... in Edern made the practice of Welsh a pleasure instead of a religious duty. I relearnt Welsh, not by grammar but by jotting down racy idioms on backs of envelopes.'

George, the youngest of the four Davies brothers, had almost lost his spoken Welsh by the first time he went on holiday to Edern, near Pwllheli, in 1888, but talking with the miller (Richard Morris Roberts, a Welsh scholar and bard) and his family and other local people revived his interest in using the language on a daily basis. In 1929, Glyn commented that although George's Welsh 'still bears the marks of an acquired language in uncertain idiom, gender and mutation, it is fluent and much more effective for its ends than correct literary Welsh'. George loved the Welsh language all his life; he read and wrote Welsh, and spoke it, however imperfectly; it would have surprised and pleased him that his only child, Jane, continued to read what Welsh she could, even in her eighties, 'dictionary in hand'; she listened to BBC Wales' broadcasts at home in Somerset, and suffered from *hiraeth*.

Sadly, Glyn's son Gwion and daughter Elin told me that Glyn had instructed his children to drop their Welsh and forget it. They regretted this in later life, and Gwion, in his eighties

Growing up in Liverpool

when I met him, was forever trying to reclaim and improve his Welsh, but struggling. Gwion wrote to Jane in 1992:

> My father [Glyn] once described a chapel service in Llyn, which he attended. It was a small country chapel, and the farmers had brought their dogs, which were tucked under their pews, with their noses to the central alleyway, for fresh air and to see what was going on. During the sermon my father got bored, and let his mind and eyes wander. He was at the alleyway end of the pew, and noticed a black beetle crawling along the coir matting on the floor, and making heavy weather of it – up one bristle and down the next, with its legs flaying out like oars missing the water. The dogs also spotted it, and unable to bear it any longer they both pounded on the beetle together – and into each other with almighty hullabaloo. The minister stopped in the middle of his sermon and shouted to the farmers to take their dogs to Hell out of the chapel, which they did. I always think of that black beetle when I try to read Welsh, and what a relief it is to read some English passage in it, like the beetle at last getting onto the smooth board floor.

Although George Davies mixed with the miller's family and friends, and the staff of the big houses in Llŷn, and enjoyed their company and respected them, there is no sign that at the time he felt they were his equals. An upper middle-class Liverpool Welsh upbringing, with servants, and living generally in upper middle-class society, would have taught the children of such families to keep 'a proper distance' from the working-class element.

There was also a gender dimension to this. Glyn maintained that boys from well-to-do families might go to Wales on their holidays and make friends with farm labourers, coachmen or grooms (playing with village children was discouraged). Girls, however, could not make friends with the farm maids, because this 'would put them on a level with a domestic [female] servant, a social cleavage that was more pronounced in their own circles in Liverpool than amongst even the most prosperous farmer class in Wales'. And there were other dangers: from the point of view of a middle-class parent, to have a daughter marry 'above her station' was a good thing, but to have a daughter possibly fall for someone 'beneath her' was to be avoided at all costs.

Relatively early in his life, George Davies began to assess the values and influences of this middle-class, respectable, chapel, suburban background. He loved his holidays in Edern, where he met the less class-ridden society of rural Wales.

An extract from George's diary (October 1894, when he was fourteen), suggests a boy who had grown up rather too fast – or perhaps simply of a boy with three older brothers, and who had been subjected to chapel attendance and influence on a regular basis. For example, George, holidaying in Llŷn, had a 'rather unsatisfactory argument' with one of the local servants, about predestination. He also speaks of fulfilling the 'time-honoured custom' at Ffynnon Fair. In his diary entry for 16 August 1905, George explains that this 'time-honoured custom' was 'to carry a mouthful of water from the holy well, 3 times round the old church, and then one's wish would be fulfilled'. Unfortunately no clue is given as to George's wish.

George and Glyn's visits were still remembered appreciatively by local people even around 1980, when Jane visited Llŷn.

George and his brothers, each in their turn, began to find the suburbs and the chapel suffocating. But he, as the youngest brother, stayed in that home until he was twenty-eight; the others had long since left. It is difficult to imagine a less natural life for a young man, with a sad and shamed father, and an extremely religious, demanding, manipulative, and habitually ailing mother. His job (at the bank) did not allow much time to enjoy life. His love for his mother, and his sense of duty towards her, meant that he tried constantly to please her, but he found it an uphill struggle.

John Davies' bankruptcy meant that instead of going to university straight after school, Glyn, Stanley and Frank started working to bring money into the family. Later, Glyn and Frank did attend the University College of Wales, Aberystwyth, but before that, Glyn travelled to Auckland, New Zealand, as a clerk. His daughter Elin told me that one day he heard a woman with a beautiful voice singing in the street, and realised she was singing a Welsh song. He rushed out to see who she was – and found many other men rushing out too – many were Welshmen! She was trying to raise enough money to buy a ticket back home; the men had a whip-round for her and bought the ticket. From that event evolved the Welsh Society in Auckland.

As life settled down after the bankruptcy, George began to work harder at school. He seems to have been quite a normal pupil, sometimes earning the praise, and sometimes the displeasure, of teachers, according to his school reports. For example, his Maths teacher in 1893 says 'Needs more energy and application'; in 1895, 'He is inclined to idleness and frivolity'; both comments are surprising in the light of his later life. In his short autobiographical book *Pererindod Heddwch*, he wrote (in Welsh):

> I did not learn much at school, and I have not the method or the gift of scholars. The best education I received was through the many-faceted recollections of my father and mother, the conversations at hearthsides and in homes, and the companionship and fellowship of the saintly of many kinds and in many places.

This open attitude to education, and George's natural honesty, explains, perhaps, how he related so well to the young people he helped when, in 1914, he worked in a home for delinquent children, and why he wrote critically about the effectiveness of conventional education, and positively about progressive education, throughout his life.

In 1896, at the age of sixteen, George Davies began working at Martin's Bank in Liverpool. He learned Pitman's shorthand, and his notes in some loose papers tucked into one of his diaries show it to be of excellent quality. By his early twenties, he was secretary to the manager, having taken at least one Institute of Bankers examination. His diary of 1903 shows him to be a reliable and conscientious working man, but very troubled. Many of the entries are on a spiritual, Christian basis, groaning over the troubles of the world, and his overwhelming feelings of inadequacy, his search for God, and his fear of death.

Glyn had been planning to go to Chile, to a clerical job he'd been offered in a copper mine, but while he was arranging his travel he was met by men from Aberystwyth who asked him to help them set up the National Library, which he did. He was always bitter about the way he was treated by the Library.

In 1903 Glyn was working hard cataloguing the Owen Jones collection of books; he wrote that he would be 'the author of the finest catalogue of Early Welsh books ever printed. There will be about 1500 to 2000 entries altogether.' His letters show his assiduous attention to the Library project, but also convey his prickliness.

One day in February 1905 he exploded in a letter to George. Glyn had had a letter from their mother in which she was pressing him to go to more revival meetings:

> Mater puts a premium on lying... This continual lacerating of one's feelings by Mater is not quite dignified... Mater takes advantage of the fact that my feelings towards her are very tender. For the last 12 years [i.e. since 1897] Mater has continually talked of passing away, and seemed to set herself out for it. If I had a child do you think I would wring its heart so?...
>
> I hope you can persuade Mater to leave me alone. I don't discuss my religion with anyone... much less can I discuss it with Mater who has inherited the hard and narrow forms of half a century ago. I did discuss these things with her some 17 years ago when I was just starting to read serious books, but she turned such a torrent of scorn and abuse on me that I have shut my mouth ever since. I was sensitive then and her attitude, unsympathetic and scornful, made a deep impression on me. The wonder is that I didn't kick the traces.

Glyn's bitterness towards his mother was clearly fierce. He suggested that rather than giving his spare money to the poor of Liverpool, George should ensure their mother got help with the housework. Glyn said he understood how George felt about poverty, but went on to say, angrily, 'I know… that Mater does not take so much interest in these things. Chapel doesn't teach civic virtues.'

Having railed against his mother's emotional blackmail, Glyn then began to pile guilt on to George himself:

> Your debt to Mater is greater than you can ever pay off, for you were but 12 years old when the crash [their father's bankruptcy] came… just think of the schooling you got, and the holidays in Lleyn, squeezed out of very small means indeed. Neither Frank nor Stan were earning their bread and butter, and just imagine how Mater must have slaved. We passed through a very tight time that you know little about.

Glyn continued this onslaught (in a large, angry hand quite unlike that of his other letters) by revealing to George that their mother had wanted George to train for the ministry, but Glyn had stopped it. Glyn had then been working, for a small salary, but had been contributing to the household, which, for a while, his younger brothers could not.

Though he loved his mother, Glyn was (like his brothers) upset and angered by her constant browbeatings and emotional blackmailing. The behaviour of parents is, however, often replicated in their children, and Glyn seems expert here at using the same strategies on his youngest brother. However, Elin and Gwion told me what a gentle, loving and excellent father Glyn had been to them and their two sisters.

George was increasingly unhappy in his job. He was unfortunate to have inherited the depressive illness that had afflicted Fanny Jones, his maternal grandmother, and others in the family. This heightened George's feelings of isolation and of dissatisfaction with his life and work. He had to contend with his bullying boss, Mr McGlashen. He did, however, have friends in the branch, and from their correspondence, it is clear that there was fun to be had there from time to time – one colleague, it seems, took pleasure in baiting George about his Welshness, but from the tone of the letters, in a friendly enough manner.

Then, in 1904 Dan Thomas, a native of Llannerch-y-medd on Anglesey, arrived to work at the bank. Dan, too, was the butt of some teasing, and George took trouble to introduce himself to Dan as another Welshman. Dan was fourteen years old at the time, and a Welsh-speaker; George was twenty-four and trying to re-learn his Welsh. A friendship began that lasted throughout George Davies' lifetime. It was Dan Thomas, as a serving soldier, who arrested George late in 1916, prior to George's term in prison as a Conscientious Objector. Dan later became a pacifist himself, and was treasurer of Plaid Cymru for forty years. When Dan's daughter Rhiannon married Gwynfor Evans, who later became Plaid Cymru's first MP, George gave an address in the marriage service.

The physical and social isolation of the Davies family's life in the suburbs of Liverpool threw the four brothers together a great deal. They grew very close, and their care for one another is obvious in their letters. The closeness continued throughout their lives – particularly between George and Stanley, and between Glyn and Frank – although Glyn, like many eldest children, was always more acerbic than any of the others. Glyn himself admitted that he and Stan were 'the most antipathetic of brothers'; Stan was the most conventional of the four.

Frank lived much of his life in China with the Merchant Navy, but his letters are warm and full of longing for his family and for Wales. Frank had departed for China in July 1904 under a cloud. It seems that Gwen Davies and Glyn had censured Frank for a career decision that they considered 'rash': he had given up the possibility of promotion in a well-established firm to go to a Chinese company. Frank spent some time with Stan in London before leaving, and Stan was dejected when Frank left. However, the four brothers continued to write regularly.

Glyn and Frank never lost their particular closeness, and any disagreements were soon forgotten. Once, while Frank was captain of a Chinese merchant ship, Glyn had a remarkably vivid dream. He and Frank were being chased down the shore by a mob of pirates. Glyn found a dinghy; he and Frank jumped in and they managed to escape. Glyn woke from his dream in a sweat, and immediately noted the time and date.

Some weeks later a letter arrived from Frank in China. He wrote that his ship had picked up cargo and some passengers, purportedly pilgrims. Once at sea, the 'pilgrims' turned out to be pirates, and stormed the bridge, with knives. Frank, a very strong man, knocked out six of them, but was close to being overpowered when the mate appeared with a gun, which put down the assault. The pirates were arrested and put in chains on the boat. When Frank and Glyn talked about this incident some years later, Gwion checked on the time his father had noted, and the times when the captain is normally on watch. With the difference in longitude between China and Wales, the time the pirates stormed the bridge would have been during the early hours of the morning in Wales – exactly the time Glyn had his dream.

Several of the Daviesses were gifted with this telepathy; Gwion told me that a sister of John Jones Talysarn once said to another sister: 'Mary, pull the curtains, Auntie has just died.' And she had.

On 7 January 1905 George, aged twenty-five, was still living at home in Liverpool; he had enjoyed a visit to friends, but when he got home, he found that his mother (then aged sixty-six) had a 'chill', and the fact of that negated the rest of the day. 'The flap of the black wing has turned all my joys into dread and darkness,' he wrote in his diary. Perhaps his anxieties about 'the transitoriness of this life' were begun by his father's business failing when George was only twelve years old, and insecurity accumulated. Certainly for a few days he was completely, and disproportionately, overwhelmed by his mother's comparatively slight illness.

By 23 January it was all forgotten, and in his diary George wrote of his shock at the news of the St Petersburg massacre. This is the first time George had written of an event outside these islands.

Soon after this, something happened in George Davies' life that was to have an immense effect on him for some time. Herbert Roberts, whom George had befriended at school in Liverpool, had stayed close to George into adulthood, even though Herbert's mother was one of those who had snubbed the Davies family following the bankruptcy. On 11 February 1905, George reported in his diary that Herbert is 'poorly... a little depressed'. On the 28th Herbert was: 'so ill... no hope... It cannot be. He my one intimate friend, my daily companion of whose companionship I never wearied, my confidant and chum who stimulated and encouraged every good impulse. We were all in all to one another.'

On 1 March, George wrote:

> Herbert died on Tuesday morning. I slept little last night thinking of it. The grief is a numb pain and to weep does not relieve it. How can I realise that our companionship is at an end for ever. How can I bear to see the old spots that we have been happy in together. The future is very blank. God help me to live – as he lived – for others. I cannot write any more.

Stanley wrote to George on the same day of his own sadness at Herbert's death, but, 'To you it is a greater loss than to me and I deeply sympathise with you in your grief'. Glyn wrote that he was 'terribly shocked... Roberts was a specimen of Christian rarely to be met with'.

Herbert's death seems to have been a catalyst for George Davies, the time he decided categorically that his life should be lived 'for others'. His agony about Herbert's death as expressed in the diary runs alongside the apparent unselfishness of his powerful love for Herbert, and his care for Herbert's girlfriend, Chattie Gallienne. He reminisced at length about his times with Herbert, even though there had been hardly a mention of Herbert in his diary before his death.

It is probable that the two men were so close when growing up that, prior to Herbert's death, there was no need to write about the friendship; that in a way Herbert *was* George's 'diary', his confidant. Perhaps his feelings for Herbert were so strong that George feared to put them on paper because they would seem more real. Perhaps he was hiding his feelings from others, and even from himself... and then later, after Herbert's death, George needed to express his grief, and could not do it, in full, publicly, so the diary was therapeutic.

The two men quite obviously had a very deep love, each for the other. It could, from the diary, be construed as a platonic romantic love – and perhaps this is why E. H. Griffiths, a Wesleyan Methodist minister, did not elaborate too far in his two-volume biography of George (1967 and 1968),which was written with a Welsh chapel readership in mind. Certain passages in George's diaries could seem, perhaps, to readers in the 1960s, unworthy of a 'saint' – as George was, and still is, viewed by many in Wales. The 'Herbert passages' indicate an intense love between two men – perhaps too intense for some sensibilities. On 18 March, George wrote about his feelings:

> Ah, Herbert, Herbert, how can I go through all the long years without you... We felt that the sunshine and open sky existed for us two and now you are gone. We used to sit on the style [*sic*] together looking towards the glowing sky beyond the pine trees, and speaking not a word, yet the scene meant more to us because we were together. I remember... how we had tea in the quiet parlour of the old inn at Stoke. The sun streamed through the leaded window frames upon the white table cloth, outside a bird was filling the quiet air with soft melody. You poured out the tea that smelt so fragrant and were so adept and motherly a bit that

> I could not help laughing. You looked up and laughed too and
> we were full of sweet merriment and contentment... Sweet spirit
> that was once my friend, art thou near me now and dost thou
> remember these things with pleasure? Sustain me until I join thee
> once more.

The final two sentences here are more like a prayer than a memory. George was deeply concerned with his own struggle to find a belief in God. Many Christians today address Christ in prayer in this manner. There is no censure, even (or especially) in fundamentalist evangelical circles, for a man having a close relationship with Jesus – indeed, a man who, in his prayers, uses expressions such as those in this passage from George's diary is looked on as having a particularly deep relationship with his God, and an admirably spiritual nature.

The Bible refers to close male friendships 'passing the love of women', like that of David and Jonathan, or Paul and Timothy. Several well-known figures had such friendships: Tennyson and Arthur Hallam, for example; Robert Louis Stevenson had a 'romantic friendship' with W. E. Henley; Rudyard Kipling had a very close friendship with Wolcott Balestier.

All these men regarded women as inferior beings. George Davies did not. Certainly both Glyn and George married very strong and capable women, not 'inferior beings' at all. However, one of Glyn's daughters, Mair, complained that her father never taught her and her sisters to make boats, as he did Gwion, even after their Uncle George had told Glyn that girls could do such things!

None of the Davies brothers appears to have been a 'team sports' person, each preferring solitary activities. All four brothers lived at home with their parents rather than being sent away to school. The gentle fathering they received, together with oppositionally controlling mothering, seemed to damage their robustness. Glyn has a lasting reputation for being generally angry (though not with his children); Frank disappeared off to China with the Merchant Navy as soon as he could. Stanley and George, in particular, were painfully sensitive souls whose lack of resilience affected their work and other aspects of their lives.

In 2003, it was suggested to me by a literary historian that, when studying George M. Ll. Davies, I should 'look under the tablecloth'. When pressed for clarification, he said he had known men who had suggested that George was homosexual. He refused to be drawn further, saying that his informants had 'probably all died by now' (as indeed has the historian). However, in spite of such rumours, I have yet to find evidence for suggesting that George Davies was homosexual.

Unitarian minister, the Rev. Emyr Evans, who, as a young man, spent some time with George in the 1940s, suggested to me that it is possible that George was (platonically) bisexual. Certainly, he seems to have been in some sort of love with Herbert, and throughout his life he enjoyed and sought out male company; but certainly he fell deeply in love with Leslie Royde Smith, and was interested in other girls before meeting her.

The one passage in his diaries which says the most about his interest in the opposite sex is the following, from 24 January 1903 (George was twenty-three). He was writing about Martha, the maid in his parents' house in Liverpool:

> Seated here an hour or more when I could hear the sharp click of the kitchen door and Martha appeared with a trowel, a basket to carry the lettuces from the garden. She stopped a moment looking down the drive when a cart rumbled past on the main road. Her arm was bare to the elbow and browned by work in the garden. The wide sun-bonnet protected her face to some extent when she put it on, which was not often. Generally it appeared hanging over her shoulder for her wealth of auburn hair she thought sufficient for protection.
>
> I tapped the window just as she was turning to the garden and she stopped, shading her eyes from the sun with her hand, looked up to the dining room window where I was standing. Seeing me she smiled merrily and pointed with her trowel towards

the garden. I smiled back to her whereat she cast her eyes down
demurely and passed in through the wicket gate.

The same deep silence again.

Then I walked slowly down the hall and through the long
kitchen resplendent with burnished pans and candlesticks. I
stopped at the door a moment. The air was heavy with the scent
of clove carnations, and then I sauntered into the garden after
Martha.

The sensuality – even eroticism – of this passage is
uncharacteristic of George's writing. There is no trace of anger,
no trace of Christianity, no trace of fear, only a total enjoyment
of life and an awareness of beauty. The lack of letters from him
to his wife is disappointing in this respect (although one or two
of her early letters to him show sensuality, if not eroticism).

The next day, George reported Martha as going about her
duties quietly, putting away the tablecloths after lunch, and
then going back to the kitchen. He returned to being the same
serious, rather self-flagellating young man, and he never
mentioned Martha again in his diaries.

George's apparently fruitless search for a personal belief in
God was of deep concern to his mother, who encouraged (or
obliged) him to go to hear some of the preachers in Liverpool
during the religious revival of 1904–5. On 3 April 1905, he
went to Toxteth Tabernacle to hear the famous Welshman
Evan Roberts. He was sceptical, however, and commented in
his diary: 'I felt at times a doubt whether we were not being
duped into letting emotion result in prayer rather than prayer
resulting in emotion.' Glyn shared George's scepticism, having
attended a similar 'diwygiad' [revival] meeting in Aberystwyth
in December the previous year. He reported to George that
the chapel was crammed full of girls, and open till 2 am. 'I
doubt that there is anything in it,' he wrote. 'They give one the
creeps.'

George did not feel that the revival experience led him any

nearer to the God he sought; nor did it ease his pain. On 20 April 1905, he wrote in his diary:

> I have no friend now like [Herbert], perhaps I shall never have. We loved each other and were contented to be in each other's company. We knew each other's secret hopes and failings and we were always sure of sympathy when we confided our troubles. Oh Herbert, Herbert, my life is very lonely without you. Be as near to me sweet spirit as God will allow you. Half my life was built on you. Death has lost its terrors now and life is more of a duty than before. But, Herbert, if we fulfil His will, He will let us meet perhaps and being better and holier our love shall be more perfect.

Again, 'half my life was built on you' could have seemed offensive to a religious readership who required life to be built on Christ, and on no mere man.

George met Chattie Gallienne, Herbert's girlfriend, regularly. Sharing memories of Herbert was a comfort to them both. It seems to have been easier for him to relate to Chattie, who was 'safe' because she still loved Herbert, than to other women who might have got involved with him. This seems consistent with the male romantic literature and other relationships of the time (for example, when Wolcott Balestier died in 1891, Rudyard Kipling promptly married Wolcott's sister). It seems a kind of 'projection', throwing the love that had been lost into another apparently very close relationship, with a common 'bond'.

George enjoyed the close friendship with Chattie, and the intimacy of their conversation. However, someone clearly commented adversely on the relationship, and in his diary on 21 April he demonstrated his annoyance:

> It is hard to comfort a girl without having one's feelings mistaken for something more than the affection of a friend. This unnatural barrier between the sexes – which a man is only permitted to cross when he goes as a lover – is absurd and wrong. The conventions of

society are the fruits of some very sordid ideas. In such a dilemma one's position is doubly awkward. One would wish to speak of the deepest things in life and it is my creed that Love is the deepest of all.

His grief for Herbert continued unabated. A few days later he wrote of 'a secret chamber in my heart, hidden from the eyes of all men... I realise now that I am alone and that there is an empty chair.'

It seems that when Herbert died, something died within George Davies, and was never reborn. Perhaps it was his childhood that died; perhaps he was so deeply hurt that he could never love as wholly again, and he feared to open himself completely to another person. It is obvious that he tried hard to be open in his relationship with his wife Leslie, whom he first met in 1911; but apart from a few years at the beginning, it seems that he did not succeed. (This may have been as much Leslie's failing as George's.) Certainly, though he was loved by many through his life, and loved many in return, he seems to have had few close friendships.

But he seemed to be progressing to a more positive state. Early in May 1905, a friend told him he was looking very cheerful and strong in the faith. George was surprised, but wrote in his diary:

> ... yes, I am happier. Before [Herbert's death] I dared not think of losing the boys or the old people. It was too dreadful to think of. And Death again and being forgotten. A stranger years afterwards, looking at one's grave; all these things filled me with the profoundest melancholy. Now, it is sweetened, for *he* has gone before, and at night I kneel and pray... with a deeper sense of the reality of it than I have ever felt before... The appalling self-consciousness that troubled me so much is leaving me.

He had gone through the situation that he feared most – personal loss – and had survived. The result was an increasing confidence, and the beginning of liberation.

George began to read more and more widely, particularly the poems of Wordsworth, 'whose works I have in a little pocket volume which I read in the train every day'. He also began to write letters to more people – a practice he continued all his life (although, inconveniently for his biographers, dating very few of them).

Throughout his life George Davies had a fascination with, and dread of, death. In the years during and after the Victorian era, extended families were the norm, and poverty all around. Death was part of everyday life, and was marked ostentatiously. It is conventionally 'Christian' to see death as a positive thing, as a meeting with God. But for George it was something terrible. In May 1905 he wrote of being 'hurried on from boyhood to youth from youth to manhood from manhood to age and from age to the forgotten grave'. This fear of the grave, and of being forgotten after death, is a recurring theme throughout George's life, and may even partially explain the manner of his own death.

After this, George's diary entries became fewer, though he did use the empty pages in following years. In July 1906 he wrote of his unpleasant boss at the bank, Mr McGlashen, whose 'rude and irritable and suspicious manners upset me altogether. I get nervous and hesitating and my heart palpitates and aches in a most distressing way'. This response to stress is interesting because the same symptoms recurred at the end of his life, and are described in detail in the medical notes around the time of his death. It is clear that McGlashen was an office bully, as George himself realised, but at that time there was little redress in such situations, and to leave the bank without a reference would have made it extremely difficult for George to find another job: his 'good character', an essential requirement of the middle classes at the time, would be in question. His description of his feelings (4 August 1906) is an excellent summary of the physical and emotional effects such a bully has on employees:

The inconsiderateness and the bullying manners of McGlashen hurt me very much at times. It either means answering back to him, which might mean dismissal, and this I have no right to risk – or else swallowing one's pride and self respect and enduring every ignominy. To have to do this breaks down one's manliness but there is no option.

The comments 'this I have no right to risk' and 'there is no option' refer to the fact that George and his brothers were still maintaining their parents after their father's financial collapse. The responsibility weighed heavily on George, but he was determined to help as much as he could. But if George had left the bank and McGlashen, would he really not have been able to obtain another job? He had risen to a high position for such a young man (twenty-six in 1906), and was clearly an extremely capable, responsible and intelligent employee. Perhaps his father's bankruptcy made a change of employment difficult in Liverpool, where the family was known. He appears to have been trapped at the bank both by middle-class conventions and by his parents' penury.

Current TUC guidelines about office bullying say the effects include anxiety, headaches, nausea, ulcers, sleeplessness, skin rashes, irritable bowel syndrome, high blood pressure, tearfulness, loss of self-confidence, various illnesses of organs such as the kidneys, and thoughts of suicide. Clearly George was experiencing a large number of these symptoms, but because of his responsibilities he felt it was impossible to confront his boss.

In February 1907, George was surprised by a new emotion. Caddie Edwards, a distant relation, confessed her feelings for George during a walk, and he kissed her:

> ... for me the first kiss of love – and my world shook to its foundations. I felt myself wondering if this was a great joy or a great disaster. What right had I to love anyone in this way or to let anyone love me. It was the sudden avowal on her part, the trust

in her eyes, the abandon of all pretence, that swept me like a tidal wave of tenderness far from my moorings. What is to be the end of this. God guide us and keep us to be wise and sincere.

George himself hardly mentioned Caddie again in his diaries, but he clearly talked with Stanley about the situation.

However, in the weeks after the kiss, Caddie wrote several letters to George. She appears to have taken things very seriously. Evidently George did not write back immediately: Caddie's next letter suggested, slightly testily, that 'probably the postmen had gone on strike in Liverpool'. In her next letter Caddie said she had had a long talk with her mother, who 'gave her consent'. However, her following letters become less and less intimate: clearly George was not responding to her wheedlings. Then it becomes obvious that George had requested a 'cooling off' of the relationship (which hardly existed at that point). Caddie agreed that they should not become engaged for a while yet – even though George had, apparently, shown no inclination to propose to her!

In a letter of 15 March 1907, Stanley Davies suggested that his brother would be marrying beneath him if he married Caddie; clearly Gwen Davies was not happy about the 'relationship'. Stan wrote:

> A man may marry above him – that is, a woman far more refined and cultured than himself, but as a rule he succeeds in elevating himself to her standard. I am sure in my mind that the converse is also true – if a man marries beneath him, he adapts himself to her status instead of her raising himself to his.

Stanley's words call to mind John Ruskin's small but influential book, *Sesame and Lilies*, which was frequently reprinted in the thirty-five years after its first publication in 1865. Ruskin's view was that 'the man's work for his own home is… to secure its maintenance, progress and defence; the woman's to secure its order, comfort and loveliness'. It would be surprising if Gwen Davies had not read Ruskin's book.

Stanley suggested that any relationship with Caddie was doomed from the start. She was clearly not George's equal socially or (judging by her letters) in intelligence; George would have been quickly frustrated and bored by Caddie.

In George's initial reaction to the kissing of Caddie, as in his writing about Martha in 1903, we see a person who is sensual, but wishes to repress this sensuality, through fear or unfamiliarity. George seemed uncomfortable with his feelings, as if unsure where they will lead him. These are George Davies' early experiences of relationships in the context of a Victorian, middle-class, religious upbringing in the Welsh community in Liverpool. His 'manliness' up to this point was shaped by these factors, and by his mother's demands on him, by his sensitivity and self-doubt, and by his inclination to fear his stronger feelings.

It is interesting that his later relationship with Leslie Royde Smith, who was to become his wife, developed outside the suffocating Liverpool Welsh community.

On 18 August 1907, George returned to his diary to report that he had been very depressed, a situation that was 'almost chronic'. McGlashen's continuing bullying didn't help. 'I fight against [the depression],' he wrote, 'but with little success for I believe that it is due more or less to being run down physically'. He was more stable in April 1908: 'The old volcanic upheavals are less frequent and less powerful, the yoke of routine is more tolerable... But my heart is not at rest. Is *this* to be the prosaic ending of all one's dreams. Is there no *man's* work for me to do.'

George added no question mark after 'dreams', or 'do', as if he is not asking a question, but making a statement. On 26 July, he wrote: 'For one who has dreamed dreams this existence is a sad disappointment. It is a disappointment to be compelled to run in a race of commercial competition when one's heart is not set on the prize.'

It is significant that George asked about 'man's work',

because at the time women were beginning to take over the kind of clerical work he had been doing. Women had been entering office work in significant numbers from half-way through the nineteenth century. In the 1851 census, just nineteen women were listed as 'commercial clerks' in the west and east of England. But as Gregory Anderson wrote in *The White Blouse Revolution*, in the thirty years between 1881 and 1911 the increase in numbers was considerable: 'from 7,444 to 146,133 in commerce and from 4,657 to 27,129 in the Civil Service.'

A clerk had to be of a better educational and social background than other workers. Qualities such as honour, courtesy, loyalty and sobriety were called for. (This, of course, is precisely the recipe for the 'respectability' to which the middle classes aspired!) Clerks needed to be able to compose business letters, and handwrite them legibly. Male clerks could expect long careers, but cultural pressures would mean that most women would have to give up their jobs on marriage, for, as Anderson wrote, the typical Edwardian career girl wanted nothing more than 'a frock-coated something in the city, to live in a suburban semi-detached villa, and carry a gilt-clasped prayer book to church on Sunday'.

Again we hit upon the notion of 'separate spheres' associated with Victorian middle-class society: the Ruskinesque idea that men took part in the money-earning and/or public activities of the home, and women looked after the quiet, domestic, 'caring' side of things. But working-class women had always had to earn whatever they could to help feed their family; upper-class women had taken part in philanthropic activities, and educated middle-class women had been, for example, teachers or nurses. The need for office workers in the new factories and service industries meant a new niche for middle-class women, and one in which they could compete with men as equals in terms of skills (if not pay). Women flocked to be 'typewriters' (as they were called at the time) – but only girls who had been educated to sixteen years old (and therefore middle class, and respectable) were considered suitable for training. By the end of the nineteenth century, some women had bought their own typewriters and were hiring out their services. Men eventually avoided learning shorthand and typing, because they felt that with those skills they would become too useful as shorthand-typists to be offered promotion to management. 'Born a man, died a clerk' was a long-held view of clerking, strongly suggesting that it was not 'man's work' at all.

In 1908, at the age of twenty-eight, still longing for 'man's work', George Davies was appointed Manager of a branch of Martin's Bank in Wrexham. He took the flat above the bank; Stanley, working in an insurance office nearby, moved in too. At last, away from Liverpool, Mr McGlashen, and his parents, George began a new chapter of his life – and soon discovered 'man's work' right on the doorstep.

4

Rise and Fall

On 17 March 1909, George Davies' father John died suddenly from pneumonia. He was seventy-one. George's diary simply stated, 'Today, dear old Pater died. Loveable, humorous, quick-tempered, quick to forgive; an old man with a boy's heart.'

After her husband's death, Gwen Davies left Liverpool, and moved in with Stanley and George, in their flat in Wrexham.

George became a popular bank manager, and his old friend Dan Thomas soon came to work at the Wrexham branch. George was as restless as ever, but he and Stanley still needed to support their mother. On 25 April 1909, George wrote resignedly: 'I must seek rather to do my duty in the uncongenial tasks of the present than neglect it for some future heroics. God grant me constancy and strength in this.'

Then, in May 1909, something caught his imagination.

In 1907, Lord Haldane, Secretary of State for War, had established a reserve Territorial Force, with the aim of avoiding the imposition of conscription in another war; his plan was to have a Territorial Force to be used initially for home defence, but which could supplement the Regulars if the need arose. The Force quickly became known as the Territorial Army.

Recruiting began on 1 April 1908. On 7 May 1909, Stanley and George Davies, being middle-class respectable men, were granted commissions as Second Lieutenants, Territorial Force, 4th (Denbighshire) Battalion, Royal Welch Fusiliers. They were expected to discipline 'both the inferior Officers and

Men serving under you', and to observe directions from their superior Officers 'according to the Rules and Discipline of War'. George encouraged young Dan Thomas to join up, too.

At that time the Force numbered 9,313 officers and 259,463 other ranks. Men between seventeen and thirty-five were eligible to join the Territorials, initially for a four-year term of service.[1] George was twenty-nine when he joined, and Stanley around thirty-two. The decision was unfortunate for both of them: George, because it made his later decision to become a non-combatant far more complicated; and Stanley, because he extended his registration, and went to war.

In 1939 George Davies wrote an article for *The Christian Pacifist* entitled 'Growing in Pacifism', in which he spoke of his reasons for joining the Territorials in 1909, and of what he had found and enjoyed there:

> The Territorial Army was established specifically for defence, and no Statesman and no Christian that I had ever heard of, save Tolstoi, repudiated the use of arms in self-defence. It was therefore a choice between voluntary and enforced military service that impelled me to take a Commission in the Territorial Army. Having so decided, there was much to appeal to one in the call and training of volunteers, the relief of willing subordination and of discipline, and the *esprit de corps* of the Battalion, the camp and the manoeuvres. The chaplains and the church parades helped to remove misgivings as to the actual morality of war. To be willing to share and to suffer together, and, if need be, to make the supreme sacrifice, seemed nobler than the normality of Christian lives, preoccupied in business or serving on Christian committees.

Clearly George Davies, future pacifist and peace-maker, was totally convinced, in 1909, of the rightness of the TA itself, and of his readiness to make 'the supreme sacrifice' in war. At the time, George was quite a political Liberal. There was a general aura of militarism, and George was swept up in enthusiasm for defending the country. He clearly believed the TA was 'specifically for defence' (though even critics of the new Force realised that in the event of a war, trained men would volunteer for service abroad). There is no guilt or regret apparent in the article, as though George had (by 1939, if not earlier) accepted that joining the TA in 1909 had been, simply, 'the thing to do'.

George continued in Wrexham through 1909 and 1910, in the bank by day, and the Territorials at weekends and in the evenings, and living with Stanley and his mother.

On 13 May 1911, George Davies' diary recorded his anger at his mother's attitude towards someone he refers to only as 'X'. This is the only time George didn't use a person's name in his diaries, which suggests that 'X' was significant.

> Of late I have been much distressed and somewhat embittered by Mater's attitude towards an affection that she thought was springing up between me and X. She has been distressed and disturbed by the thought and says she is entirely unsuitable. The grounds seem to be that her parents are poor, that she is English and Anglican, and that a sister has separated from her husband. If in marriage and love one is to carry out the principle of self-sacrifice as in other things these considerations should not weigh and it has distressed me beyond anything to feel that my mother (in a natural enough ambition from a worldly-wise point of view) should attach so little weight to the voice of the heart which is after all the deepest department of one's life.
>
> Fortunately our acquaintance has not been close enough to ripen into anything more. She is a sweet, impulsive young girl very much of the temperament of Dorothea in *Middlemarch*, but, in any case, one's desire for love and matrimony are checked by the hope of emancipation from the present mode of life; the country and the Church still remain almost the only other worldly ambition I have but its attainment is next to impossible unless God designs otherwise.

'X' was Leslie Eleanor Royde Smith. She had been working as a schoolteacher in Wrexham, where she taught Domestic Science. Later she moved to a school in Barnet, London. When she returned to Wrexham to visit friends, who also knew

George, the two met. It is said that she fell in love with him when she saw him in his uniform. This would have been easy: photographs show him as a beautiful, grave and wistful young officer. George describes her as a 'young girl', but she was only four years younger than him. He was thirty-one. When George was born in 1880 John Davies was about fifty and his wife forty-one; it seems as though the combination of being born to quite elderly Victorian parents and growing up with a bankrupt father and a mother with a 'chapel mind' had conspired to make George feel older than his years. Leslie's energy and liveliness would have thrown his staidness into sharp relief.

George seemed to expect 'self-sacrifice' to be a part of everything in his life. Certainly he was unable to leave the job he hated because over the years he had been giving financial support to his parents. But what was 'self-sacrifice' going to entail within marriage? Or within love?

The ambitious Gwen Davies had wanted George to marry Gwendoline Davies, one of the sisters of the industrialist and philanthropist David Davies, later Lord Davies, of Llandinam. These Davieses, too, were related on their mother's side to John Jones Talysarn, George's grandfather. George's mother approved of Gwendoline, who was described by a close family friend, Thomas Jones, as 'a shy, timid, modest religious spirit'. This may have been true, but she was also highly complex. Neither she nor her sister Margaret (known as Daisy) ever married, though Gwendoline became very fond of George's cousin Edward Lloyd Jones (known as 'Dolly', for reasons best known to his friends and family), who was the son of David Lloyd Jones, George's uncle, the Presbyterian minister in Llandinam.

Gwen Davies was predictably prejudiced against Leslie Royde Smith. Even though Leslie had (acceptably) been to a finishing school in Switzerland (and Gwen had been sent to one in London), Leslie was a confident working woman, neither shy nor timid, and from a family of free-thinkers, not at all the quiet woman providing a homely atmosphere for her man that

Gwen would have favoured. Leslie's mother was Welsh, from Penybont, but perhaps Gwen did not know this. One of Leslie's sisters, Naomi Royde Smith, had indeed separated from her husband, was the Literary Editor of the *Saturday Westminster Gazette*, and lived a somewhat avant-garde life in London, on the fringes of the Bloomsbury Group. Leslie lodged with her from 1904. The poet Walter de la Mare was a regular visitor between 1911 and 1915: though married with children, he had a passionate but probably platonic relationship with Naomi. Naomi also had a 'close friendship' with the writer Rose Macaulay. When she was fifty-one, Naomi married Ernest Milton, an Old Vic actor fifteen years younger than her – he worshipped her, but was not interested in women in a sexual way.

Leslie's lifestyle had been very different from George's narrow, chapel-regulated family life. This, together with the other 'negatives', meant that Gwen Davies' mind was set against her.

In a letter to Glyn and his wife, George said Leslie was:

> ... clever, quixotic, fastidious in manners and metaphors, perfect sangfroid: that was the devil to get through and a volcano underneath, sweet when won, sweet through and through. Interests – literature, especially French and German and latterly Welsh, wild country, motoring, music and myself.

One wonders whether someone who was 'quixotic', having both 'sangfroid' *and* 'a volcano underneath', was the best partner for the emotional George Davies. But he was besotted with her. He was a man with a strong 'feminine side' (as were his brothers), and perhaps Leslie's independence and capability were part of the attraction. Throughout his life George seems to have enjoyed the challenge of getting underneath a person's 'mask' to the feelings beneath it, whether politician or preacher, child or miner. The one person who did not seem to keep his interest, after the age of eight at least, was, sadly, George and

Leslie's daughter Jane Hedd. As a result of this fatherly neglect, Nancy White told me, Jane rejected all religion for the rest of her life. When Nancy and Peter were growing up, nothing biblical or religious was ever mentioned by their mother.

The investiture of Prince Edward as 'prince of Wales' in Caernarfon castle was set for 13 July 1911. Gwen Davies was delighted because (as George told Frank in a letter dated 9 July 1911) Mrs Lloyd George had sent her a ticket; but she disapproved of the occasion and told off her Territorial Army sons for 'dressing up to kill people'. There is no concrete evidence to show exactly why Gwen Davies disapproved of the investiture (or, indeed, whether she used her ticket), but it is known that one of the reasons she disliked Leslie Royde Smith was because she was an Anglican. The investiture was an Anglican ceremony, which would have greatly displeased Gwen Davies.

George was not yet a socialist, and at that time was a sentimental, rather than an angry, nationalist. He was looking forward to taking part in the ceremony:

> ... the greatest pageant Wales has witnessed for centuries... I am to carry the Regimental Colour. What appeals to me most about it is its significance as a recognition of Wales and its nationality and its language. There will be thousands of old country farmers from Lleyn and Snowdon and the district in Castle Square, and it brings a lump in one's throat to think of the old Welsh hymns being sung by such a congregation and to such an audience.

By that time, he and Leslie had, in spite of his mother's opposition, agreed to have just a short engagement before marriage. They went on holiday in Llŷn to visit George's childhood haunts. But it did not go well, and ended with a row on the slopes of Madryn, with Leslie berating George for (as she saw it) blowing hot and cold with his love. Leslie was not so sure by then that they had anything except affection in common. Clearly she did not appreciate that George's depression often got the better of him.

About this time, Leslie wrote a poem that conveys her impression of the argument:

Forgive me but I did not understand
    The deeper meaning of the love you swore.
Forgive me that I thought it this, no more:
A comradeship, when hand may cling to hand
In awe of the blue silence when two stand
    On bare, wide hills; of souls that kneel before
    Earth's mystery of colour, at whose core
Glows the white truth for which men plough the sand.

It was your way. Even so. Be mine the blame.
    Only, another vision glows for me.
Narrow and cold you call me; by this same
Token, I call your lusts, captivity.
    Then, since for each such different beacons shine,
    Follow your star in peace. I follow mine.

Leslie's words seem consistent with comments she made in later letters to George, to the effect that she wanted more of a deep spiritual 'comradeship' relationship with him, rather than a physical one. Her upbringing, and perhaps Naomi's influence, meant she had a rather unconventional view of marital sex.

Looking back to his writing about Martha in 1903, George seems to have been a much more sensual and sexual being than his later diary entries or letters show. The Bible exhorts its readers to 'Beware of the flesh', and to strive to be above earthly lusts. This aim, evidently, had been uppermost in George's thinking for most of the previous few years. However, those 'lusts' are normal human feelings, and in spite of denying or repressing them, George did not lose them altogether. If this feature of Leslie's thinking, and their subsequent sexual incompatibility, lasted throughout the couple's marriage (and from my conversations with George and Leslie's granddaughter

Nancy White, there is evidence that it did), it is hardly surprising that they lived apart for long periods from 1930 onwards. This led to accusations of George 'neglecting his wife and child', which are still heard in Wales today. Nancy recalled Jane telling her of these accusations. I, too, have heard from those who, far from considering George a 'saint', are of the opinion that he was a 'monstrous' person for 'leaving his wife'. (However, as we will see, this is not the whole truth.)

On 21 August 1911, George wrote to Frank about love and marriage. He spoke of how delightful it would be to receive £100 a year from somewhere, and to be able to give up the bank and live in the country, and how impossible it would be to do that if he were married. The next extract says much about George's emotional state and his somewhat patronising view of the working classes; it also predicts the last two decades of his life:

> Of course I grant that love is the highest thing in the world – but man-and-woman love often turns out to be a pretty sordid thing. If we could only manage to love our fellows – especially the more unfortunate ones – with something like the ardour we are prepared to bestow on perhaps a shallow pretty girl, our love would be a better and nobler thing and not a passion based to a large extent on animal instincts.
>
> What a life it would be if one could become... the confidant and friend of simple country people, prepared to help and console and advise them and to carry the burdens of their human life. You would both give and receive love that would be the real thing.
>
> Apart from matrimony it is not easy (especially as one gets older) to enter into an absolutely intimate affection with another – especially if the 'other' be a woman. And so we tend to draw into ourselves and become superficial in our attachments... This state of mind is intolerable to me. I must have affection or else life is a desert.

George was busy in Wrexham with his work at the bank and the TA. But he wrote to Frank again on 1 October 1911 saying he had been made Secretary of the Welsh Housing Association, one of the many projects initiated by David Davies, brother of Gwendoline and Margaret. The Association aimed to improve housing conditions in Wales, and to reduce the death rate from consumption and cancer, which 'is the heaviest in Europe'. Lord Kenyon, the President, had newly obtained the patronage of the King and Queen, and George adds, perhaps naively, 'and this ought to serve to make it a movement in which all classes and parties can join'. (But a political patron, such as Lloyd George or Keir Hardie, would also have excluded other 'classes and parties' from participation.)

In his 'spare time', George was running a club for 'poor boys' in the town, with a reading room, gymnastics, military drill, and camping expeditions in the hills, and enjoying riding and driving his newly-purchased and beloved bay mare, bought for £11. He was sad to have to sell her before the winter to save the 6d a day he paid for her upkeep.

In his next letter to Frank (undated), he wrote:

> I have been simply off my head with work – early and late. Two nights a week for the Boys' Club, the Secretaryship of the Welsh Housing Association, the building of a Garden Suburb near Wrexham, the Treasurership of the Excavations committee and of the Voluntary Aid Detachment, two Eisteddfod Committees, the management of Tanycastell [his grandfather's house in Dolwyddelan], the Old and New Estate, the Territorials and incidentally the Bank.

Perhaps all this busyness was a method of hiding from himself; perhaps it simply put a great strain on him. Whatever the cause, George Davies suddenly felt life was too much. In a state of great emotional upheaval, he told Leslie that he released her from their engagement.

Soon after, George asked Stanley to bring Dan Thomas to meet him in his room. Dan found George in deep distress. He tried to persuade Dan to leave the Territorials, saying that he had come to believe that it was against God's will to kill other people, and he blamed himself for Dan joining in the first place. He said he would buy Dan out. Dan failed to convince George that he had made his own decision about joining, and he refused to leave the Territorials.

George decided to leave banking, declaring that banks were almost anti-Christian. In May 1914 he resigned his commission (his officer status) in the Territorials, 'less from a specific objection to war than from its irrelevance to my positive purpose in life', George wrote in retrospect.

From the glamour of the investiture in July 1911, and the excitement of falling in love, it seemed that George had lost his job, the Territorials, and Leslie. A lot of bridges had been burnt. It was the first of several significant periods of turmoil and change in George Davies' life.

But most of the turmoil at that time was caused by the fact that he was beginning to tear himself away from his mother's influence by his personal decision to turn pacifist, and by being involved with someone his mother disapproved of. In a way, perhaps this was something of a late 'teenage rebellion', at the age of thirty. To his credit, though, even in his most fragile state, he did not allow Gwen Davies' manipulation, browbeating and emotional blackmail to deflect him from his path.

George's breakdown had begun in late 1911, and he was not completely well until the end of 1914. In the meantime, he sought to be as useful to his fellow-man as he could. Initially, he became more involved in trying to improve the housing situation in Wales. He had been the Secretary of David Davies Llandinam's Welsh Housing Association (WHA) since 1911, and now threw himself deeper into the work. He also wrote regularly for a new monthly magazine, *The Welsh Outlook*, founded by David Davies in 1914 to promote progressive Liberalism and cultural nationalism.

David Davies of Llandinam (1880–1945) was a millionaire, a coal-owner, and a philanthropist. 'Institutions' were an expanding field at this time: philanthropists wanted to see (and have others see) the fruits of their generosity. Apart from the Housing Association and the *Outlook*, David Davies had another project in mind: the King Edward VII Welsh National Memorial Association for the Prevention of Tuberculosis (WNMA), set up in 1910. Funds of £300,000 were raised by public subscription and David Davis contributed £150,000, for 'dispensaries, residential institutions, a propaganda department, and a research department'. George Davies was asked to be Secretary of the WNMA. The Secretary of a company or association is a key directorship post, with everyday responsibilities and legal obligations; the former bank manager was experienced with budgets and accounts, and in assessing the viability of projects.

In 1912, David Davies used £1million of his own money to set up the Welsh Town Planning and Housing Trust (WTPHA), and asked George to become Secretary of that Trust, too.

The WTPHA was a direct descendant of the England-based Garden City Movement, the vision of Ebenezer Howard, a stenographer and shorthand writer with a vision. In 1898, Howard published his seminal book, *Tomorrow: A Peaceful Path to Real Reform* (later reprinted as *Garden Cities of Tomorrow*). Howard wrote of the 'marriage' of town and country in an ideal society, with town supporting country and vice versa, 'and out of this union will spring a new hope, a new life, a new civilisation'; he envisaged a good social and economic balance, common land ownership, co-operative living, and a wide choice of employment; no terraces of houses, larger plot sizes but smaller social units, and sufficient light and water in the houses.

George is very likely to have read Ebenezer Howard's books, being involved professionally in the field, and being very much in sympathy with Howard's idealism. Since his childhood, George had seen how towns and cities affected particularly the working classes, and how the physical stuffiness in the slums replicated the metaphorical stuffiness of the suburbs.

The first draft Constitution of the London-based Garden City Movement was written in 1897 by W. St John Hancock, a Welshman from Dolgellau, who drew in two other London Welshmen, Thomas Idris and Aneurin Williams. In 1907 Thomas Idris became the first Chairman of the Council of the Garden City Movement.

The first Garden City was Letchworth, in 1903. Although its image was somewhat 'cranky', businessmen like George Cadbury and newspaperman Arthur Harmsworth became interested and began to exemplify Howard's principles. Cadbury developed Bourneville in Birmingham for his workers; Lord Lever, who also provided material support for the Garden City Movement, built Port Sunlight on Merseyside for his.

Gradually, Garden City principles were then applied to existing towns, and it was realised that Garden Suburbs and Garden Villages (as in Wrexham, which became one of George's projects) were more practicable than completely new Garden Cities. Of the fifty-seven projects originally planned, only one Garden City per se – Letchworth – was ever built. But the Garden City Movement was the inspiration for many smaller projects from 1890 onwards, and influenced the Settlement Movement, with which George became involved in the late 1920s.

In 1911, David Davies invited St John Hancock, Thomas Idris and Aneurin Williams to be part of the Welsh Town Planning and Housing Trust Ltd (WTPHT), with the objective of improving housing 'in the Principality of Wales, the County of Monmouth, and elsewhere'. (The 'elsewhere' extended, during the inter-war years, to projects with the Great Western Railway, of which David Davies was a Director – rented accommodation for railwaymen, using GWR funds and the Trust's expertise, in London and the west of England as well as in Wales.)

The Trust was registered under the Joint Stock Companies Acts. David Davies was himself the Vice President, and Lord Kenyon the President. George M. Ll. Davies was Secretary. The

first Board meeting was held on 3 May 1913, at the offices
of the Barry Railway, in Westminster. (The Trust was still in
existence in some form until the 1970s.)

George himself reported that he had decided to leave the bank
in Wrexham at the time of his breakdown, but an unpublished
account written in 1956 by T. Alwyn Lloyd, George's boyhood
friend and co-worker on several housing Trusts' Boards, says
that David Davies had 'induced' George to leave the bank in
order to become the 'promoter' and Secretary to the Trust. It
may be that David Davies, being an old friend of George's, had
covered up the real reasons for George leaving the bank – or
perhaps Alwyn Lloyd put a gloss on events to protect George's
reputation.

Llyfr Coch Cymru (written by St John Hancock in 1911)
lists the officials and members of the Council of the Welsh
Housing Association (evidently coterminous with the Welsh
Town Planning and Housing Trust Ltd). Hancock listed himself
as 'a bilingual native of Dolgelley [*sic*]' – the only one in the
list described as 'bilingual', inferring that the others, though
Welshmen, were not Welsh-speakers. (George was, of course, a
Welsh-speaker, but possibly at this time he spoke more English
than Welsh.) George is listed as Secretary of the Wrexham
branch of the WHA.

The book gives statistics showing how overcrowded some
areas of Wales were at the time. The Rhondda had an average
of 5.7 people to a house – a 'house' being, often, a two-up, two-
down, with no sanitation. In one area of Merthyr Tudful there
were 300,800 people to a square mile. The author pointed out
that there were problems in north Wales too, when summer
visitors flocked there in their thousands.

The 1911 census showed a shortage of 250,000 dwellings in
south Wales. In 1913, David Davies formed the South Wales
Garden Cities and Town-Planning Association, again with
George as Secretary. David Davies said he would contribute
£100 per year to the Association for the following three years,
provided that sum was at least matched from other sources.

63

The Council deemed it necessary to have a full-time Secretary and Organiser (George again), and decided they needed £300 p.a. for that purpose. George's salary, therefore, a single man, was to be around £6 per week – about six times the normal income of working-class men at the time.

In order to work more effectively with David Davies and his trusts, George Davies moved initially to Cardiff, to live in the Creigiau Hotel in Pentyrch. He then went into lodgings with his old schoolfriend T. Alwyn Lloyd (the architect to the Trust) and Mrs Lloyd. George later moved to 70 Bute Street, in the Tiger Bay area of Cardiff, a dockland area which was at the time full of sailors and families from all over the world.

George's administrative work for the Trust brought him into contact with the people he had always wished to help, but at that time his relationship with them was that of a kind benefactor. When he'd lived in Liverpool it was certainly not in close proximity to the working classes. While noticing the life taking place in Bute Street, he was not involved in it, and did not wish to be. His task in 1912 was to help the philanthropists, not to relate to the people actually living in the houses he was helping to build.

In 1942 George wrote an introduction to a pamphlet about Quaker 'social work' in the Tiger Bay area of Cardiff, issued by the Quaker Peace Service during the Second World War. The pamphlet included photos of Iorwerth John, who was involved in the QPS during his time as a Conscientious Objector. The introduction begins: 'I have known Tiger Bay for over thirty years, and Iorwerth John for half that time.' George admits that when he had lived in Tiger Bay he had not been in what he later called 'feeling-touch' with the local residents:

> In 1912 I occupied a room in the offices of a great Colliery combine [David Davies' Ocean Coal Company] in Bute Street, and was formulating a scheme of Town Planning and Housing for Wales, with the support of peers and millionaires. I was preoccupied with Plan rather than Man, and so had no time for

those thousands of Arabs, Negroes, Lascars, half-castes, dagoes, Scandinavians and 'lesser breeds without the law' as I then considered them.

Yet here was a Corinthian market-place of all nations, a crucible for sympathies or antipathies that might be carried to the ends of the earth: but peace-making and understanding this No Man's Land was not profit-making to the Combines.

Initially, the WTPHT planned ten projects. Lord Davies put in the money and management skills, Alwyn Lloyd the design, and George worked on the financial and administrative side: he also wrote the initial memorandum and articles of the Trust. They built a Garden Village in Wrexham and houses in Llanidloes, Machynlleth, Burry Port and Barry. David Davies liked appearing to be 'up to the moment': he was determined that his WTPHT houses would be pleasant and convenient to live in, each with a garden and with open land in front, and they would have water, gas and electricity laid on.

In spite of their earlier problems George and Leslie Royde Smith were still planning to get married. They had been looking for a house in Cardiff or Barry. Early in 1914 Leslie wrote to her mother:

> There is a prospect of a small house in a garden village (not one of George's) which may be built by the early summer. So far that is all. George is fantastically busy – and at present in Wrexham looking after the housing there, which is so far the most important and the most advanced of all the schemes. Consequently private affairs suffer, and no-one house-hunts.

This garden village might well have been Rhiwbina, which was not one of the Trust's projects initially, though they invested in it from 1915 onwards.

George was indeed very busy in Wrexham, where the development was proving problematical. He was also travelling around Wales visiting the Trust's projects and reporting to Council meetings. The huge amount of work involved was

65

beginning to tell on him: he was still quite fragile from his recent mental breakdown. In November 1913, in the Minute Books of the Board, the words 'The Secretary reported...' are at the start of the majority of the items, including site visits and reporting progress on sites, as well as his own administrative and accounting duties. George asked for a Deputy to help him cope with the growing activities of the Trust.

In June 1914, the Wrexham Housing Association produced a booklet, *Some Interesting Facts about Wrexham Garden Village*, almost certainly written by George. The first annual report of the WTPHT (1913–14) detailed forty-four inhabited houses, built at a total cost of £12,000; a further 200 were due to be ready for occupation by November 1914, with five large villas also planned. Rents were between 4s. 9d and 8s. per week.

Certain rumours, said the author, needed to be addressed. For example, the Village was being built specifically to house colliers and families (the new Gresford pit was potentially the employer of 3,000 men); nevertheless, amazingly, a rumour had been put about that 'The Society does not care to let houses to Colliers'! Two more petty rumours were that 'All blinds in every house have to be of the same material, colour, pattern, etc' (this was discounted as 'Absurd' by the author), and that tenants would not be allowed to hang out their washing: the booklet states that clothes could be hung out to dry 'every week-day, if necessary' (by implication, not on Sundays).

The Village, said the writer, would have sewers and lit roads; each house would have water, electricity, and a bath. They would be well-equipped, some with fitted furniture. Recreation grounds, playgrounds, and an Institute (community hall, library and education centre) would be provided, and space was reserved for a future shopping centre. Tenants would invest the equivalent of a year's rent into the Housing Association, either as a lump sum or in instalments.

The Society, the booklet went on, had negotiated favourable terms for the supply of electricity to the Village. Every Monday, with the rent, the rent-collector would also collect one penny

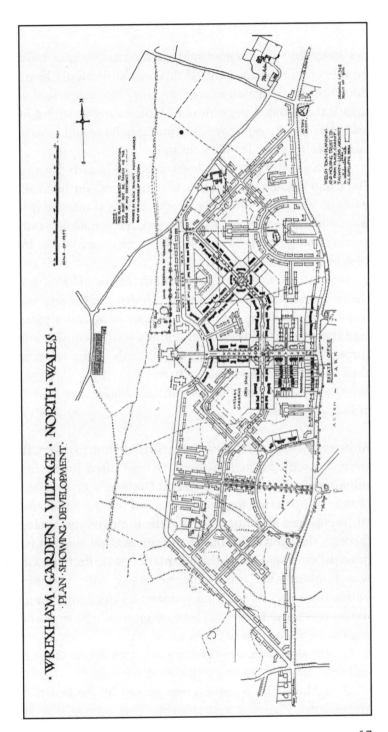

· WREXHAM · GARDEN · VILLAGE · NORTH · WALES ·
· PLAN · SHOWING · DEVELOPMENT ·

per lamp. But the booklet said sternly that tenants 'must not be wasteful or extravagant'. If this was 'suspected' (the author does not offer suggestions as to how this 'suspicion' would arise), there was a possibility of fixing a meter in the house, and 'the tenant would probably find that he would have to pay considerably more for his lighting'.

Tenants could take in lodgers, with the Board's permission. Dogs and cats could be kept. Allotments would be available; gardens would be dug over by the Estate Gardener prior to a tenant moving in, so that the ground would be ready for sowing and planting. There would be an annual prize for the best garden.

Drying facilities were very important for colliers' houses: many would have a drying grate, to dry the colliers' clothes away from the living room. 'It is neither healthy nor pleasant,' said the author, 'for the collier and his sons to come home wet through and to have to sit down to meals in the room where their clothes are steaming in front of the fire'. (And not too healthy or pleasant for the woman of the house or her daughters either, of course.)

Although George and Leslie were still intending to marry, things were not settled between them. George often found himself thinking about Gwendoline, David Davies' sister, and because of this, was worried that he had committed the 'unforgiveable sin' mentioned so ambiguously in the Bible (many theologians through the ages have sought to explain what this sin is, and have differed widely in their explanations). Perhaps George was thinking that life would be easier with Gwendoline, outwardly a sweetly spiritual woman and less demanding than the more intense Leslie. His turmoil grew, and he broke off the engagement with Leslie again.

George started reading Moffat's new translation of the Bible, still searching for the peace that eluded him.

On 7 May 1914, a motion was passed by the Board of the Welsh Town Planning and Housing Trust saying that 'it was absolutely necessary that the Secretary, who had been seriously overworking, should be immediately pressed to take a sea-voyage extending over several weeks'; the necessary leave of absence was agreed. George joined a sea voyage at the end of May 1914, accompanied by his cousin. He returned to Cardiff by the end of June 1914, but the trip had not had the desired effect. He wrote sadly to Glyn:

> Life has been hell for three months. It has coincided with a great rush of anxious and confusing work. Things are quieter now in one's head, but something vital to life seems to have been smashed.

On 12 June 1914, Frank, serving with the Merchant Navy in China, wrote to George:

> Poor old Tiger, you have had an awful time of it but I hope by this that time has alleviated your suffering... Don't worry, George, look ahead; let the past lie in oblivion – Better, far better to break off your engagement than marry without love. The human heart is a complex thing – erratic, and prompted by passion and sentiment when a woman comes into one's life. But my dearest boy, does it not make one feel thankful that although our hearts respond to ideas and whims at times, we realise after all that our love for each other as a family remains untouched by adversity, or prosperity.

George saw a Harley Street specialist, and then went for a while to the psychiatric hospital at Roehampton (latterly The Priory). He wrote to Stan from the hospital in July 1914: 'I alternate between periods of calm and deep depression.'

On 15 July, his mother wrote to Glyn that George was 'going under treatment. Be sure to write a cheerful letter to him.' A little later she wrote to Glyn, 'It is quite evident that poor George is in a serious condition, he has been writing to me every day but there is nothing since Saturday. I am in the depths of anxiety, the suspense is terrible.' Mrs Davies did not seem to realise that if George was 'under treatment' – possibly an early electric shock treatment – he would be needing time to rest and sleep, without feeling obliged to write to his mother every day.

While recovering from his treatment, George wrote the first of many articles he contributed to *The Welsh Outlook* between 1914 and 1930: this was 'Houses and Hovels of Wales', commenting on the implications for Wales of John Burns' Housing and Town Planning Act, 1909:

> Disease, destitution, intemperance, immorality are the consequences and, in turn, causes in a vicious circle of degradation. In the more recently developed districts, where the houses have hardly had time to degenerate into actual slums, a new evil has grown up, the baneful effect of which is incalculable. The characteristic of urban cottage building is perhaps its deadly monotony, and monotony here, as in other things, is the devil's best ally. The long row of drab brick cottages, the wide barren street with gloomy and dingy back yards in endless repetition, make the heart sick.

George voiced his frustration that Welsh local councils were not putting the Town Planning Act into action, and called for 'not only more houses, but better houses' with gardens and adequate open space. 'Rarely has there been such an opportunity for social reformers and the Churches to get to grips with one of the deepest social evils of our time,' he wrote.

George's writing style in this article is, in spite of his depression, fluid, passionate and colourful, but derivative. It is a 'rallying call' rather than any kind of personal account. The whole 'feel' of the article, eloquent and excellent though it is, is that George sees himself as one of these 'social reformers'. There is no evidence that he had visited these homes and got to know the people in them. And yet after 1931 he became well known as someone who would walk round the hills in the Rhondda, visiting the poorest families in the area, sitting, talking and laughing with them, enjoying their company, and they his.

There is a contrast between what George feels about people

having to leave their rural homes (sadness, sympathy, identity, understanding, bereavement) and what he feels about people having to live in the urban slums (with their 'disease, destitution, intemperance, immorality'). It is almost as if his compassion turns to judgementalism half-way between the rural and the urban. There is no stated fellow-feeling for the people who have arrived in the towns; simply for those who are leaving the countryside. But perhaps George, having enjoyed his holidays in Edern in Llŷn, was sentimental about life in rural Wales: in 1911, for example, Edgar Chappel, in his *Gwalia's Homes: 50 points for housing reform*, had exposed the unsanitary and overcrowded state of housing in both urban and rural Wales, and by 1918 Anglesey's 'quaint' rural houses were said to be 'in a very grave state of decrepitude'.

By the end of 1914, Europe was five months into the First World War. George Davies was still not well enough to resume his duties with the Welsh Town Planning and Housing Trust. In March 1915, though, he still appeared on the list of administrative staff, with a salary of £500, his original salary: clearly he was getting paid in full despite having been off sick for so long.

But around that same time, after decades of searching, came a kind of epiphany for George, which some Christians would call a 'conversion'. Looking back on this time, he wrote in an article in *Y Dinesydd* (The Citizen), published on 16 April 1925:

> When you and I come to great darkness, when our world is falling to pieces, when our own hearts are like a quick-sand to build upon, when we feel we can bear anybody but ourselves – then there is nothing less than the terrific unreasonable love of God in Christ that can meet our need.

Somehow, through an unreported combination of influences, George found the personal relationship with his God, and the personal friendship of Christ, for which he had so long craved.

For the rest of his life George promoted his 'policy of personalism': personal friendships and communications between men, between men and their god, and through communion with the beauty of humanity and all creation. He regarded this simple policy as the solution to the problems of the world, and to a large extent he shunned organised religion.

Now, at last, George M. Ll. Davies had the focus for which he'd been yearning.

5

The Coming of War

By August Bank Holiday Monday 1914, war with Germany was inevitable. Sir Edward Grey made his famous remark to a friend about the lamps going out all over Europe. Lord Haldane of the War Office had started to send call-up papers to members of the Territorial Army – including George Davies, who, although he had resigned his commission, was still, officially, a private in the TA. On 4 August German armies invaded Belgium. By midnight, the war was a reality.

A conference had been arranged in Konstanz in Germany later that August with the aim of setting up a 'World Alliance for Promoting International Friendship through the Churches'. After only one day the conference had to disband due to the international situation.

Back in Britain, Henry Hodgkin and his wife, both Quakers, were appalled at the amount of pro-war feeling abounding, even amongst those who had been at the conference. They paid for an advertisement in the papers in Britain and circulated it in Germany too, affirming 'the Quaker loyalty to the principle of peace'.[1] Hodgkin gave the same message in a Quaker-run conference at Llandudno in September 1914.

About that time, Richard Roberts, originally from Blaenau Ffestiniog but minister of a Presbyterian church in London, realising that some of his young German church-members were absent from the congregation, was horrified to think that they might soon be viewed as 'the enemy'. At that point he knew he could not support the war. Roberts arranged a meeting at his house, and Hodgkin and various others attended. Late in 1914, Hodgkin and Roberts arranged a meeting in Cambridge, attended by 130 people, most of whom were finding themselves at odds with the pro-war attitudes of their churches. The Cambridge Conference reduced their sense of isolation, and the Fellowship of Reconciliation (FoR) was born. A five-point statement was drawn up, which became the basis of the FoR, and defined inter-denominational Christian Pacifism for the first time (the Quakers had defined Christian Pacifism in their own terms about 300 years earlier). One of the founder members of the FoR was George M. Ll. Davies.

From the start the FoR sought to promote itself as proactively anti-war and pro-reconciliation, rather than simply a passive peace movement. The five-point 'Basis' emphasised the response of the individual member to war, rather than involving them in group demonstrations. It did not use biblical texts, or injunctions against specific activities; rather, it stressed 'Love' as 'the only power by which evil can be overcome, and the only sufficient basis of human society'. The hope was that members would live 'a life of service for the enthronement of Love in personal, social, commercial and national life'. It is probable that the lack of a strong biblical element, and the emphasis on individual conscience, came out of the influence of the numerous Quakers at the inaugural meeting, who would not wish to be too prescriptive about how people should live their lives.

However, even with the 'Basis' set out before them, such a definition of Christian Pacifism was unlikely to pull together all the individuals in the Fellowship. Martin Ceadel's observation in his *Pacifism in Britain 1914–1945* is that the FoR was too 'heterogeneous' because of personality clashes, and

> ... reconciliation in its own ranks was embarrassingly hard to achieve in practice during its early years... what leading members had most in common was confidence in their own spiritual

intuition and the courage to stand by it even to the detriment of their careers.

Four decades later, the pacifist Canon Charles Raven (himself a fairly complex individual) wrote:

> In the First World War far more than today pacifism was apt to be the creed of uncompromising individualists, men or women inheriting the fine tradition of independence which its critics were apt to stigmatize as the Non-conformist Conscience.

Looking at the lives and characters of other prominent members of the FoR at that time, it could be argued that what some of those 'uncompromising individualists' had most in common was, to take Ceadel's words further, 'confidence in their own spiritual intuition and the courage to stand by it even to the detriment' of the FoR itself.

These personality clashes distressed George Davies. But as he wrote in an article for the *Christian Pacifist* (June 1939), he found in the FoR a place where his own uncompromising position on pacifism was welcome, even in the 'refreshing and very mixed salad of humanity' that 'made the first demands on our pacifism'. He found that he could usefully employ the strength that had been born during his father's bankruptcy to make a stand against the establishment. He also found at least a few like-minded people he could get on with.

George liked walking, reading, and riding his horse, but does not seem to have been a 'team' player. Early in the Second World War, evidence collected by Mass-Observation from Conscientious Objectors showed that most had solitary hobbies such as ornithology, painting, and cross-country running. None of those interviewed, who came from a wide range of backgrounds and had very varied occupations, mentioned taking part in team sports.[2] It is likely, then, that a Conscientious Objector – an 'uncompromising individualist' with the 'fine tradition of independence' – is a personality type. It is interesting to note that before the First World War, schoolboys at English public schools were being prepared, in their rugby and cricket teams, to be good soldiers – Sir Henry Newbolt's 1892 poem 'Vitaï Lampada' says it all – and in this 'schoolboy' mindset, those who decided not to 'play the game' but become Conscientious Objectors would have been seen as 'letting the side down'.

At the time, George was still the full-time salaried Secretary to three housing organisations (the Welsh Town Planning and Housing Trust Ltd; Wrexham Tenants Ltd; Barry Garden Suburb Ltd), whose Boards of Directors included military men. George told them he was considering resigning from his job and working for the Fellowship of Reconciliation. George wrote in 'Growing in Pacifism': 'It was not easy to explain one's fledgling pacifism to noble Lords and Major-Generals, to whom it must have seemed like religious mania'.

On 6 October 1915, the new Secretary of the Board of Wrexham Tenants Ltd wrote to George saying how deeply they regretted losing him as Secretary, but 'we all admire you for undertaking new work in a cause that your conscience tells you you ought to do'.

Early in the war George wrote an essay – later published in his book *Essays towards Peace* – telling of a train journey when he met soldiers who had been invalided out of the Army. Their banter and laughter attracted him, and he joined in the conversation. He enjoyed the fact that they considered the Germans, their 'official' enemies, to be 'chaps like ourselves... all right when ye passed a word or a joke with them'. Then they told of the death of a lieutenant, 'as nice a little toff as ever walked', and George realised that this lieutenant was the son of a rector he knew.

This essay is written in George's own style. Although it has a Christian basis, it is not a sermon, and it is not self-righteous or didactic. It is beautiful in its humour, its sadness, and its humanity, speaking movingly of the soldiers, of the Llŷn landscape and people, and of the restlessness of mankind, and asking what is the meaning of life. It is as if George is expressing what is in his own soul. It is, at last, also as if the joy of writing has come to George – or, perhaps, returned to him, for there is the liveliness of the 1903 diary entry about Martha in this essay, and in others in the collection in which it appeared.

The essay is entitled 'Est nihil vobis, O viatores omnes?' (Is it nothing to you, all ye that pass by?). It begins, 'What first attracted my attention was their astonishing expletives and capacity for beer'. George listened for a while to their conversation, and their complainings about the Depot Medical Officer, their declared 'common enemy, a miscreant of unspeakable turpitude', then he joined in the conversation:

> and soon I was in the midst of it all – the long marches in the heat of September with 96 lbs of kit to carry, 'la belle France' with its sunshine and vineyards... then the debacle and tremendous retreat from Mons when the end seemed near. They told me too, of the utter misery of the water-logged trenches, of the slimy clay, of the wet and cold and vermin, when a wound would have been a welcome relief and even death appeared an easy release.

The essay describes the rectory where the lieutenant had lived, which George had often passed when he was younger. The way the mood of the piece changes from exuberance to emptiness is masterful. Somehow, between 'Houses and Hovels' and this article, George had found his own voice, and the ability to paint pictures and convey moods with words.

This writing shows George's love for, and enjoyment of, his fellow man, and how he could turn his anger, sorrow, and passion against the war into a positive work of peace. It shows his tolerance and respect of people. He is self-questioning and ready to learn. Even after his stultifying upbringing under the influence of his mother, there seems to have been no bigotry in

George Davies. These qualities, and his gifts as a writer, have so far been under-appreciated.

On 24 October 1914, Gwen Davies wrote to Glyn in some consternation because George had been in touch with Leslie again:

> ... he says that Leslie is the only one who ever tried to help him in his difficulty but he is not writing to [win] her back. What steps he may take I cannot tell. Just the fact that he cannot keep a wife and family will I hope be sufficient to keep her from [mentioning] such a step.

(The words in square brackets are so because Gwen Davies' handwriting is next to illegible, and often it is impossible to be sure of a word.)

George still had a good position with the Welsh Town Planning and Housing Trust, so presumably Gwen meant that George could not 'keep a wife' because of his mental illness, rather than his financial position. Leslie's letters to her mother did not mention receiving a letter from George – perhaps she kept it quiet because the Royde Smiths, too, disapproved of the relationship, partly because of George's pacifism and partly because of his mental ill-health.

On 4 December, Gwen wrote again to Glyn asking him to write to George and 'cheer him up. He is very lonely there.' Perhaps Leslie had written a less than friendly letter in reply to George's. George carried on for the time being with his work for the Trust, but leaving was always on his mind, much to the distress of his mother. On 21 April 1915, she wrote from Cambridge to Glyn:

> George left here for London on Saturday. I did all I could to avoid speaking of his plans, but he told me he had told D. Davies that he may give his work up and go to the ministry. *I told him I could not stand more mental strain at present.* [Italics mine.] He said D. Davies wanted him to go on with the business... He seems very

confidentially with Dolly, and Dolly gave me to believe that it
would be the right thing for a man to give up his career for a year
and go to the ministry if he felt he was called to it. I told him that
those that are called are always qualified for the work. I tried to
sound Stanley but can get nothing out of him.

It is obvious, then, that Gwen Davies still wished to control
everything that George thought and did. Equally obviously,
neither Dolly, nor Stanley, nor George, wished to engage her
in dialogue on the subject, so she was trying to call Glyn into
her game. Her comment about her own 'mental strain' is
manipulatory, and astonishingly self-centred given that George
himself was still recovering from a fairly catastrophic mental
breakdown. It is also obvious that George by this time had
found a way of being able to ignore and resist his mother's
control to some extent. The irony of the juxtaposition of her
comment before the investiture about 'dressing up to kill
people' (for patriotic reasons), and her subsequent opposition
to George's pacifism (for religious reasons), could not have
been lost on George: neither path found favour with her.

George and his brothers loved their mother, although they
found her difficult at best. It is very likely that learning to get
on with his own life in the face of her disapproval and her
obstructiveness contributed to the necessary stubbornness and
steadfastness which later enabled George to make a stand as a
Conscientious Objector.

It is interesting to note that Glyn, the eldest of John and
Gwen Davies' sons, was the angriest of them throughout his
life, and married a formidable woman who, though a good
mother, was described by her youngest daughter Elin as 'very
– well – *ambitious* for her children'. Frank Davies disappeared
to Shanghai with the Merchant Navy after his mother had
damned him for a career decision; he eventually married an
extremely nice woman, Enid, with whom he was very happy
until her death. Stanley was always quiet and nervous, with
a tendency to depression; his first wife was an overbearing

woman. After her death, however, he married a much gentler person and was very happy; and after she, too, died, his third wife was another very warm woman. Gwen Davies seemed to make it very difficult for her sons to make a good initial choice of wives.

As an officer with the Royal Welch Fusiliers, Stanley Davies joined the Mediterranean Expeditionary Force, and wrote to George on 23 July 1915, on headed paper from the Anchor Line Twin Screw Steamer *Caledonia*, saying he expected to reach their (secret) destination the next day, and that the heat was intense. The destination was, in fact, the Gallipoli peninsula, on the Aegean Sea. In the nine months of battles in that area, 48,000 Allied and 66,000 Turkish men lost their lives, and nothing was gained.

In July George received a letter from 'Dolly', also at Gallipoli with the Royal Welch Fusiliers. Before he left, Dolly had told George that he understood the pacifist stand George was taking. The cousins had always been close. In this letter Dolly wrote:

> One longs to look to the Church for guidance, but even the Church seems to be divided in its attitude towards the present strife... Is there any honest Christian who believes that the problems of life will ever be settled by force of arms?... For pity's sake keep one clear light shining throughout this terrible darkness. Surely Christ stands, as He always did, an eternal monument of peace and goodwill towards men.
>
> There is a cry to-day for men and munitions. Will not someone strive with equal emphasis for a purging of the spiritual life of the nation, for a wholesale break from the paths of the so-called 'progress' which has brought on such a terrible calamity. Is there not only a striking but an overwhelming need for a return to the first principles of our Faith without modifications to suit the clamourings of an infidel Press. We are still in the throes of Old Testament theology; the New Testament might never have been written. All praise to those who are striving towards the dawn

amidst the jeers and derision of a populace who play while Rome is burning.

Dolly's father, David Lloyd Jones, was Gwen Davies' brother, the Presbyterian minister in Llandinam who had written such unforgiving letters when John Davies went bankrupt. Dolly's remarks are interesting in the light of his father's profession. His letter increased George's determination to work for peace, and to 'keep one clear light shining'. George quoted it in many articles during, and after, the First World War.

In September 1915, George received a very distressing letter from Stanley at Gallipoli. It is on seven sheets of very thin paper, in tiny writing in purple pencil, much of it illegible:

Fy Machgen Bach [My dear boy]
This morning I was out with an NCO and 8 men trying to clear up the battlefields of several days ago. It was a sight to make one deeply sad... How proudly many of these poor lads put on their helmets at Rushden. Now they lie about the place. Many of them have Welsh names written on them from such familiar places as Penygroes and Pwllheli. Where are the poor lads. 'Killed, Wounded or Missing Other Ranks' is all we make of them...
Men lying here and there, in some cases swollen up into hideous things with faces that have blackened. The later stage brings the stretcher bearers carrying wounded and dying men. The sights saw, my dear boy, I would [give] my right arm to forget. One poor young lad had his foot completely traversed and a great hole of blood and flesh where his ankle had been. Another poor lad with his cheek almost gone and a hole as large as a hen's egg in the side of his face and his whole body drenched with blood. Lines of people passed them every day with never a thought.
...
Above all to me – I saw our dear lad [Dolly] lie for more than a day before his Colonel put him to sleep.
If anyone talks to you about the field of battle as an ennobling place, refining and strengthening character and exalting human sacrifice – take it from me – ... it is a horrible and damnable deception.

I have felt quite incapable of thinking or feeling normally. Not more than 300 yards away the Turks have buried themselves in the ground and a little this side a lot of lads from Lleyn, Penygroes, Dinas, Portmadoc are also dug in the soil, all waiting to murder each other. What *have* they to do with each other and what is the scoundrelly influence that has brought them face to face with murder in their hearts. Every soul I have met *longs* for peace... but much more abandoned rifles and equipment must be collected before the tale is told and many a lover and many a wife must shed scalding tears over the scrap of paper that tells her that Pte – James No 4372 is on the roll of honour. (An aeroplane is humming overhead. One does not trouble to go outside to look at it.)

...

I write sadly. I have none of the... spirit of Major Rome who was watching a furious cannonade through his glasses and said simply and emphatically, 'It's a damn good fight'. Dolly's death and many – oh so many others – have made me sorrowful.

It would be surprising if George, loving his brother Stan and his cousin Dolly as he did, did not experience deep grief and anger on receipt of this letter. According to Glyn's daughter Elin, the war 'wrecked' her Uncle Stan; she said he was a bundle of nerves for years after. Stanley's love for Wales, his pain at seeing the Welsh boys in the trenches, and his anger at the attitude of '*Dulce et decorum est pro patria mori*' (It is sweet and right to die for your country), are all clear here. Stan was discharged from the Army on medical grounds in March 1918.

Stan also commented in this letter that Dolly had become very close to Gwendoline Davies (of Llandinam) before leaving for the Front, and that 'Gwenny will be stricken into the very dust' by this news. Dolly had left notes with George for Gwenny and others in his family; George travelled to Llandinam to deliver them.

Writing from Park Place, Cardiff, George told his mother, 'In [Dolly's] last letter he told me that he felt that the way of war was wrong and that he was praying for me that I should be kept strong in the way I was taking'. George calls Dolly 'almost my most intimate friend and I knew his heart', words reminiscent of those written after Herbert Roberts' death in 1905.

Gwen Davies wrote to her son Glyn, 'I feel sick with the constant anxiety about Stanley. What he has seen is terrible, poor Dolly being dead on the ground for a whole day without being found.' It seems George did not (understandably) tell his mother that Dolly's Colonel had had to shoot him – a form of 'battlefield euthanasia', which was sometimes necessary.

In spite of his deeply-held pacifist beliefs, George never opposed Dolly or Stan, or other friends, if they felt going to war was what they should do. In another letter to his mother, and in what might be regarded as a gentle hint, George wrote:

> It is a deep consolation to remember that Stanley's heart is against it all and that he is still full of the old kindness and love of others. In the last count I think that is what matters... I have seldom seen anyone who is so simple and affectionate in his judgements of other people... I am realising more and more that that is the essential thing in Christianity... Christians have so often substituted church-going for Christian conduct.

Throughout his life George always attempted to give unconditional support and respect to other people's decisions about their own lives, and perhaps his mother's controlling nature had helped him learn that lesson.

Gwen was still writing regularly of her distress at George's decision to give up his prestigious job and work for the Fellowship of Reconciliation – perhaps because of his stand for pacifism, but perhaps also because, through working for David Davies' enterprises, he had become very respectable and was about to give it all up to be unconventional. In a letter to his mother on 6 August 1915, George wrote:

> I am distressed that you are so distressed. I... feel that the moral perplexity and agony of the world is so great at present that

everyone must do his part to bring light and peace. If I could only feel it to be right, I should enlist at once and be glad and relieved to do so, but the more I reflect the more am I convinced that war is utterly against the spirit of Christ. I cannot remain merely a spectator. I must do my utmost to work for a better way, and there is an increasing number of people who feel as we do. It is bound to be very unpopular for some time but the dawn will come.

Do cheer up for my sake. Codwch eich calon, Mam bach. [*Lift up your heart, Mother.*]

Gwen Davies seems to have brought up her sons with the belief that 'the family who suffers together stays together'. Time after time in their letters each one of them 'suffers' for one of the others, over and beyond the call of duty. From their letters it is obvious that this was happening after John Davies' bankruptcy, but perhaps it occurred before that too. It had been a part of Victorian life to align with the mourning Queen, as a show of solidarity. Gwen Davies seems to have sought to bind her sons to her by her suffering. In some instances it is clear that the boys were in fact simply writing the words they knew would placate their mother. Failure to do so usually resulted in a reproachful, guilt-instilling letter from her, documenting how the situation was affecting her health. But there were times when Gwen Davies' sons genuinely felt for, and suffered with, one another.

In 1915 George again wrote to Gwen saying again how difficult it was for him to make decisions which upset her so much. 'I am convinced,' he wrote, 'that the only way by which one can kill a wrong idea is by a right idea, and in time it will do its work if it is advocated with courage, patience and persistence'. It might be that George was trying to sow a general principle here, as much as to prevent her nagging on this specific issue. However, he continued his work in Cardiff with the Trust, 'purely,' as he wrote to his mother, 'in deference to your entreaties and to allay your fears'.

By the summer of 1915, the FoR had moved to a new office

in Red Lion Square in London, and there were around fifteen local branches in existence, several of them in Wales. Richard Roberts became General Secretary. He had been minister of a church in Crouch End, but in 1914 his pacifism began to cause problems with his congregation. He left to work for the FoR but was unhappy in an administrative role.

After Dolly's death in 1915, and against the pleadings of Gwen Davies, George finally left the Welsh Town Planning and Housing Trust and went to London to become Richard Roberts' assistant, receiving £10 a month for expenses – a considerable drop in earnings. George went to the role experienced in office work, financial affairs, and administration, leaving Roberts free to travel and to oversee new branches.

In December 1915 Roberts left for a pastorate in New York. Now George was both Secretary of the Fellowship, and his own assistant. He enjoyed his work and the simplicity of his life.

On 3 February 1916, Leslie Royde Smith wrote to her mother:

> This letter is about George. I discovered about a fortnight ago that he was living in London. He had thrown up his Housing work and offered his services free to the Fellowship of Reconciliation. He has no kind of salary, but only living and travelling expenses. Moreover he believes in being quite poor and does not wish to have any money. How do I know all this? Because about 10 days ago he came to see me. He is very well and active and happy, and looks entirely different from the pitiable wreck that I parted from two years ago. From a prudent and worldly point of view he is quite impossible as a husband; but if he came to live at Midholm, and if I went on working, and we fed on beans, and decided that we need never have new boots or toothbrushes, we think we might be very happy if we got married – so we probably shall.
>
> You always said that poverty was the least of all evils, didn't you! I'll go further than that to say that in some conditions it is a very blessed state. Don't you… worry because you think I'm going to commit a desperate indiscretion. I'm not!

So, then, George's mother disapproved of Leslie's nationality, religion, and her sister's marriage problems; Leslie's father was unhappy about George's pacifism and his mental health problems. Despite these objections, there was clearly something special between George and Leslie, and they were married quietly on 5 February 1916 at St Luke's Church in Finchley. Dr Fearon Halliday, a psychotherapist, was best man; only four other people were present. From the date of Leslie's letter it seems that the marriage had already been arranged when she wrote to her mother, and that the timing of the letter was such as to prevent any interference. Gwen Davies and the Royde Smith family did accept the marriage after the event.

George moved into Leslie's house, 10 Midholm, Hampstead Garden Suburb. Leslie carried on teaching Domestic Science; George continued working for the FoR. With his £10 a month expenses from that organisation, plus the little he had saved, Leslie's earnings, and a bit of financial help from her family, the couple managed to survive. George wrote to his mother:

> Leslie is quite well and working hard. She does the washing herself too. Her knowledge of cookery comes in very useful. She used to lecture in various parts of the country on economy in cooking.
>
> On Saturday [Leslie's] aunt and uncle and cousin – the Whitley-Thompsons – came to tea and liked the little house very much. They were very nice and kind but far too prosperous. They are very rich and the daughter's husband is heir to a peerage. How empty wealth and titles seem in these days. I realise their danger more and more.

In his diary George listed his personal expenses as:

Old Man 3s
Tramp 2s 6d
3 lbs Margarine 1s 10½d
Haircut 6d
Telegram Leslie 2s
Socks 3s 6d

Charity 1s
[Welsh] Outlook 6d
Stamps 2s

The list above adds up to 16s 10d, with George giving a total
of 6s 6d to the Old Man, the Tramp, and a Charity. The former
bank manager clearly kept meticulous records of every penny
he spent, but even though he was now far from rich he still
gave to the poor. Leslie, who had initially fallen in love with a
bank manager and TA Officer, was beginning to find out how
much George Davies' priorities had changed.

The couple knew that they would have to face the possibility
of George going into prison because of his stand against the
war. They would, of course, have discussed this before marrying
– it was part of the work of the FoR to furnish young men
with information about becoming a CO. But even with this
preparation, neither could have foreseen how dramatically the
next four years would change George.

6

The Peaceful Route to Prison

ON 2 MARCH 1916, the Military Conscription Act came into force. Not enough volunteers had gone to the front (vast numbers were being killed or wounded), and it was considered necessary to compel men to go. On 15 August 1915, all single men between eighteen and forty-one were called up. Some were exempt: clergy of any denomination, those medically rejected, those in reserved occupations, men who supported relatives, some civil servants, and Conscientious Objectors.

Many people in Britain deplored conscientious objection. Even the Quakers, who had been against war for centuries, were condemned. As Martin Ceadel says in *Pacifism in Britain*, until conscription, many people believed that pacifists were merely cowards who wished to avoid fighting. Conscription brought pacifists head-to-head with the government, and absolute pacifism into public awareness. 'Indeed,' Ceadel wrote, 'the martyrdom of the absolutists has created a mythology which has coloured most accounts of pacifism in the Great War.'

Certainly, later in his life, George Davies became known as a 'saint' in Wales, and was a hero to many young men. He was not the only Welshman to be incarcerated as a CO during the war, but came to represent, to Welsh Christians at least, the highest ideal.

As well as the Fellowship of Reconciliation, another British anti-war organisation was formed in 1914 – the No-Conscription Fellowship (N-CF), headed by Fenner Brockway (later Lord Brockway of Eton and Slough) and Clifford Allen (later Lord Hurtwood). Both these men ended up in prison. The N-CF's statement of principles required members to 'refuse from conscientious motives to bear arms because they consider human life to be sacred': thus it was more able than the FoR to be a catch-all for religious and secular objectors alike. In spite of the press referring to them as the 'save their skins brigade', the movement grew rapidly. There was so much opposition to the organisation that it became 'an extraordinarily efficient underground movement', with a code to mislead police about the locations of meetings, and a printing press that was moved to a different house each night.[1]

Conscientious objection was claimed by around 16,000 men in the First World War. Some were Quakers or Non-conformists from the FoR. Many were members of the No-Conscription Fellowship, or various religious groups including the Salvation Army and the Jehovah's Witnesses. Some Conscientious Objectors were from the Independent Labour Party, and there were other Socialist COs too. Many were not connected with any organisation, but simply hated war. All were called before tribunals, which decided whether they should be accorded 'unconditional exemption' from any war service (even civilian service) or be given some kind of wartime work. The tribunals were decentralised, and individual panel members were often confused about government policy. The main problem was that many tribunal members could not believe that some men simply objected to the whole concept of war.

Martin Ceadel reports that 64 per cent of the objectors co-operated with the rulings of the tribunal system; 5,944 initially resisted the terms of their exemption. Some 'absolutist' COs defied the tribunals' decisions; many later found that compromises could be made. But George Davies was not a compromiser. He knew that eventually he would be imprisoned.

The tribunal of George Davies (No. 16719) was held on 6 May 1916 in Finchley. His tribunal statement begins:

> I cannot take part in either combatant or non-combatant war service, as all war services are to me a negation of the plain teaching of Jesus Christ that we should forgive, help, and love even our enemies, as we expect God to forgive us, and that it is vain for us to call Him Lord and Master if we do not obey his chief commandment to love.

Further, George explained that he had resigned from the Housing Associations because, although he had enjoyed the 'philanthropic work of social benefit, with friendships and opportunities which I valued deeply', he felt sure there was a more urgent duty towards his fellow men. George said that his decision to work full-time for the FoR was made after 'a conversation in June 1915 with a group of former fellow-officers who were leaving for the Front, and who were also distressed by the difficulty of reconciling war with Christ's teaching'.

George believed his 'work of national importance' during the war was to 'advocate to men [Christ's] way of life', adding that this was even more important than usual because of his fear that 'the revulsion against war, which is spreading so rapidly among the people, should become a revolution and plunge the country into civil, industrial and class wars', and because of the Fellowship of Reconciliation's view that men should be reconciled to each other 'by advocating a practical belief in love'.

The tribunal required George Davies to undertake 'alternative service'.

First of all, he went to the FoR's newly-established experimental home for delinquent youngsters, the Riverside Settlement, Melton Mowbray, to oversee the financial side of the project, and get involved with the work. From the minutes of meetings of the FoR it seems this 'Delinquents' Colony' was set up out of a kind of enthusiasm for 'doing' reconciliation wherever possible, rather than with any careful business plan, but the general idea was excellent, and based on the ideas of Homer Lane, the complex American who had (in 1913) begun a similar experiment known as The Little Commonwealth.[2]

It was an era of increasing interest in 'alternative' methods of educating children, and of working with young offenders. The school system developed by Maria Montessori (1870–1952) was being applied through Europe (George's brother Glyn's four children, Gwen, Mair, Elin and Gwion, were educated by their mother on Montessori lines), and others were beginning to implement the ideas of Freud, Marx and Jung. Johann Pestalozzi (1746–1827), the Swiss educational reformer, said, 'I knew no order, no method, which did not rest upon the children's conviction of my love for them. I did not care to know any other'.

Homer Lane was thrilled by these words, and applied the same approach in the Little Commonwealth. His work with young offenders was important and forward-looking, but his avant-garde methods were controversial. Lane was always difficult to work with, and eventually, he was ousted in disgrace when he took Pestalozzi's words to the extreme; former residents in the Little Commonwealth levelled accusations of sexual abuse at him.

In an article, 'Growing in Pacifism', in *The Christian Pacifist* (June 1939), George Davies described part of his role at Riverside thus:

> Actually to live and eat and work day by day with a dozen young criminals and to meet violence, cruelty, laziness and lust, face to face, was something entirely different from the cloistered study of theories of freedom and forgiveness. It meant learning the difference between organising and improvising, between impersonal ideas of pacifism and personal peace-making.

This demonstrates George's flexibility, his readiness to learn and change, and his ability to relate to people in the personal way that became his 'trademark' for the rest of his life. He admitted that contact with the young people at Riverside changed his outlook on many things. According to George:

> The delinquents... included A, the leader of a criminal gang which had attacked and robbed men at the London Docks, D, who had had several convictions for theft, and whose last escapade was to steal £500 worth of silk bales by jumping on to the driver's seat while the driver was in a shop; L for shop-lifting and fighting with knives; E, who had spent five years at a Reformatory for being beyond control, and on release had half-killed her mother; and so on.

The first youngsters were released from prison into the care of the Riverside warden, who refused a police escort and walked with them to the station. When they arrived at Riverside, George was gardening. They helped him for a while, then got bored and started testing boundaries. No action was taken. Then one girl, 'Flash Lizzie', was found with pad and pencil, 'making rules' for them all, and the rules they chose were kept to. The staff were unflappable. When one child swore, one member of staff decided to swear too, to make it less fun.

Riverside was a progressive and brave project. For several of the residents, it worked well. Unfortunately, however, the Settlement suffered from the staff's personality clashes. Russell Hoare, the warden, was a CO who had received 'complete exemption'. Like Homer Lane (though lacking his charm and charisma), Hoare seemed to go out of his way to be difficult to work with, and to sabotage his own best efforts. He had a 'desire to produce rebels'.[3] This made it difficult for middle-class Quaker intellectual 'progressives' (i.e. most of the staff) to work with him. Hoare eventually became disillusioned and joined a closed Roman Catholic order.

During his time at Riverside, George learned something more about living among working-class people, and enjoying their company; he also had a chance to see that this way of working with young offenders chimed with his growing vision for non-violence, love, reconciliation, and peace-making. The 'child-centred approach' to education became very important to George. Most importantly, his philosophy of 'personalism' was first put into action at Riverside, both with staff and with the young people.

Nine years after leaving the Settlement, George was sad to discover that Riverside was in financial trouble. He had attempted from the start to establish the Settlement on a sound basis; after he left, nobody even reasonably able seems to have taken over. It seems that the FoR's idealism, and their initial enthusiasm for the project, was greater than the vision for the whole, and long-term, picture. In this, Riverside had much in common with other Settlements around this time, many of which suffered from the same triumph of optimism over realism: founders and participants tended to have rose-coloured and high-minded dreams, which fizzled out when ugly practicalities, such as division of labour, spending constraints, or the difficulties of living with other people, intervened. In December 1925 the Committee sent out a circular letter asking for the signatures of three-quarters of FoR members in order to dissolve the Settlement. Apparently this was achieved.

George had learned painful lessons that he could take to future projects. As an example of co-operative working, Riverside looked at the start to be extremely worthwhile, but it was a gamble with faith. Too many things seem to have been done by idealists without a strong guiding hand. Some of the FoR members were themselves needy people whose common sense seems to have been overruled by the necessity of the project. These errors tended to be repeated in other Settlements, as George discovered a few years later.

While George worked at Riverside, Leslie, still in London, was pregnant. In late September 1916, her anxious husband told his mother that he was afraid of Leslie being alarmed by Zeppelins, which were bombing England. He went on: 'It seems very strange and unreal to think of having a child to care for and we both feel it a glad and great responsibility to try and guide his [*sic*] feet into the way of peace.'

Leslie decided she would go into a nursing home in Colwyn Bay to have the baby, and stayed with her sister Maude there for a month meanwhile. Jane was born on 20 November 1916 in Tandderwen Nursing Home in Colwyn Bay. Her parents were overjoyed. Jane was given the second name of Elinor, but at some stage it was replaced by Hedd ('peace'), which, Jane told me, she later disliked intensely. A few days after the birth Leslie wrote to her mother: 'She's more ridiculously like George than you can imagine. He thought her very lovely.'

A few weeks later, George's term at Riverside came to an end. He returned to his beloved Llŷn hoping to get work on a farm, but many people were reluctant to take on a 'Conshi'. Eventually, early in 1917, he started work as a farm labourer with Robert Hughes at Uwchlawffynnon. It is interesting that Robert Hughes gave George – by his speech and manner (and probably by his faulty Welsh) clearly a 'gentleman' – the parlour and the best bedroom in the farmhouse.

George wrote to Gwen Davies of his joy: 'It is a wonderful experience to be on the hills in the evening light. The glory of the colours and the silence are beyond description. Already I have rescued several sheep from the brambles.'

In the same letter George said that he and Leslie had decided to give his mother about £100 of shares to reduce Gwen's anxiety: 'It is part of my creed that I ought not to save money but to trust to God and do my duty by serving my fellows. If anyone offered me a bit of money I feel I should refuse it.' Again George demonstrates his lack of trust in money, and his active desire for simplicity of living.

After a few weeks George moved farms, and went to work for Huw and Ann Roberts at Moelfre Fawr, Llanaelhaearn, as a shepherd. This was to prove a happy development in

George's life. Leslie and Jane were still living with her sister in Colwyn Bay. Leslie's mother wanted George to find some work nearer London, but Leslie listed the reasons why he could not:

1 He must do either dock-labouring, forestry, or agricultural work.
2 Agriculture is best-paying.
3 English people/farmers have a very strong prejudice against conscientious objectors.
4 In Llŷn they welcome him whole-heartedly, and he loves them ditto.
5 It is his native heath.
6 He doesn't want Jane and me to be anywhere in Zeppelin radius.
7 He says that when peace is declared the towns will not be safe places after the soldiers are back, etc, and as he couldn't live with us in London if he were farming, he prefers that we go to him now for good.
8 We may decide to settle on the land.

The former bank manager was employed, officially, as a shepherd, at 8 shillings a week:[4] at £20 a year, this income is tiny compared to his FoR expenses, and even more so compared with the £500 a year he earned as Secretary to the Housing Associations. George learned how to work with a sheepdog on the mountains, how to care for a flock of sheep, and how to train horses with love and kindness. Huw and Ann's daughter Gwladys Japheth (née Roberts) told me that George was prepared to do any job on the farm, and would do a job that needed doing without being asked, but he was not a very good shepherd, and her parents didn't like to give him too much to do because he hadn't been born to the work and had been a bank manager. She told me her parents had come to love George very much.

Gwladys said George was 'A *clean* man. No evil thoughts. He thought the best of everyone, and got the best from everyone.'

(In Welsh, the word '*glân*' is used to describe someone who in English might be called 'clean' or 'pure', or even 'holy'.)

George continued to preach the message of peace. He would speak anywhere – in the market-places and town squares, and in the chapels, if they would have him. This was against the terms of the tribunal's decision: it was considered that preaching against the war would undermine national morale.

In the first volume of his autobiography, *Pererindod Heddwch* ('pilgrimage of peace', published in Welsh in 1943, though not the same as the book *Pilgrimage of Peace* published in English!), George Davies wrote of going in fear and trembling to Pwllheli Fair hoping to declare his message of peace. There were many soldiers and sailors there, and policemen, but when they had heard him speak some of them shook his hand warmly. Thereafter he went from village to village for a week, and to his surprise, he found that the local people felt as he did, and their response was 'more of welcome than of hostility'.

On one occasion he visited Aberdaron, at the tip of Llŷn, and preached to the villagers from the steps of Gegin Fawr in the village centre. An English officer went up to him, saying, 'I am the ADC to the GOC Western Command. I'll have you in clink for this.' He marched George off into the Ship Hotel, and took George's name. George told him that he had duties to his own king. The officer 'went a bit quiet, and I heard nothing further'. When George stepped out of the hotel he saw some of his old friends, Huw Felin, Wil Gegin and others, who had gathered to wait for him, and who were threatening to throw the officer head-first into the river! George persuaded them not to, saying that it would be completely at odds with all his beliefs, 'but I couldn't fail to feel warmly about them for their protectiveness'.

Interestingly, in other versions of this story, people have said that George emerged from the hotel with blood on his face, having been roughed up. George himself does not say this in *Pererindod Heddwch*; perhaps, after so long, he did not wish to; perhaps it did not happen.

It was ironic that at the same time as George Davies was preaching peace in the north of Wales, the Rev. Dr John Williams (from Brynsiencyn on Anglesey), who had been the Davies family's minister at Princes Road Chapel, Liverpool, from 1895 to 1904, was also touring villages in Llŷn, sometimes even conducting chapel services in army uniform and clerical collar, and in God's name recruiting men to fight in the army of the King of England. George went to Llithfaen once to hear him speak, and afterwards the two men, whom many would have considered to be in opposition, sat by someone's fire in the village, talking about the way Lloyd George had forgotten Wales, and how disappointed 'Wilias Brynsiencyn' was with Winston Churchill. The two men listened with respect to each other's views. Wilias Brynsiencyn was especially interested in what George had been doing at Riverside, and the philosophy of the place. He observed, 'This is what we need for the future, but the world is not mature enough for it yet'.[5]

George wrote in May 1917 to his old friend Thomas Jones, by then Assistant Secretary to Lloyd George's Cabinet in London: 'How far apart our paths have led, yours to the confidence of statesmen and the direction of vast enterprises, mine to a mountain farm and labourer's life.' He continued by saying how lovely was the area where he was living, and how much he respected the local people 'who bring up their families on £1 a week'. He went on:

I have seen the lads get notices to join up. They hardly conceive of any other course than to obey though they loathe the whole business especially that of being compelled to kill other lads against whom they have no quarrel. It is the mothers in the twilight, and the fathers as they follow the plough by the hour, on whose hearts the pain of it falls most, drop by drop in the silence... By now there has spread a deep and most bitter

GEORGE DAVIES: PILGRIM OF PEACE

disillusionment. I doubt if any man is so suspected in these parts as Lloyd George. Everywhere the sense of it is: 'Y mae o wedi gwerthu ni i fod yn fawr.' [He has sold us to become great.]

This was in 1917; at the start of the war, however, according to historian Dr John Davies, 'Lloyd George's enthusiasm for the war was one of the most important factors in inducing [Welshmen] to join the army'.

George travelled once from Llanaelhaearn to Cricieth, to Lloyd George's home, to try to persuade him to consider peace negotiations, but Lloyd George would not listen. A story was told (in *Crynhoad* [Digest], April 1951) about the rest of that journey, by the stationmaster at Afon Wen. This is one of the earliest recorded elevations of George Davies to something other than 'normal':

> 11 o'clock, a knock at the door, and I saw a tall, handsome man, who, in a melodious voice asked if he might sleep the night in one of the waiting rooms! I noticed that his knees were wet, and after inviting him in, with the wife making him a cup of tea, he began his story. He had walked from Llanaelhaearn to Brynawelon so as to try the way of the Lamb since the way of the lion had failed. His plea to the Prime Minister was in vain, and near Bontfechan, in spite of the dew, he fell to his knees... to pray for a new dawn. Following his heartfelt prayer, he felt too weak to proceed with his journey that night, so when he saw a light at Afon Wen he made a beeline for it, and we had the privilege, unknowingly, of giving lodging to an angel.

The period working on the Roberts' farm was perhaps the happiest time in the whole of George Davies' life. He was living in Wales, and specifically in Llŷn, in his view the best place on earth. He was living a simple life in the country, with good friends, and with Leslie and little Jane. He was working hard physically, and also able to preach in some of the local chapels. His mental health appears to have been good. Prison was inevitable at some stage because, by preaching peace ('undermining morale'!) he was not keeping to the terms of his exemption from military service. But George doesn't appear to have lived in fear of the future. There is much evidence that he and Leslie had discussed and read about prison, to prepare them both for what lay ahead. On 27 March he wrote to his mother about how much he was enjoying the life he was leading, but he felt he should be doing more. He was finding a lot of sympathy among the ordinary people; the 'deadness', he said, was 'mostly in the Ministers and deacons, especially the older ones'. He saw a danger in membership of churches and chapels: 'People get deceived into thinking that it is enough to behave and to believe like other people instead of trying to obey the teaching of Jesus quite simply.'

George showed unending care for his mother, sending her frequent letters, money, and gifts of food when rationing was tight. She was no doubt 'sick with anxiety' about him, as usual. George was concerned about what would happen to Leslie and Jane while he was locked up. He was spending more and more time going round Llŷn, to fairs, markets and villages, 'preaching for peace and goodwill among men'. Many people believed as George did about the war, and many shared his views about war in general, but he also discovered other attitudes. He wrote to his mother that he had found 'kindness and love and sympathy' from the ordinary people of the area, but:

> Church and Chapel teaching is the greatest barrier to overcome. Listening to sermons and attending services has deadened people's minds to the teaching of Christ. The teaching is principally set forth in the Sermon on the Mount, which no Church observes.

This is another damning indictment of the religious bodies of Wales, particularly the judgement that they ignored Christ's Sermon on the Mount, which includes such pronouncements as 'Blessed are the peace-makers, for theirs is the kingdom of heaven'. Later in the year, George wrote to Gwen Davies that he was quite prepared to face prison, but he felt compelled to continue attempting to 'awaken people to love each other (which is to believe in God)'.

In September 1917, George went to the Hiring Fair in Pwllheli, and told his mother how sadly he watched many agricultural workers, instead of being employed for work on farms, being conscripted into the army. Presumably by definition they were not, on that specific day, actually 'employed' in an agricultural job, and therefore not considered – on that day – to be in a 'reserved occupation'.

George knew he was putting himself in an untenable position by continuing to work for peace, but he knew that was his calling, and he faced his fate.

George, Leslie and Jane next moved to a cottage, Tancelyn, on the estate of Mr and Mrs J. Henry Jones at Ty'n-y-Maes, Nant Ffrancon. Henry Jones had heard about George, and was in sympathy with him. He knew George's brother Stanley, too.

Inevitably George was summoned to the Central Tribunal in London to explain why he had continued to preach against the war, contrary to the terms of his tribunal. On his way to London he visited a peace conference held by the FoR in Llandrindod Wells,[6] and was instrumental in wording a resolution calling on governments to try to end the war. Also at that conference, George made a friend of the pacifist, schoolteacher, novelist and nationalist, D. J. Williams (always known in Wales as DJ). Although George attended the conference in Stan's old clothes (much too short for George!), and penniless, to DJ 'he looked like a prince among men with his handsome face lighting up the gathering'. George and DJ met many times thereafter.

In London, George went before the Marquess of Salisbury (Chairman of the Central Tribunal) to explain why he had broken the terms of his exemption. George said he had to obey God's will. Lord Salisbury referred George's case to the War Cabinet where, ironically, George was defended by an old Anglo-Boer War soldier, Lord Milner, but opposed by his fellow-Welshman David Lloyd George, the Prime Minister.

Lloyd George declared, 'We must win the war', and said that preaching reconciliation undermined national morale.

George had thus succeeded in putting his case not only to a tribunal but also to the War Cabinet. He forced these war leaders to face, personally and directly, the reality of the principles of conscientious objection.

George was given another three months to mend his ways, and went back to Nant Ffrancon. On 13 November, Leslie wrote to her father:

> George was called up last Tuesday – 6th – but as they allow 14 days before posting them as deserters he probably won't be arrested till next Monday or Tuesday – Jane's birthday, no doubt! I hope they won't try torturing him in prison like they have some of the others. Solitary confinement is a sufficient form of torture, I believe.

Leslie demonstrated an amazing calm and matter-of-factness in the face of her beloved husband going to prison. Mrs Jones insisted she and Jane should stay on at Ty'n-y-Maes.

George sent the call-up form back, unfilled, with a covering letter saying that he could not fill it in because he had obeyed the call of the 'Higher King'. George was told that he would be taken to court in Bangor the next morning. The judges at Bangor sent him to the military. He travelled, unescorted, by train to Wrexham, where he was met by the Arresting Officer – his old banking friend Dan Thomas – and a few other friendly Territorial Army officers known to George. Private Davies was sent to the guardroom.

The court martial was held in December 1917. Leslie wrote to her mother:

> [George] is to be court-martialled tomorrow – Monday – then I must find out the rules of whichever prison he is sent to before I can say whether he will be allowed parcels. I should think not, because they punish conscience with the hardest sentence (like the worst criminals) and they have solitary confinement and are only allowed one visitor once every 2 months, and one letter ditto,

I believe. There are about 1500 conscience men in prison. 12 of them have been committed to asylums. One died 2 days ago and one was removed to a nursing home, the hardiest of them are still alive through very much undermined in health and mind by the confinement and the tortures that some of them have been put to. The record is unspeakably shocking. The commandant of Wandsworth Gaol was dismissed because of the way he had allowed one of them to be treated. And we pretend that we are 'fighting for liberty'...

I write to G. every day as so far he is still in the guard-room (no furniture, no lights – they sleep on the floor and have to go to bed at 5, because walking about then becomes dangerous!) and have sent him some things – he is allowed visitors, so except for the dark and dirt he is not so badly off, especially as he has made great friends with the 3 other men who are shut up there.

Leslie reported that she and Jane would be spending Christmas with 'the old lady', Gwen Davies, 'who is pathetically fond of Jane... I think she's quite fond of me now – at any rate she has forgiven me heartily'.

Perhaps Gwen Davies could see that George was happy with Leslie. All the evidence at this time is that the couple were very much in love, while also being very strong-minded and independent people. Writing to her father, Leslie commented that she was glad she had done things with her life prior to settling into marriage. Having been something of a career woman, Leslie was strong enough to face George going into prison, and to survive it, whilst bringing up their daughter. George seemed to draw from Leslie's strength. There appeared to be no resentment on Leslie's part, at that time, about living in poverty with a farm labourer in a tiny cottage in the Welsh countryside.

Up to the time he entered prison at the age of thirty-seven, George Davies had suffered a difficult childhood, long-term mental illness including two major breakdowns, a broken engagement, the deaths of family members and friends, and a significant change in status and income – from bank manager and Territorial Army officer to shepherd. But all the changes seemed to have made him more emotionally robust, and altogether stronger in spirit. He had escaped from the suffocation of the bank and suburbia. He was living in his beloved Wales, in the countryside, a working man respected by other working men, at a healthy distance from his mother and her neuroses, with a strongly independent-minded wife and small daughter. He had decided not to fight in the war. Many saw fighting as the truly brave (and masculine) thing to do, while the Conscientious Objector was often seen as 'shirking, lazy, spineless, un-Christian, unpatriotic, and un-English/British... sometimes he was perceived of as womanly... or was suspected of sexual inversion'.[7]

But George, who had found 'man's work' in the Territorial Army and had then decided for pacifism, had the strength and integrity to carry his decision through to the end.

While waiting for his court martial, George was put in a cell with three others on various military charges, all Expeditionary Force men (the first to go to the Front in 1914). He wrote about them in an essay, 'Letter from a Guardroom' (published in *Essays Towards Peace*, London, 1946). Initially, the men told their stories with 'a careless, riotous abandon', but then George found 'that there is a hypocrisy of evil, no less than a hypocrisy of good; the swashbuckler is often only the outer man'. For George, used to the middle-class chapel-goers of his youth, fond of promoting their own goodness while snubbing and persecuting the less well-off, it was quite a revelation to him to see that the opposite existed.

George began to appreciate these 'toughs' as people from whom he could learn – not simply about 'prison deportment', but about life itself: 'These days... have been an extraordinary revelation to me of man's unconquerable mind. The goodness of [the toughs] blooms like wild roses on brambles, and the real man in them has often the heart of a child.' In the light of George's struggle to find 'man's work' in the middle-class world a few years before, it is interesting that he could now see in these working-class men the juxtaposition of the rose on the bramble, of the child in the real man.

Something within George began to relate in a deep and happy way to these men. He missed this masculine camaraderie between 1919, when he left prison, until he went to work with unemployed miners in 1931. This lack was to be the biggest problem for him in those intervening years, when he was far more rudderless even than he had been before 1914.

George's court martial was held in December 1917. He reported it with a certain angry irony:

> My three judges solemnly repeated the oath 'to administer justice according to the Army Act' concluding 'So help me God' and kissing a copy of the New Testament. My defence was simply that even though 'deemed to be a soldier' I was faced with the obligations of a higher obedience – to my conscience and to another King's regulations – Christ's, whose help they had invoked – whose written teaching their lips had kissed in reverence. My sincerity had been admitted by the three tribunals before whom I had appeared…
>
> The sentence was not promulgated for some days, when I was marched to the parade ground, and in the presence of all sentenced to 112 days' hard labour. It might have appeared more solemn had not one of the soldiers winked encouragingly at me. Meanwhile the dawn flushed its splendour over the eastern sky, 'the clouds were touched and in their silent faces did I read unutterable love'. Against such a background, the panoply of human justice and the pride of armed force seemed rather trivial.

The Lieutenant-Colonel, sentencing George to prison, said, 'George Maitland Lloyd Davies, I must condemn you to the cell because you have refused to obey an order issued on behalf of His Majesty King George V, but God knows that I condemn a far better man than myself' ('Letters from Prison I', in *Essays Towards Peace*).

George Davies spent Christmas Day 1917 in the guardroom. On Boxing Day he left for Wormwood Scrubs prison, 'my last recollections of the army being the sergeant of the guard pressing me to take a cake that his wife had sent him, and the escort's whispered encouragement at the prison gate to 'keep a good heart'.

The sentence of 112 days of hard labour would have taken George Davies up to about 16 April 1918. In fact he, in common with most COs, was to be imprisoned until June 1919, long after the war had ended.

7

Prison

LATE IN DECEMBER 1917, Prisoner Number 3158 George Davies entered Wormwood Scrubs prison in London. He wrote to Stanley later that 'The Scrubs was an experience for which I shall always be grateful. It showed how love and faith overcome the unkindness and brutality of human punishments.' Despite these brave words, George Davies seems, judging by his own writings, those of others, and from the evidence of friends and family, to have suffered mentally during and after his time in prison. His philosophy and values were also changed, and his physical health was permanently damaged by the regime of near-starvation.

During George's time in prison he managed to get essays and letters smuggled out to Leslie – mostly by visiting Quakers. In 'Letters from Prison II', he wrote of his arrival at Wormwood Scrubs:

> Here was no smile nor word of human sympathy – only orders, rough and peremptory. One's clothes were stripped and a convict's rough, unsightly garb was substituted. A pint of porridge was handed to me and then I was marched to a great hall with gallery after gallery of cells, turned into one of them, the iron door slammed and locked behind me – I was in prison.

George found the prison system dehumanised both inmates and warders:

> ... men who had apparently been schooled out of all gentleness, or sympathy or compassion – who roared threateningly at one for

any mistake or omission, who slammed the doors on one, who said nothing to one that was not an order or a complaint.

In 'Letters from Prison III', he described:

The... pyramid of fear... Prisoners, warder, chief warder, governor, prison commissioners, Home Office, and, behind them, Parliament, the public – each layer pressing the layer beneath, each delegation of coercion becoming more official and inhuman, sharper and heavier, until at the last the Legislative Act ushered in, as statesmanship, with due perorations that promise 'a world safe for democracy', created what the prisons of England are today.

Of the Fellowship of Reconciliation's 1,269 members of military age in 1916 – including George M. Ll. Davies – only 296 were imprisoned, and sentenced to 'hard labour'. Many of these were traumatised mentally and affected physically by serving their sentences;[1] Stephen Hobhouse, later one of the authors of *English Prisons To-day*, was totally broken by his time in prison and never recovered from his experiences.[2]

There were many reasons for men becoming Conscientious Objectors. Not all were pacifists. Even the pacifists differed widely from one another, and many were not 'pacifistic' in their personal lives: Bertrand Russell said that 'in some men the habit of standing out against the herd had become so ingrained that they could not co-operate with anybody about anything'. In *Reconciliation* (1932), George Davies himself said he was astonished at hearing that when another CO had been asked at his tribunal if he had any objection to killing, he answered: 'I've no objection to killing the likes of you,' and he shoved the table at them.

In February 1919, by which time they considered they should have been released, COs caused huge problems for the prison service – and for their less radical fellow-prisoners – by going on hunger strike in ten prisons, and by causing a disturbance throughout the night in others. This forced the

The CO in Prison: two cards, found in George Davies' papers.

government's hand; by April 1919 all COs who had served a minimum of twenty months were released; by August the rest had gone too.

The 'Silent and Separate Systems' in British prisons (one person per cell, and no communication of any type) were implemented in the eighteenth century, with the intention of keeping prisoners apart so they could not corrupt each other, and giving the offender time to contemplate his crime. But these systems increased the incidence of insanity amongst prisoners. After the Prison Act of 1898, a new principle was expressed: that prisons should be for reformation of criminals and deterrence of crime, rather than simply for punishment. Unproductive labour was to be abolished; books and educational facilities were to be more widely available; aid and care were to be extended to prisoners before and after release; the sentence of 'hard labour' was the most severe category of punishment available to the courts, and was meant to be less commonly used than 'penal servitude'.

In practice, though, reforms were slow to be implemented. The courts still used 'hard labour' more than other categories, and after sentence a lot depended on the particular prison, and the particular governor. Certainly the prison system was ill-equipped to deal with prisoners incarcerated only for reasons of their own conscience.

Judging by George's experiences, and those of other COs in the English prison system between 1916 and 1919, not much had changed since Oscar Wilde was in Reading Gaol in 1898. In 'Letters from Prison II', George quotes four stanzas of Wilde's 'Ballad of Reading Gaol', without comment. One is:

> Like ape or clown in monstrous garb
> With crooked arrows starred,
> Silently we went round and round
> The slippery asphalt yard.
> Silently we went round and round
> And no man spoke a word.

Stephen Hobhouse's powerful pamphlet *An English Prison from Within* reported that 'In March 1919 there are still 1500 Absolutists doing hard labour':

> Most of them have been sentenced more than once to the severest form of imprisonment known to the law, over periods extending in some cases to nearly three years, and they are continually being sentenced now, even after the Armistice. Of the 54 men who have died since arrest, 8 died actually in prison, 1 in an asylum, 11 in Home Office camps, and 6 committed suicide. 37 have become mentally affected, while 189 have been released from prison because of their shattered health since Lord Curzon made (on December 4th 1917) his promise that this should be done.[3]

Hobhouse described himself as 'a recent convert [to Quakerism] of unusual intensity: a repressed and idealistic product of Eton and Balliol, who had renounced patriotism, capitalism and Anglicanism under the influence of a nervous breakdown and the works of Tolstoy'.

Hobhouse reported that from April 1917 particularly, prison rations – never generous – were severely curtailed. The total daily rations during a man's first week in prison were 24 oz bread, 2 pints gruel, and 1 pint porridge (with occasional potatoes or suet pudding). From that first week the rations increased, but were still 'wretchedly inadequate'. Many men suffered seriously from under-feeding. 'Nearly all of us constantly knew what hunger means,' he wrote. When a man was seen by a warder passing bread to another, both were reported to the Governor; both were penalised by extension of their term of imprisonment by a few days, and three days' solitary confinement on bread and water. Conscientious Objectors were treated in exactly the same way as others doing hard labour, except that COs who had been inside for twelve months were 'permitted to have books sent in from the outside, and the provision daily of two periods of exercise, at which talking in pairs is allowed'.

The Prison Commissioners' report to the House of Commons

on 31 March 1917, about the treatment of COs, remarked that 'dietary restriction is the principal instrument of punishment'.

In his autobiography George says that as he approached Wormwood Scrubs prison he remarked, 'It's huge!'

'Shut yer marth!' the warder barked. He pushed George into an empty cell, where he waited for over an hour, then he was put in another room to wash and put on convict's clothes, with the broad arrow on them, and 'socks that had never been twins, and shoes that had been worn before by many an old pilgrim'. He was then led to his own cell.

The first word on the Prison Rules' card was 'SILENCE'.

Emrys Hughes was another Welshman in Wormwood Scrubs, and described it as 'the most terrible place I had ever been in'. Hughes differed from George in that he was not religious, was an Independent Labour Party member and close friend (and later, son-in-law) of Keir Hardie. Unlike George, Hughes relished 'leaving human beings behind and going into prison'. He enjoyed, for a time, the 'quietude, serenity and beauty' of his work making mailbags, before being transferred to a larger prison, where he felt as if he was 'among hundreds of caged, restless, thwarted spirits who could not even feel lonely in their misery'.

It was to this that George M. Ll. Davies, with his history of mental illness and breakdowns, was admitted in December 1917.

The 'hard labour' sentence for Conscientious Objectors began with a month of strict confinement to one's cell (apart from exercise and chapel), with a plank bed. After a month, good conduct won the inmate 'associated labour' – that is, work with others, but with very limited conversation. From the beginning, names were changed to numbers. Nothing could be done except under orders. There was a weekly bath (rushed), a weekly change of socks and towel. Underclothes were changed once a fortnight. Cells were inspected every day.

Very little personal property was allowed: spectacles, some letters (censored), four small photographs, two books, and for Quakers, the Weymouth version of the New Testament, and the Fellowship hymn book. George's Weymouth New Testament contains many pencil notes in the margins.

Hobhouse reported that the men decorated their cells around the large card listing the prison Rules. Rule 1 read: 'Prisoners must observe silence,' and Rule 2: 'They must not communicate, or attempt to do so, with one another.'

'Communication', depending on the warder in charge at the time, could be reported even if one prisoner had simply smiled at another. However, in *Pererindod Heddwch*, George said that while in Winson Green prison, Birmingham, he learned a prisoners' version of Morse Code. This was taught to him by the old soldier in the next cell, who related by knocking on the partition wall how he had come to be imprisoned: a long tale of injustices, which he ended with, 'If there's another war I'll fight for the Germans!' Although communication of any sort was absolutely forbidden, men did find ways to 'talk' with their fellow-men.

A half-hour visit once every few months was all some prisoners could expect, and their family or friends had to shout to them through a wire grating, and in the presence of a warder. 'No such brutal or torturing degradation exists in any Continental prison system,' wrote H. J. B. Montgomery in a booket, *How to Reform our Prison System*, published by the Humanitarian League (Criminal Law and Prison Reform Department) in 1907. The effect was to dehumanise and demoralise men – and their relatives: often women had to travel hundreds of miles to see their relations in prison, for a half-hour visit.

One prisoner's report, 'Through Guard Room and Prison', substantiated what others wrote about the brutality of the system: 'It is the almost universal testimony of prisoners with whom I have conversed,' he wrote, 'that the deliberate policy of the warders is not to tell the new prisoner what is required of him, but to abuse him for the inevitable mistakes which he makes'.

According to this prisoner, the prison timetable was:

5.30	Light on, bell for getting up. Fold up bedding, place it over bed board, rear it against the wall. Tidy cell, clean utensils.
6.00	Door unlocked, fresh water, slops emptied. Applications for doctor etc to warder who comes round with a slate. Cell locked; prisoner finishes cleaning cell.
7.00	Breakfast is brought round.
8.00	Door unlocked; to yard for exercise, ¾ hour. Back to cells.
9.45	To fender shed; work till 11.35; return to cells. Dinner brought round, 'rather before the official hour of twelve o'clock'. After dinner prisoners resume work in their cells. Door unlocked at 1.30 to empty slops.
2.00	Work resumed in shed.
4.00	Return to cells; 'supper'.
5.30	To fender shed.
7.00	To cells. Free to read till bed time.
8.00	Warning bell to get bed ready; light extinguished.

Hobhouse and Brockway reported that prisoners spent seventeen hours out of twenty-four locked in their cells. They had only one hour for reading, and only three-quarters of an hour for exercise. Breakfast was a pint of tea, a pint of porridge and six ounces of bread. 'Dinner', the main meal of the day, consisted of some kind of meat, veg, a suet or rice pudding, and seven ounces of bread; 'Supper', a mug of cocoa and some bread, was brought at about 4pm; the prisoners then ate or drank nothing until 7am, fifteen hours later. At first glance this menu would seem to be verging on adequate for keeping men alive and working, but the porridge was often 'thickened with mice droppings', 'the potatoes diseased, the meat leathery or bad'. At one prison the COs complained that the oatmeal was 'contaminated with rat excreta', and it was removed from service; when the 'politicals' were released, the same oatmeal was brought out again to be given to the 'ordinary prisoners'.

A prisoner on an outside working party picked up stumps of cabbage and carrot to supplement his rations; he was found out, and punished. A vegetarian diet, implemented at the behest of the suffragettes who had been imprisoned before the war, was still available, and perfectly adequate to keep people alive, but it took a lot of effort to get it, and most vegetarians simply ate bread, potatoes and porridge.

The exercise ring was two oval concrete paths about 3 feet wide, outer and inner, around which the prisoners trudged for three-quarters of an hour. Warders stood on raised blocks around the ring, 'to see that the prisoners did not talk or communicate with one another in any way'. But, says this unknown reporter, the prisoners managed to communicate, nevertheless, with a smile or a nod; it had to be done with great care, since it was against the prison rules to communicate at all. But, he wrote, it was at least possible to look above the prison walls and enjoy the sunrise on frosty mornings, and birds flying across the sky, and sometimes 'warders and prisoners alike would peer upwards striving to catch a sight of [an aeroplane]'.

Sometimes the prisoners would be told to 'double' [run] round the exercise ground, but some men could not do this. 'One of the saddest sights at exercise was to notice the increasing pallor and feebleness of some prisoners whose health was suffering from confinement.'

There were 'observation cells' in which people showing signs of mental distress were placed, on their own, with an iron gate so that the warders could watch their every movement; the prison chaplains made cursory 'visits'; the writer himself had broken prison rules by hiding mail bags behind his cell door so that he could give himself extra warmth at night. His report ended:

> ... a prisoner who has undergone a long sentence, during which all power of personal direction has been denied to him, emerges as a free man with an impaired sense of responsibility. Accustomed merely to acquiesce in a rigid and soulless regimentation, he is

little fitted for the self-determination which ordinary citizenship
demands of him.

But another prisoner was surprisingly optimistic:

> COs in prison are not to be pitied, but envied. To see them one
> would imagine them the happiest of people. And so they are. They
> will emerge stronger and better equipped for the great struggle
> that is yet to come than those who have not had their experience.

Hobhouse wrote that warders were spied on by their
superiors, and were reported to the Governor if they engaged
in 'familiar' conversation with prisoners, or said anything to
them that did not bear on the prisoner's work or the prison
rules. 'I have heard... warders... denounce the present system
as 'tyranny' from their point of view also, and express regret, on
grounds of humanity, that they ever entered the prison service'.
The system drove some of the warders to break the rules and
risk losing their jobs, or be fined up to five shillings if found
'talking familiarly' to a prisoner.

In the 1930s and 1940s a series of pamphlets was published
by *Heddychwyr Cymru* [Peacemakers of Wales]. In one of them,
Triniaeth Troseddwyr [Treatment of Criminals], George told of a
Welsh warder who worked at Wormwood Scrubs when George
was there. When it was 'safe' – that is, when the warder was
sure no-one was observing the illicit conversation – the two
talked together. After George had left prison, this warder wrote
to him:

> Governors can, of course, organise things to run smoothly, if they
> wish, but there are also Governors and senior officers who delight
> in making the lives of those in their care as uncomfortable as
> possible... I would love, dear friend, to impress on your mind the
> fact that you must reform the officers who handle the prisoners
> before you can reform the prisoners... but how to reform them is
> beyond my comprehension... If they were to recognise the Union
> of Police Officers and Wardens it would be a big step towards

humanity. At present we can't hold a meeting to discuss matters without the threat of losing our jobs, and many a brave and honest man has paid the price for that.

And, George wrote:

... warders and governors were like so many cogs in a vast machine... this vast pyramid of torture and cruelty, driving men into insanity and crime – this prison system of England, with its scores of prisons and reformatories, was founded on an *idea*, and this idea, in turn, founded on a conception of God – a God who punished men and who countenanced and even commanded men to punish and penalise one another, in order that righteousness might be maintained on the earth. So one came back to the fount and origin and teaching of an established and terrible idea, which on battlefield and prison and slum is doing its deadly work in the world. It was that *idea* then which was the enemy, the great illusion, the negation of Christ, the liar and murderer from the very beginning.

George's awareness of structures and injustices in society was growing. At Riverside, a regime without punishment had worked for the young criminals; here, it was very different. His perceptions were sharpening, and his analysis consequently became more cutting and passionate. In 1922, in 'Politics and Persons', he wrote about his perceptions of 'the Truth' while in prison:

Six months' solitary confinement in a cell had some advantages. At least you escaped the newspapers. As an amateur photographer I learnt that the narrower the aperture of the lens, the clearer its focus became. The apertures [in a prison cell] were certainly narrow enough – 1 sq. yard of window, 20 sq. yards of floor, and 40 minutes per day of seeing one's fellow-men – at a safe distance. Still, there were books, memories and thoughts. After re-reading your few precious letters for the tenth time, and trying to recall mile by mile that mountain tramp to Snowdon five springs ago, to remember the sweet, plaintive call of the yellowhammer by

GEORGE DAVIES: PILGRIM OF PEACE

the mill pool, you returned to your preoccupation of star-gazing – upwards and inwards. There are always those two directions of vision which filled Immanuel Kant with awe – the starry heavens above, and the moral nature of man. Sometimes you peered out upon the future and then even prison life had for you a feeling of safety and settledness which you were almost loth [sic] to leave, to face once more the conflict of ideas and the tumult of the Truth. Then the real hard labour would commence.

While in solitary confinement, George began to re-read the Bible 'with an especial purpose and intentness', reading it 'not as true because authoritative and revered, but as to be revered and authoritative where true'. This is an important distinction, and indicates an increasingly analytical approach. The majority of Christians were taught that the Bible is the Word of God and to be believed *in toto*. George's new way of reading gives a significant clue to his change of emphasis in the latter years of his life, from a conventionally Christian gospel to the 'gospel of personalisation' – his principle and practice of seeing the individual as more important than belief, or rule, or dogma.

But prison chapel services were anathema to George. In *Pererindod Heddwch* he relates how the men were 'herded in hundreds to the chapel', the door was locked, and there were prison officers sitting on high chairs around the chapel and watching for any sign of even a whispered word between the men. George found the greeting 'Dearly beloved brethren', which started the services, cold and empty. He could not find peace in his heart, and decided to protest against this 'religious service'. He went to a morning service but was so nervous he could not breathe, let alone speak. He was afraid he would be labelled a crank, or mad. But in the afternoon service, in a second of silence, he managed to say, audibly: 'Remember, brothers, that Christ asks us to be forgiving and merciful to each other, and not to punish and imprison each other.' A ripple of surprise ran through the place. He heard the prisoners repeating his words 'through the windows'! The next morning he had a visit from the prison doctor, who took him to the Governor.

'Do you have anything to say?'

George answered, 'Nothing, but it is true.'

'That's hardly the point. You could have set off unrest through the whole prison.'

George was sent to the punishment cell, unable to go to the chapel or the exercise yard. 'The punishment cell was the lowest place in the prison – a cold and dark place.' Bread and water diet; picking oakum as work. They took George's handkerchief away from him to prevent him from hanging himself; but 'on the contrary, I felt a wonderful relief in my heart, and I knew that I could do a lot better than hang myself'.

While in the punishment cell George heard a muffled knock on the door, and a voice said quietly, 'There's a crack in the glass in your window; a piece will come out, and I'll put some bread in through the hole'. George never saw the face of his kind fellow-prisoner but they had several quiet conversations through the hole in the window. When he got back to his usual cell, George reflected how fear and punishment contaminated the whole prison system and engendered deceit and cunning, making the men conspire and whisper with each other.

George decided to take further action. He asked to see the Governor again, and told him that in order to 'save his own humanity' he had decided that he would no longer try to talk secretly, but intended to communicate openly and naturally, without disrespecting the Governor or his staff. The Governor's surly answer was, 'You will take the consequences'.

That evening in the work room, with an officer watching to see that nobody spoke, George did so, openly. He was taken straight to the Governor again; two days in the punishment cell; but the punishment had lost its power. This happened repeatedly. Shortly before Christmas 1918, a JP asked to see George in the punishment cell:

He said courteously that he felt uncomfortable going to his home without asking me to reconsider my disobedience to the prison rules, and my attempt to set myself against the system.

I thanked him for his geniality, but told him I had already considered the step very carefully. After further conversation, he then said, 'May I shake your hand?' It was difficult to hold back the tears in the face of such a brotherly greeting and the acknowledgement of the human unity between us. I never saw him again, or knew his name, but his generous humanity laid my heart and the cell wide open.

They summoned me in the end to appear before the Justices, who had the right to give me the most extreme punishment: flogging. The Chief Warder said, 'Why can't you be like the others? It makes no odds to me if you speak, but don't do it in my presence.' I pointed out to him that we were all in prison, including him; everyone is in fear of the person above them.

Before the Justices, I referred to the fact that I'd read that the appointing of Justices was carried out according to the Prison Reform Act that was introduced in Westminster by their famous [Birmingham] fellow-citizen Joseph Chamberlain. The intention was to safeguard prisoners against inhumane treatment. I said that the imposition of total silence for many months, on hundreds of men, was totally inhumane, and created cunning and deceit, and polluted the spirit and morale of prisoners.

The Chairman asked me, 'Would it not be more sensible for you to obey the rule for now, and try to reform it when you have been freed?'

I replied that I couldn't escape from the duty to do what I had the chance to do, and urged them to consider deeply what they could do, according to their rights.

With a smile, the Chairman asked, 'How do you know we aren't?'

'Then I've achieved my goal,' I answered.

Soon after, George Davies heard that the Birmingham Justices had taken the matter to the Home Office; in time the inhuman silent system was reformed.

During his re-reading of the Bible, George became 'distressed' by the 'brutal and bloody history of men who assumed for themselves the title of chosen people, or priests or oracles of God'. He became thrilled by the humanity and fallibility of the patriarchs. He saw the books of Kings and Chronicles as 'an arid desert of bigotry and cruelty', and churches as 'the mummy of a historical Christ', but in 'Letters from Prison III' he expressed hope:

> The Wesleyan Chaplain General was reported recently to have said that the consensus of opinion of the 'boys' at the front was 'that the churches had failed and should be thrown on the scrap heap, but that Jesus Christ had not failed'. The Christianity of the churches has been tried for centuries with war, and law, and prisons, and judges for its allies... The religion of Christ remains to be tried – the new commandment that men should love one another in the way that Christ loved men.

From Winson Green, George was moved to a CO Settlement attached to Dartmoor Prison. It had been taken over for accommodating COs in March 1917 and renamed the Princetown Work Centre. The *Manchester Guardian* (21 February 1917) said that only a few of the original staff remained, including the Governor, Major Reed. Around 1,200 Conscientious Objectors were interned there. According to one of them, Horace Shipp, some of the prisoners had shattered nerves, and had been sent from other prisons to the Camp. 'We were,' Shipp says, 'be it confessed, a slightly neurotic crowd'.[4]

In 1918, George wrote to a friend that the Dartmoor camp was 'a change of degree rather than kind':

> Being pampered criminals, we were sent out in gangs under warders only. Real convicts were escorted by civil guards armed with carbines, with mounted guards patrolling the roads, were watched from an observation tower, were fenced in by telephone wires in all directions to prevent escape.
>
> The work imposed was mainly wasteful and useless, just penal in fact and intention; hundreds of men with heavy spades

were engaged in digging peat land at a cost of hundreds of pounds per acre, sixteen men set to turn the crank handle of a cumbrous oat-crushing machine of which the total work output was said to value 2s. 6d. per day; scores of men were employed at haymaking and scattering the hay with their hands – and all this futility under the guise of 'work of national importance' ... I think it was the waste and foolishness of it even more than the constant threat of punishment that inevitably made malcontents... The warders were as much in prison as the prisoners, the governor perhaps more so than anyone.

However, George continued, reassuringly:

I have everything I need in the way of mackintosh and leggings and hat for the sun. We work on the moor all day. The hours are rather long but the work is not very heavy, only tedious. Please do not have any anxiety about me. Perhaps I may be moved somewhere else before long. We never know. In any case how much better off I am than all those poor fellows who are in the trenches.

It may be that George was part of a work party engaged in the 'reclamation' of some of the Prince of Wales' land near Princetown. A letter published in the *Manchester Guardian* on 16 May 1917 reported that fifty or so of the COs were involved in this work. All the work at Princetown, the correspondent said, was 'penal in character... the object was to make work, the harder and more physically tiring the better'. He saw eight men pulling a roller across a field: 'work that one man and a horse could have performed in a third of the time.' It had taken three weeks for men to dig a field, when it could have been ploughed in three days. 'No-one,' said one man, 'can pretend that it is work of national importance'.

Soon George and others were moved from Dartmoor to a camp at Caeo in Carmarthenshire, south-west Wales, to work (breaking stones) on the road between Llanwrda and Pumsaint (now the A482). The prisoners were allowed to travel by train, in their prison uniform. George's train was waiting at Cardiff station when, he later wrote in *Pererindod Heddwch*, he saw an old friend on the platform, and stepped off the train to shake her hand. It was Mrs Lloyd George, the Prime Minister's wife. She was amazed to see George, in those clothes, and asked where he'd come from.

'From Dartmoor prison,' George replied. She was as cheerful as always, he wrote, and full of kindness. One wonders whether she reported the meeting to her husband, who had been personally instrumental in George's incarceration. (George later told Gwynfor Evans that Mrs Lloyd George asked George, 'Who has done this to you?', and George replied, 'Your husband, Madam'!)

In his essays 'Bottom Dogs II and III', George wrote of his time in Carmarthenshire as a member of a road-making work party of COs. The men, mostly former clerks and students, worked from 6.30am until 5.30pm, even in the summer heat, living 'on nominal wages and short rations and seven in a tent'. But they enjoyed being under the open sky, hearing the murmur of brooks and 'the kindly talk of Wales'. George told of the attitudes of local people to the group of men who were, to all intents and purposes, 'a group of dusty navvies... just navvies to the rich, and just men to the poor':

> The other navvies pass by with a jest, the little farm servant maid
> with a smile, the children look up wonderingly and unafraid, the
> little farmers or their wives passing by in their carts have generally
> a friendly word, the better-off farmers in their gigs have their
> status to preserve and just nod condescendingly, the Priest and
> the Levite pass by on the other side, the Council official (a heavy
> portentous man whom the other navvies have christened 'The
> Hun') comes by once or twice a day to find fault, and to look it.
> He does not speak to the men, but is heard to mutter to the ganger
> – 'Keep them at it, or they'll have to go back to prison'.

George found that in rural Carmarthenshire there was yet another version of the pyramid idea: 'economic coercion and fear'. In prison the pyramid had the convicts on the bottom and the government of the day at its apex; here, the convicts were again on the bottom, and the ascending order was 'the Ganger, the Time-keeper, the Contractor, the Council Surveyor, the Committee, the County Council'.

At this point, we find a major clue to his change from the middle-class bank manager and Territorial Army officer, to the person he became after his prison years. He wrote: 'the lower in the social scale one goes the more humanity and compassion one sees.'

In prison, George himself went down the social scale. He was effectively 'de-classed'. As prisoners, COs lived alongside 'common criminals', suffering the same privations. That they were former bank managers, theologians, artists, academics, and not 'criminals' was irrelevant. They were treated as 'criminals' by those aware of their prisoner status, and viewed as 'navvies' by the local people.

George's own humanity and compassion enabled him to see humanity in others, including people that formerly he would have been kind to, or tried to help, but not valued as equals. He tells of 'Old Cockey, the Ganger, whose gruff voice and unrivalled profanity might seem forbidding, but his philosophy is as candid as his heart is kind'. Cockey was good to his workers, and put 'the frail theology student on to a soft job'. Cockey's 'working creed' was that 'It's the poor that's the friend of the poor, sonny. Parson blokes ain't no use for the likes of us. They've got their living to make. The navvy's best friend is the navvy.' Cockey said that when he'd been walking for fifty miles looking for a job, and was broke, it was usually a fellow-navvy that recognised his plight and helped him out with a few shillings.

George wrote that one navvy had given him a shilling, and another two eggs. 'These rough men are very tender with little children and kind to each other in need. They will be the first in the Kingdom of Jesus – many of them, while the learned and rich and eloquent may be outside.'

This comradeship of the poor was new to George. Perhaps, indeed, this whole concept of a support system of peers was new to him. His brothers had been supportive to one another, true, but the chapel people in Liverpool had not been when John Davies had gone bankrupt, and George never forgot that. He wrote little about his time in the TA, but he would have come up against the pyramid structure of authority there too, and likewise in the banks. He had had the support of Ann and Hugh Roberts on the farm in Llŷn before his prison days, but not quite as equals: though he was their employee, they revered him.

One Saturday evening, after a day on stone-breaking duties in Carmarthen, George went for a walk. Wishing to find his ancestral home, Rhos-y-bedw (near Ffarmers), and also feeling 'a sentimental protest against being treated just as "labour" or "a hand" in this county of my kin', he walked for several hours, but found no trace of his family there, the house having recently been sold, and the church rebuilt, with no epitaph. Only the initials of a Governor-General of the Punjab, one of the members of his father's family, were found on a part of the wall. Even the woodlands that had stood there for generations were being cut down for the war effort. Dispirited, George began his walk back to the work camp. As had happened so often in his youth, 'the sense of the precariousness of all earthly relationships lay heavy upon me... All was so transient'.

As he continued walking into the evening, he rounded a corner at Bwlch Cefn Sarn and saw a Romani camp, with their horses and dogs. They invited him to stop for a 'paned' (cup of tea) and a sandwich with them. He sat for hours by the fire, talking with them. He told them he was a prisoner. 'What did you do?' they asked.

George told them he didn't believe in war, and that he believed Christ's way could make peace on earth.

'And they put you in prison for that? The dirty rascals!' was the indignant response.

George sat with them 'till the glow of the fire reddened the faces of the boys and girls, and flashed in the eyes of the dogs'. He said he would like to go with them on their journey. 'Yes, do come,' said one of the boys, 'and we'll teach you to catch rabbits and eels, and you can teach us some things.'

After hours of conversation George left the camp: 'I walked onwards, confused and thrilled as one who has been near some holy core of being, or had walked unwittingly on holy ground... I felt as if I was full of new wine. I had found my family and my fatherland.'

In that one evening George bade farewell to the ancestral home and the illustrious antecedents at the upper end of the social scale, and found a deep appreciation of those with no permanent home, but with the warmth, humanity and compassion that he craved: 'my family and my fatherland'.

(George's brother Glyn was involved with researching the languages of the Welsh Romanies around the beginning of the twentieth century,[5] and later, one of the best-known of them, Hywel Wood, became a dear friend of George in the 1930s, after they met at Pant y Neuadd, Parc, near Bala.)

Towards the end of the war, many COs, including George, were sent to the work centre at Knutsford in Cheshire, where there was a much more relaxed regime. There were discussion and education groups, informally arranged by the prisoners, and George was asked to run classes on Crime and Punishment. He wrote to Ann and Huw Roberts, in Welsh and with a thick fountain pen (rather than the pencil allowed in other prisons), saying Knutsford was a much freer regime than other places. From his words it seems that he had not been able to write to them before.

George wrote to his mother:

I wouldn't have missed the prison experience for anything. It was a great opportunity for seeing the inside of these cruel systems of punishment which kept men locked up for years like animals for their sins... I sent some photographs to Leslie showing what these places are like. Here it is a vast improvement. We work on odd jobs from 8.30 to 5.00, and then we are free to do as we like. There are a number of Welshmen here... On Sundays we are free all day. Every evening there are meetings in the Prison of various kinds and we meet for talks in each other's cells. We learn a great deal from coming into contact with all sorts and conditions of men and it is very *cynhesol* [heart-warming] to speak Welsh with a few.

George's work was washing floors: 'It makes one's knees and hands pretty sore but it gives more opportunity of leisure than some of the other work.'

One day George's brother Frank visited him, and George showed him round; then they had tea together, which, George wrote to their mother, 'was delightful'. On another occasion he walked to Durham Lawn, Bowden, 'where one of Leslie's rich relations lives'.

It seems Leslie also had at least one whole-day visit to see George at Knutsford; she wrote to him in 1918:

I've had a very absorbed and happy day with my husband today.
Marriage seems quite perfect when you can forget all about
the flesh – in fact rather hate its fleshliness and just be entirely
peaceful and content to know that there is a heart always warm
and understanding, always exacting and inspiring.

Was this to reassure George in this time of enforced celibacy, or was it Leslie's ideal of marriage? She had seen her sister Naomi's relationships functioning in an unconventional manner, and perhaps wanted the same for herself.

Mr H. G. Jones, a friend of George, visited the prison on 28 February 1919. He wrote to Thomas Jones to say that he had spent:

40 minutes behind 2 grilles and a foot apart. [George] was in
wonderfully good spirits. He has grown a beard and his hair is
quite long so only his voice was really recognisable. I spent most of
the time telling him current news as he sees no papers at all. It was
a most weird experience.

It is not known why Leslie and Frank could meet George
freely, while Mr Jones had to stay behind a grille.

From May 1918, the FoR set up a Committee to oversee CO
members' convalescence after release from prison on grounds
of ill-health. In 1919 the work was expanded to cover all COs.
Donations of £6,000 were received to set up a befriending system
after prison: post-release support was not generally available to
prisoners at the time. Release was especially difficult for single
men with no family, and one FoR member bought a large house
in Kent for them. Help was also available for finding work,
hospitality, accommodation, clothing, training, holidays, light
work, and general assistance. For many, rehabilitation would
not be easy: *English Prisons To-day* reported that the silence
rule, and the total obedience that was expected, had grave
mental consequences, and some men left prison 'mentally
defective' [*sic*]. The editors commented: 'The whole regime is
devoid of soul, of tenderness, of mercy, of sympathy.'

Some members of the FoR believed that all Conscientious
Objectors would be released from prison when the war ended,
but George Davies, for one, was not released until June 1919.
Keeping COs in prison this long, it is popularly believed, allowed
men of the armed forces to be brought home, and for those still
able to work to find jobs as they became available. In reality,
however, the decision about what to do with Conscientious
Objectors still in prison was not made by the War Cabinet until
well after the end of the war.

Early in June 1919, George became extremely anxious
about his wife and daughter. He had not heard from Leslie
for some time. He wrote in English to Mrs Jones, Ty'n-y-maes,

Nant Ffrancon, where Leslie and Jane were staying, to ask for news:

> In the solitariness of the cell my thoughts are constantly about
> them and the strain of hearing nothing day after day becomes very
> great... I do not know when release may come. Probably when they
> sign peace – if they ever do. We are only at the beginning of times
> of unrest, of tumult and dismay throughout the world which will
> become worse and worse.

News was more easily to be had at Knutsford than at the other prisons. The world was, of course, in tumult after the war, with the Russian revolution and attempted revolutions elsewhere, the collapse of Austria-Hungary, the smaller nations claiming independence; the peace treaties were not signed until 1919, or later. But George's words suggest he was suffering clinical anxiety, and not simply feeling dispirited with the world.

It turned out that Leslie had been seriously ill with bronchitis. George appealed to the authorities for release. This was turned down, but he was given permission to go to see Leslie on her sick bed. Then suddenly, at the end of June 1919, George was released from prison.

In January 1919, the Prison System Enquiry Committee was formed at the behest of the Executive of the Fabian Society's Labour Research Department. They had realised there had not been a systematic enquiry into the prison system since 1894–5, and there seemed to be no prospect of one. But there was a substantial resource to draw upon – the large number of intelligent, articulate and educated political prisoners (Conscientious Objectors, suffragists, Irish nationalists, and others) who had experienced the system at around the same time. It was felt that an unofficial enquiry would be more objective than a government 'official' one. The initial committee was formed of many with experience of law and the prison system, including some ex-prisoners, including Stephen

Hobhouse and Fenner Brockway. At its foundation, the committee was linked with the Labour Research Department; after January 1921 it became independent.

The committee had to contend first with the intense secrecy surrounding government reports on the prison system, and a point-blank refusal by the Home Office to discuss the system or give access to the reports. The committee formulated a questionnaire that was handed to prison staff directly; some gave consent to be interviewed. Soon after, a Home Office memorandum forbade officers of any kind to communicate with the committee. Before – and after – this memo, however, the committee received testimonials and questionnaires from:

> ... 50 prison officials – Anglican chaplains, Roman Catholic priests, visiting ministers, medical officers, and warders of different grades. To this official testimony we were able to add evidence from 34 agents of Discharged Prisoners' Aid Societies and other persons having supervision of, and intimacy with, ex-prisoners, from 22 visiting magistrates, and from 290 ex-prisoners. Among the ex-prisoners were a large number of men and women who had been sentenced to imprisonment (mostly for terms of hard labour) for political offences, but it included also a number of ex-prisoners committed for criminal offences who had had experience of both Local and Convict prisons.

English Prisons To-Day was published in 1922, selling at 25/-.[6] (The volume is marked 'Special Edition for Subscribers' but it gives no record of those subscribers.) Hobhouse and Brockway, who compiled the Report of the Committee, had both been in prison themselves as COs. As mentioned earlier, Stephen Hobhouse was released because of the breakdown of his health. Fenner Brockway, a Socialist journalist, had founded the No-Conscription Fellowship in 1914, and was imprisoned as an absolutist. Notwithstanding the likely emotional effect on the two men of carrying out the task of editing the Report, it is a balanced and thorough record of the prison system from around 1914 to 1919.

Fenner Brockway was contacted by Beatrice Webb, one of the Fabians, who said her nephew, Stephen Hobhouse, was 'buried under documents' from the prisons, and Webb feared he would never finish the report (Hobhouse was in fact suffering from a mental breakdown exacerbated by his time in prison).[7] She asked Brockway if he was prepared to help; he gladly agreed. Brockway wrote: 'I had great admiration for Stephen... He was still far from well, but worked untiringly. It took about a year to convert the mass of evidence into a report... Several reforms followed our exposure, including the abolition of the Silence Rule.'

It is admirable that *English Prisons To-Day*, over 700 pages long, took only 'about a year' to compile. Also in 1922, a companion volume, *English Prisons under Local Government* was published: a history of English prison administration, by Sidney and Beatrice Webb. (The book has a 66-page Preface by George Bernard Shaw.) The prison system of the time, then, was under public – and informed – scrutiny. When *English Prisons To-day* was published there were long and shocked reviews, which were kept and filed by George. One was headlined: '"Living death" in prison: stinging report of Inquiry Committee: Dehumanising: High rates of suicide and insanity' (*Manchester Guardian*).

George's 'pyramid idea' is substantiated many times in *English Prisons To-Day*. At the apex, reported Hobhouse and Brockway, was the Home Secretary, with the Home Office staff and the Prison Commissioners just below him. All 'subordinate officers' were appointed by the Prison Commissioners, who also nominated the higher prison staff to the Home Secretary, and recommended their promotion or dismissal. The system was open to corruption and nepotism, and the 'old boy network' was used to appoint Commission members.

The Report argued that a fresh approach both to prison government and to the philosophy of the prison system was urgently needed. As Hobhouse and Brockway reported:

The evidence given by political offenders has a greater completeness, consistency, and accuracy, and it has the special value which arises from the relative simplicity and uniformity of the conditions under which it is obtainable and the comparative normality and moral responsibility of this class of offender. It has fortunately been possible to find among such offenders many whose accounts constitute a carefully weighed and balanced judgement, free from any serious degree of distortion on the score of prejudice or resentment.

There was widespread belief that imprisonment would be more painful to 'political offenders' than to 'ordinary criminals'. This was refuted by the political prisoners themselves. Many who gave evidence (including George) were, wrote Hobhouse and Brockway, 'poets, idealists, and men of refined susceptibilities; it is probably fair to assume that such are endowed with a specially sensitive constitution'. But many political offenders asserted that the sufferings of 'ordinary offenders' were worse than their own. The Report analysed the mental effects of imprisonment. Most prisoners who contributed to the questionnaires and interviews had been on hard labour for twelve months or more. Most were between twenty and forty years old; most were COs. But it was found that the effect of imprisonment on these men was much the same as on the 'ordinary offender of average mentality'. A diet of poor nutritional value combined with hard labour caused long- and short-term malnutrition, in addition to the negative mental and emotional effects of the rest of the regime.

The authors of *English Prisons To-Day* found there to be four stages of mental deterioration. The first, 'Excitation', happened in the first few weeks of imprisonment. During this stage, most prisoners went through an intense experience of 'acceleration of mental activity and of emotional response', ranging from a 'condition distinctly hysterical' to 'an intense curiosity in the novelty of the situation'. Occasionally it was not experienced as painful, but usually it was 'a great intensity of suffering'. The risk of suicide was higher during this time, and many of the political offenders made explicit mention of the symptoms of a serious nervous breakdown. These included religious mania, 'a militant semi-insanity', morbidity and moodiness, and the refusal of all discipline.

Then came the 'Making the best of it' stage. During this period, conscious attempts were made to occupy the time profitably, with either self-culture, or physical exercise. In the silence and solitary confinement of the system, this could lead to self-centredness and introspection. There was most evidence on this stage from the more educated prisoners; the 'ordinary offenders' moved quickly on to the third stage.

Stage Three was 'Deterioration'. During this stage, a decline in profitable reflection arose from the exhaustion of resources. The men suffered from day-dreaming and vacuity. Mental activity decreased from lack of stimulation, lack of discussion, lack of criticism, constant repetition of thoughts: 'Thoughts of food, of liberty, of all the unsatisfied desires tend more and more to occupy the mind.' Memories of childhood wandered through the mind, side by side with emptiness and depression. Resisting this process led to more pain and breakdown than giving in to 'the torpor and indifference in which prison discipline ceases to be a pain'. The Report discovered that from time to time, there were states of heightened irritation, in which men breached discipline, had violent fits of rage, or quarrels, which led sometimes to assaults and sometimes to the destruction of their cell furniture. This seems to be the stage Emrys Hughes described when he mentioned 'caged, restless, thwarted spirits who could not even feel lonely in their misery'.

Stage Four was 'Apathy': a settled torpor, when the routine became mechanical, and the prisoner, appearing externally to be calm and free from suffering, was considered by many to be 'reformed'.

In their analysis of the reports of the political prisoners who responded to their request for information, Hobhouse and Brockway found that 50 per cent of them believed that the 'silence system' and the lack of free association with other men in the prison were the worst aspects of the prison system.

Another CO wrote about the effects of imprisonment on mental health. He said that he adapted to prison life by going into a sort of mental and nervous hibernation. After eighteen months of imprisonment his concentration span was very short and his memory feeble. His powers of observation suffered, and that carried on after his release. This CO asserted that since his release in April 1919 he had gradually recovered from the mental ill-effects of prison. But his attitude to his former occupation (insurance clerk) changed as he became 'convinced of the immorality of the present competitive commercial system', and he decided to become a school-teacher. He observed that since leaving prison, he had had a 'contempt for the law and for the opinions and moral code of society'. He ended, 'After two-and-a-half years in such a morally venomous atmosphere, I do not claim to have come through unscathed'. One wonders what kind of school-teacher he became.

In October 1916, Morgan Jones from south Wales (later MP for Caerphilly) wrote to Clifford Allen, whose health had been completely broken by his prison experience, saying that he had just been moved from Wormwood Scrubs to a camp at Warwick. 'The effect of prison upon my mind,' Jones wrote, 'has been to entirely deprive me of the power of... concentrating on any subject for any length of time... I have a perpetual feeling of falling headlong into space. It makes me quite miserable.' Morgan Jones had been arrested only at the end of May 1916; his mental collapse was the result of just those five months in prison.

The physical and mental effects of prison on George's life were very similar. George's eyesight, hearing and digestive system were permanently affected, and he was never again to achieve the robust good health he found when working on the farm in Llŷn. His attitudes and values also changed. He often referred to being imprisoned – especially in 1921 when meeting Irishmen who had been incarcerated – and he was involved with penal reform for the rest of his life.

In Wales in the 1920s and 1930s, George became something of a hero for having gone to prison for his principles. Indeed, many young men were influenced to become Conscientious Objectors in the Second World War because of his inspirational presence among them.

His months in the prison system (January 1918 to June 1919) were a catalyst for him in many ways. He observed the 'pyramid hierarchy' in the system, and saw that it existed in other areas of society. In spite of that, he found humanity in prison.

Perhaps most importantly, he learned that 'the working classes' consisted of human beings worth listening to, and learning from.

In an essay 'In Forma Pauperis', published in *The Welsh Outlook* in June 1922, George wrote:

And so, in time, men who were born free, awake to find themselves in chains… Already in school and college, shades of the prison house begin to close upon the growing boy, as he finds himself equipped not for service but for servitude, not for freedom but for conformity. The sufferings of the imprisoned life and the agonies of breaking free are all around us – the girl who *has* to marry for money, the parson who *has* to preach for a living, the judge who *had* to imprison Gandhi, the warder who *has* to bully his convicts, the schoolmaster who *has* to 'maintain order', the Prime Minister who *has* to lose a peace in order to seem to have won a war – all these entanglements are the consequence of having accepted at some stage a creed or a position or policy of Power which simply *does not work*, is disruptive and destructive of life, both physical and spiritual.

8

Gregynog

AFTER HIS TIME in the prison system George Davies should have been given time to convalesce and get his bearings. Instead, he found himself being thrust towards his next occupation.

In August 1919, about ten weeks after George's release from prison, his old friend Richard Roberts (the former Secretary of the Fellowship of Reconciliation) had been to see him, and was worried about him relying on voluntary gifts to keep himself and his family. He had suggested to Dr Thomas Jones (TJ), George's old friend, Assistant Secretary to the War Cabinet in London, that it might be possible to make some 'more regular provision' through Mrs George Davies (Leslie). TJ was not convinced that George would accept anything 'in the way of an interest or an annuity', but told Richard Roberts that he would mention it to John Owens of Chester (a JP and stockbroker to Gwendoline and Margaret Davies).

John Owens replied on 30 August that he had discussed TJ's letter with Mrs Lloyd Jones, George's aunt in Llandinam. She had said that Stanley Davies, George's brother, had put £100 a year at Leslie's disposal, but Leslie had never called upon it, and if she hadn't accepted help from Stanley, she was unlikely to accept it from others. Mrs Lloyd Jones pointed out that Stanley had a good job and his wife private means, and that they could look after George if he was in need. 'There is a good deal of sympathy for [George] here on account of his many good qualities,' Mrs Lloyd Jones had told Mr Owens, 'but you will see the difficulties of the position'.

Presumably neither John Owens, Thomas Jones, Richard Roberts nor Mrs Lloyd Jones Llandinam were party to the information that Leslie's sisters – Maude, and particularly novelist Naomi – had been providing financially for her during George's imprisonment, and that Stanley and his wife were providing emotional and other support to Leslie and Jane. It seems that Leslie, a resourceful woman, who had lectured professionally in catering on a low budget, was also a proud woman, and had mentioned her needs only to her immediate family.

It is also possible, of course, that Thomas Jones, John Owens, and Mrs Lloyd Jones, all of whom moved in the circles of the political and social elite of Wales at the time, were uncomfortable with the fact that George and Leslie Davies were accepting these 'voluntary gifts', rather than having a more 'respectable' income.

David, Gwendoline, and Margaret (Daisy) Davies of Llandinam, the grandchildren of the self-made millionaire David Davies (1818–1890), had all inherited his philanthropical inclinations. The family owned the Ocean Colliery in the Rhondda. David Davies (grandson) was Colonel in Chief of the Royal Welch Fusiliers, and was also involved in the setting up and running of the Welsh Council of the League of Nations Union. As we have seen, George had worked for David Davies in the Welsh Town Planning and Housing Trust, *The Welsh Outlook* journal, and other ventures.

In 1920, when the two sisters were obliged to leave their home in Llandinam, they bought Gregynog, a large house in Montgomeryshire, from their brother David.[1] The two sisters had worked voluntarily as nurses near the Front in the Great War, and wanted to contribute beauty and art to post-war Wales. Gwendoline wrote to her great friend TJ: 'it provides a glorious opportunity… I love beautiful things and I want others to share them too.' The two sisters set about collecting art and holding cultural events such as music festivals; Gwendoline also set up the Gregynog Press, producing beautifully bound and illustrated books. The sisters donated 'The Gregynog Gift' to the University College of Wales, Aberystwyth, to be used to develop the College in TJ's way – they assumed he would obtain the Principalship in 1919; though he did not, the money was still given to the College, on condition the authorities continued to develop using TJ's ideas. And TJ persuaded David Davies to set up the Woodrow Wilson Chair of International Politics at Aberystwyth, rather than at Oxford as David Davies had originally intended.

This was the hot-house of elite culture into which George was being invited, only a short time after spending eighteen months in prison, and after finding the working classes to be his 'family'. Although he had known David, Gwendoline and Margaret Davies all his life, it is not surprising that he took his time making up his mind whether he wanted to participate in their world.

At the beginning of September 1919, Leslie Davies wrote to her mother from Ty'n-y-Maes in the north of Wales, where she, Jane and George were still living. She said that they were 'in a state of transition at the moment which is occupying all our minds'. She told Mrs Royde Smith that she and George had been to Pwllheli to see a small-holding, 'but it was such a hopeless sort of house that I decided definitely against it before knocking at the door'. (From 1919 onwards the government offered small-holdings to injured soldiers, plus training, so that they could become self-sufficient. It is possible that the FoR had a similar scheme for its members who had been imprisoned.)

In the same letter, Leslie hinted to her mother that there might be a forthcoming move, to somewhere not too far away, but without going into any details. George had already started to undertake speaking tours around Wales.

Daisy Davies wrote to Thomas Jones on 3 September 1919, saying that George and Leslie would be visiting Gregynog to see a cottage in the grounds the following Monday. It may well have been TJ's idea that George Davies should be recruited to the Gregynog enterprise: as well as being an old friend of George, TJ was advisor to Daisy Davies, and had worked with George (and David Davies) on various projects before the war.

On 5 November 1919, Leslie wrote to her mother with more concrete news. George had at last made up his mind about going to Gregynog, and they were to move early the following month. Leslie explained that the Misses Davies were starting 'a kind of Social Centre for Wales', and wanted George to go there for a year, be their advisor, and help get it going. Leslie wrote, 'They wanted him to be Secretary – but he won't take any fixed job that interferes with his liberty – he doesn't want to accept a salary and be bound to them by money'. This was one of the effects of prison on George's mind and principles.

An arrangement was made that Leslie, George and Jane would live free of charge in a cottage – new, well-built, modern, but isolated, Leslie wrote – on the Gregynog Estate; they would be given free coal, and their removal would be paid for. Rather than the 'Social Centre' Leslie mentions, George wanted Gregynog to be 'a Centre for Reconciliation in every sphere, not excluding the Davieses and the miners'. Perhaps Leslie foresaw the conflict between the Davies sisters' vision and George's principles.

Leslie added that she was looking forward to having friends to stay in the cottage, because she had had more than her share of loneliness while George was in prison. She accurately predicted that he would be away from home a lot in the future, on speaking tours and at conferences.

This 'cottage' is in fact quite a sizeable house, a short walk from the Gregynog house, through lovely parkland. Perhaps it was too distant for Leslie, however; Jane was three, and Leslie would be short of adult company when George wasn't there. Frank wrote to George from Shanghai saying he'd heard George and Leslie were living 'at a cottage umpteen miles from anywhere... Poor old Leslie... try and get her fixed near human beings, George bach'.

In many of his letters, Frank complains that George's letters gave little news of Leslie, and that Leslie's letters gave little news about Jane. Leslie's letters do, though, tell us much about George's state of mind after his release from prison. Just as soldiers had come back from the Front changed, and unfamiliar to those they had left behind, so the former convicts were changed and traumatised. The effects on George are clear. Leslie sounded impatient at his inability to make the decision about Gregynog just a few weeks after leaving prison, but I suspect he felt a deep need of 'time-out' and adjustment.

Before 1922, when the Conscientious Objectors' reports on the prison system were published, there was little pre- or post-release help. The effects on prisoners' minds of that 'morally venomous atmosphere' were hardly understood. The FoR probably had no resources to work with prisoners' families, which would have been profoundly worthwhile. Leslie, and perhaps George too, had expected his homecoming to be joyful. Now they were facing reality: George's changes were deep.

Leslie had fallen in love with a Territorial Army officer and bank manager. She had understood his anti-war feelings and had gone along with him working in a home for delinquent children, and with him being a shepherd, and then a prisoner, presumably expecting that they would return to a kind of 'normality', with George in some responsible and salaried job, and the family living in relative comfort. Now she began to see life as it would be – George something of a hero (especially in Wales), away a lot, and in great demand as a speaker; and Leslie living in isolation with Jane, longing for intelligent adult company. George, because of his experiences as a CO, had become a public man, not the private man Leslie had married.

But alongside the 'public man' role, and necessary for George's survival, ran a strand of post-prison avoidance of close contact with people, due to solitary confinement and the Silent System; also, returning to any kind of comfortable, salaried, official, middle-class existence was anathema to him.

Leslie faced a future without a secure income. She had grown used to that while George was in prison: her sisters sent money to her, and of course Stanley was supportive in many ways. In her letter to her mother (5 November 1919) Leslie seems to be trying to understand why George refused the post of Secretary to the Gregynog enterprise. It must have been puzzling to her. George had been earning well while working for David Davies with the housing associations prior to 1914. But post-prison, George, like the CO who was reported in *English Prisons To-day*, had a deep wish to stay independent of the 'present competitive commercial system'.

George had misgivings about the Gregynog project as a whole, and about the ethics of his role in it. Early in 1920, he wrote to TJ from Ty'n-y-Maes, near Bethesda, speaking of Gwendoline and Daisy Davies and of his ponderings about their scheme: 'The proposals appeal to me very much but I feel I should not be honest in helping the girls to carry out these excellent intentions while neglecting the far more urgent responsibility of making Peace with their Employees.' If they were willing to look at this, wrote George, 'I will be their servant as loyally as I try to be their friend. They may lose their millions but they will save their lives by finding new fellowships and freedom.' George wanted the Davies sisters to look fairly at their workers in the Ocean Colliery in south Wales. He (perhaps judgementally) saw their riches as an obstacle to their salvation.

In December 1920, a mutual friend, art collector Winifred Coombe Tennant, wrote to George saying 'Gwen is a tragic figure – I long to know her better but she is not easy to get near... How glad she is to have you within reach, and available as an element in Gregynog gatherings'.[2] Winifred was disturbed by Gwendoline Davies' unhappiness, and the 'bitterness and pain that has burnt into her mind' – no explanation of this, but presumably Dolly's death was part of it, and perhaps she was still hurt by being 'evicted' by her brother from her home in Llandinam.

George's frustration with the Misses Davies, however, continued. Despite the later claim of Eirene White, TJ's daughter, that the Llandinam Davieses were among the 'very few coal-owners who spent [their] great wealth with some consciousness of the needs of those who had toiled to produce it',[3] this 'consciousness' of their employees' needs did not go far enough for George. He wrote to Thomas Jones in January 1921: 'The whole scheme is morally suspect as long as the means by which they obtain their wealth is morally suspect.' Clearly George's part in the Davies' scheme – a Christian socialist working for millionaire coal owners – was doomed to failure.

At the end of March 1922, after just over two years there, George, Leslie and Jane Davies left Gregynog for some rented rooms in Maenan Hall Farm near Llanrwst. George wrote to TJ of his relief at being out of Gregynog, and said that he felt he'd failed to be of any help to David, Gwen and Daisy Davies, or to persuade them to have any better attitude towards their colliery workers, 'whose labour gives them all their power'. George added:

> … even with the workmen building [renovating Gregynog] there
> is no attempt at real reconciliation – although these men are very
> decent fellows – Welshmen and ex-servicemen, many of them.
> It is the old fallacy of attending to the machine before the men,
> and the shell before the soul. Poor things – the tragedy of the
> imprisonment of wealth is an awful one.

This comment about the 'tragedy' of the Davies' 'imprisonment of wealth' seems consciously ironic, in the light of George's actual imprisonment. Although it is clear from various comments that prison had affected him mentally and physically, he never referred to it as, or seems to have considered it, a 'tragedy'. Again and again he said that he learned from the experience. Perhaps the 'tragedy' of the Davieses, in George's eyes, was that they were not learning from theirs. With their opportunity and resources, they could have been pioneers of social justice in post-war Wales.

Even in the late 1920s, when George was a minister in Tywyn, he wrote a rather jaundiced letter to TJ asking if TJ knew anyone who could give money to a minister in Tonypandy who was helping miners: George said he would have asked the Davieses of Llandinam, 'but my [Tonypandy] friends are probably deemed too Socialist'. He added that it made him sick 'to see money thrown away on those damned old pictures of Augustus John' when people in the Rhondda were trying to help the miners.

There seems to be no documented record of George's contribution to Gregynog. But Gwendoline and Margaret Davies, in spite of the obvious differences in priorities between them and George, later became Trustees of the Maes-yr-haf Educational Settlement where George lived and worked for the last two decades of his life, and they often visited George there, in the tiny hut in the garden where he chose to live. George had invited them to become involved, and TJ had supported the invitation. George and 'the girls' remained good friends; but he continued to argue with Lord David Davies throughout his life for the rights of the Davies' employees at the Ocean Colliery. In September 1931, George wrote to Pierre Cérésole (1879–1945) of Service Civil, the international voluntary service for peace, who had spoken graciously at Gregynog. George confessed that he had not been that gracious when he had lived at Gregynog with the Misses Davies, and only after Cérésole's address there did he realise he had been too hard on them, 'denying their moral right to their wealth until they sought reconciliation with their ten thousand employees'.[4]

Even while living at Gregynog, from 1920 to 1922, George was concerned with reconciliation elsewhere. He became known by trade unions as someone who could mediate effectively between employers and workers, which must have been much more satisfying for him than his Gregynog duties. Throughout the 1920s, he travelled to peace conferences in continental Europe, many of which were organised by the International Fellowship of Reconciliation, which had first met in 1919. One of those at the first meeting of the IFoR was Pierre Cérésole.

George also went to Germany, and saw the terrible conditions resulting not only directly from the war, but also from the punitive Versailles Treaty. Afterwards, George wrote a pamphlet, *Reparations and Industrial Ruin*, which was published by the Quakers in 1932. In it he correctly predicted that the harsh treatment meted out to Germany under the Treaty would have a dire effect on the industrial life of Wales: for example, German coal, which, as part of reparations, had to be produced well below the cost of production, would undercut coal produced in the Welsh coalfields and create unemployment in Wales.

In his pamphlet, George suggested that the Treaty was the source of the current 'bitter fruits of disillusionment and disaster' in Germany, and accurately prophesied that 'insisting on Germany making debt payments was engendering hatred, which would be turned on Britain and America'.

George wrote about the economic and political consequences of the Versailles Treaty on Britain and Europe. Herr Simon, then Secretary of the League of Nations Union in Germany, had said in 1923 that the hope that Germany could restore itself after the war had turned to 'disappointment and bitterness and reaction by the breaking of the terms of surrender and by the demanding of only one question, "How can Germany pay?"'

George's pamphlet has many quotes about the economic results of the Treaty, from contemporary economists including John Maynard Keynes, and from passages from political and economic journals. It is clear that George (the former bank manager) had read widely on the subject, and Keynes' work would have chimed well with his views and experiences.

George's daughter, Jane, remembered the family's time at Maenan as very happy, on the whole. She and George enjoyed

Two of the 'Welsh Streets', Elwy and Madryn, Toxteth, Liverpool. At the end of Madryn Street can be seen the back of the houses on Devonshire Road, where George Davies lived from 1891 to 1902.

38 Devonshire Road, Toxteth, Liverpool, where the Davies family lived from 1891.

Second Lieutenant George M. Ll. Davies (centre, behind gun barrel) training with his men around 1910.

George Davies around 1911.

Leslie Davies shortly after her marriage to George, in her home in London. The tiny photograph was found in the Weymouth Bible George had with him in prison.

George with daughter Jane Hedd in 1917. He was arrested and imprisoned a few weeks after Jane's first birthday.

George and Leslie's daughter Jane. When I met her in her 80s she had the same direct gaze.

George in his cell in Knutsford Prison, 1918. The message to George on the back of the card reads: 'In memory of many happy little tea parties!'
By permission of the National Library of Wales

L–R: Rev. Richard Roberts from Blaenau Ffestiniog, founder of the Fellowship of Reconciliation; George; Rhiannon Thomas and her father Dan. Rhiannon later married Gwynfor Evans.

George M. Ll. Davies
MP, 1924.

George (right) on one
of his annual visits to
his beloved Bardsey
Island.
By permission of
Myrddin ap Dafydd

Work on Brynmawr Pools – this appears to be a posed photograph!

George Davies (centre, in white shirt) helping with the work at Brynmawr.

The Pools almost completed.

All that's left of Brynmawr Pools today.

The international student workers at Rhosllannerchrugog, 1932. George is in the back row, on the right.

Inge Christensen from Norway, who painted houses in Brynmawr and Rhosllannerchrugog.

Lunch break at Rhos, 1932. George's talks were popular with the international volunteers and the local people.

Gardening was one of George's greatest pleasures – here at Maes-yr-haf in about 1935.

The Malthouse, Wick, during the Second World War, when women and children were sent there from London's East End for a holiday. Gwynfor Evans was in charge of peeling 'tons of potatoes' for them.

The Malthouse, Wick, as it is today – converted into flats.

A Heddychwyr Cymru conference, possibly at Tretower, in the early 1940s, George centre front, behind boy. Immediately behind George is Mrs Dan Thomas; to her left is Dan, then Gwynfor Evans. Just behind Gwynfor's left shoulder is Emyr Evans, whose memories provided valuable insights.

George Davies (second row, centre) in typical pose, pipe in hand, with unemployed miners, Wick, late 1930s.

Hywel Wood, of the well-known Romany family, one of George's dearest friends.

The kitchen at Pant-y-Neuadd, Parc, near Bala. George's friend Meinir (later Burden) sits next to Hywel by the harp; at the end of the table, with Meinir's brothers, sits Kurt, a German prisoner of war. At the other table, Mair, Meinir's sister, serves their Mam with a cup of tea.

George M. Ll. Davies in his 60s, before his decline in health.

L–R: Rev. Dafydd Ll. Jones (George's uncle); Ieuan Ll. Jones (George's cousin); Stanley; George.

George's headstone on his grave in the little cemetery on a hill in Dolwyddelan.

The view from the cemetery at Dolwyddelan, Gwynedd.

It was a privilege to be asked by Dr D. Ben Rees to unveil a plaque, in October 2004, on 38 Devonshire Road, where Glyn and George lived for a while. Both men, however, would have preferred the inscription to have included all four brothers!

each other's company. She remembered the practical jokes he played on her. He seems to have been remembering his brothers and their high jinks, but forgetting that Jane was a little girl. One day they enjoyed an excursion to the woods with a wheelbarrow to collect some firewood. But 'the wheelbarrow' tipped her into a stream… Jane was not impressed and roared her protests all the way home to Leslie. Yet a postcard from George to Jane urges her to 'Look after Mummy and be very loving to her when she asks you to do things so as to be the loveliest girl that ever was'. His expectations of his daughter were always somewhat high.

Jane wrote to her cousins that George made elderberry wine once, 'which was duly bottled – too early, I imagine – and parked in the *tŷ bach*, where it went off in a series of ferocious reports, its potency due, according to Leslie, to the fact that George strained it through his vest'.

Throughout 1920, as well as working at Gregynog, George was busy with reconciliation work on farms, and in quarries and mines, whilst writing a number of articles published in, for example, *The Welsh Outlook*. In one piece, 'Church and State', George called for 'the Good News of the Politics of Love' to be restored to its proper place, which, he felt, would revolutionise the Church, politics, and national government, but also criminal justice, education, industry, and animal welfare. This demonstrates George's knowledge of and interest in the latest developments in many fields. He aimed to bring peace and reconciliation into every area of personal, political, and public life.

9

Ireland

Towards the end of 'Church and State', George mentioned another area of conflict that was on his mind: the War of Independence in Ireland. Following the chaotic Easter Rising of 1916, the brutal actions of the British troops had turned public opinion in Ireland in favour of the 'rebels', namely Sinn Féin and its military wing, the Irish Republican Brotherhood, which later became the Irish Republican Army (IRA). James Connolly (1868–1916), Edinburgh-born, was a Marxist-Communist and Trade Unionist in Dublin, leader of the Transport and General Workers' Union, leader of the Citizen Army, and co-leader (with Patrick Pearse) of the 1916 Easter Rising. He was shot in the leg by the British during the Rising. He contracted gangrene and was executed tied to a chair in Kilmainham Gaol. The shock caused by this act, and by the shooting of Mac Diarmada, who had had polio, contributed significantly to the rise of anti-British feeling after the Rising, and led to the War of Independence.

In his essay 'Extremists' (found in George's papers, but there is no evidence that it was ever published), George spoke of his first visit to Ireland in September 1902. He had enjoyed the fishing, but he also spoke with people who remembered the famine of 1845–50, the huge loss of life, and the subsequent cruel evictions of Irish tenants from their land. It was the beginning of George's sympathy with the Irish nationalist cause.

Prior to the First World War, David Lloyd George had been

a passionate advocate of Home Rule for Ireland and Wales. Many had hoped for progress in these directions when Lloyd George rose to ministerial power in Westminster. They were disappointed.

In 1915, Captain Jack White, a Protestant Irish nationalist from Ulster, visited the Fellowship of Reconciliation office in London. Jack White was the son of Field Marshall Sir George Stuart White, who had earned the Victoria Cross fighting for Britain in the Anglo-Boer War. Jack White told George that he had helped to organise and train[1] the Citizen Army led by James Connolly (in fact he had founded it), and that they were preparing to seize Dublin.

Jack White was a fascinating character. Whether he was totally mad or totally brilliant is still a matter of debate. Leo Keohane (Galway) wrote a PhD thesis on anarchy and Jack White; his view is that White *considered* himself a pacifist, and so joining the FoR would not have been out of character.

George tried to persuade Jack that an uprising in Dublin would be a mistake. Jack said he agreed, and joined the FoR. When over Easter 1916 the Citizen Army, together with the Irish Republican Brotherhood, stormed the General Post Office in Dublin, Jack White called at George's home in the Garden Suburb. In an essay 'Ireland and Peace Politics' (1924: possibly unpublished), George wrote:

> I remember pacing the quiet road with him late at night trying to dissuade him from following his impulse to throw in his lot with the rebels and finish fighting, though, intellectually at any rate, he felt its futility and immorality. Finally he travelled... to South Wales and there tried to persuade some of the Miners' Leaders to demand the cessation of the Court Martial executions of the Sinn Féin rebels... For this he was arrested and imprisoned in Swansea gaol.

This meeting with Jack White in 1915 was George's first direct experience of the Irish nationalists. He saw more of them when he was with them in Winson Green prison in Birmingham, and particularly in Knutsford Camp in 1919, when he discussed with them their aims for a free Ireland. George Davies was therefore known and trusted by several IRA members. This unique status was to prove useful later on.

In 1920 the Fellowship of Reconciliation met to discuss the Irish situation. The situation post-Rising was appalling. The 'Black and Tans' ('irregular' troops) had been sent in by the British government to put pressure on the nationalists, and were terrorising the people of Ireland. An Irish Reconciliation Committee was set up. The FoR sent an appeal to the religious and secular press of Britain and Ireland for the abandonment of violence on both sides, and for a conference of the heads of Anglican and Non-conformist churches. On 27 August 1920, George Davies received a reply from the Archbishop of Canterbury, who rather coldly said he did not wish to get involved; George wrote angrily at the top of the letter: 'NOT replied to.' In his article 'Extremists', George said that the English Free Church leaders and the Archbishop alike made it clear that they would not co-operate in any conference which would discuss Irish independence.

On 3 June 1920 the North Wales Free Church's annual conference passed a resolution sympathising with the government's difficulties, but appealing to them to adopt in Ireland 'methods in accordance with Christ's teaching'. Clearly, though the Free Church leaders in England felt they could not co-operate at all, the Welsh Free Churches were more open to discussions.

Then, 'after having made contact with Lloyd George again in a personal approach', George Davies went to Dublin representing the FoR, having first arranged to meet some of the Sinn Féin leaders. It was a dangerous mission: the Black and Tans were at liberty to shoot anyone they merely suspected of being a supporter of the nationalists; talking with the leaders would certainly endanger George Davies' life.

In 'Ireland and Peace Politics' George said he met Desmond Fitzgerald (later Sinn Féin Minister for Foreign Affairs), and was surprised to see Fitzgerald looking up and down the road before leaving the house, in case a policeman (or one of the Black and Tans) had tracked him down. Fitzgerald told George he slept at a different address each night, for safety. In one of his last articles, 'Poles Apart' (in *Reconciliation*, the FoR newsletter, January 1949), George commented: 'Our talk was so very human that it was humiliating to think that the British Prime Minister of the day was himself a Celt who had been a nationalist leader of revolt in Wales, and that General Tudor of the Black and Tans was also a Welshman.'

Later, Arthur Griffith, then Acting President of Sinn Féin (Éamon de Valera was in America), told George that he personally disapproved of violent actions, but that he 'couldn't repudiate them without splitting the Sinn Féin movement, just as Mr Lloyd George could not repudiate Black and Tannism without alienating English Die Hards' (who were holding out for Northern Ireland to stay British). George pointed out that talking with Sinn Féin might mean political ruin for Mr Lloyd George as well as risk for Mr Griffith.

George did not know that the Dáil Department of Propaganda had set up this system – Dublin Castle (British army headquarters) called it the 'republican scenic railway'[2] – in which foreign journalists and others would first make contact with Fitzgerald, then, 'with an elaborate show of secrecy', with some of the Sinn Féin leaders, and then ladies 'who described atrocities they claim to have seen'.

Around the same time George suggested to 'one of the most extreme of the Irish Republican leaders' (perhaps Michael Collins) that Lloyd George might risk his whole career in a bid for reconciliation. The reply was: 'If he did so he'd go down even now in Ireland as the greatest Premier England [*sic*] ever had.'

Late in 1920, Lloyd George asked Joseph Clune, Archbishop of Perth in Australia, to visit Éamon de Valera, the President of Sinn Féin, in Dublin, with a brief to sound the leadership out about a truce and negotiations. At the time, with de Valera in America raising funds and support, and Arthur Griffith, president of Sinn Féin, in prison (much to Lloyd George's annoyance, because he saw that Griffith's imprisonment was turning Irish public opinion towards Sinn Féin), the temporary leader was Michael Collins, the charismatic commander of the IRA, and Minister of Finance in the Provisional Government. Instead of the surrender Lloyd George had hoped for, Clune went back to London with Collins' terms. Lloyd George's reaction to this assertive response was to step up Black and Tan action in the south of Ireland – where Collins' family lived. Their home, Woodfield, was razed to the ground and his family thrown out.

Collins let Lloyd George know that the IRA would not be broken. The British government further hardened their attitude. Collins wrote in 1922, shortly before his assassination, that he felt that if certain Irishmen had not been over-keen for peace, thus indicating weakness rather than keeping up the pressure on Lloyd George, the eventual Truce of July 1921 could have been signed in December 1920, avoiding several months of violence.[3]

David Lloyd George had once been a vociferous Welsh nationalist, who had spoken to the Welsh Nationalist Society in Liverpool (around 1900) on 'Llywelyn and Welsh Nationalism'. George attended, and remembered 'this pale and passionate man – he had not lost his Welsh accent then – portraying the struggle of this lonely Prince against the might and power of England'. Lloyd George ended his talk: 'But the spirit of Llywelyn is abroad in the land and the race which followed him so gladly unto the Gates of Death is even now awakening and responding to his call.' George walked home 'on air', and 'a consciousness of nationality, a passion for its freedom became, as it were, part of my very being'.

But Lloyd George found his role as Prime Minister was

complicated by Irish nationalists. As George Davies wrote in 'Ireland and Peace Politics' in 1924:

> The momentum of the Great War mentality had hardly ceased when Mr Lloyd George found himself faced by the Little War in Ireland, and with this additional moral embarrassment: that the demand for a full measure of self-determination had already been advocated by himself and passed by Parliament [in 1914]... The conflict between old ideals and new confederates must have been bewildering, if not agonising, at times.

George Davies wrote to TJ from Gregynog on 20 December 1920 saying that a mutual friend, Winifred Coombe Tennant, had appealed to Lloyd George to initiate talks with de Valera and the Irish nationalist leaders. Lloyd George had blurted out that he knew it had to be an act of faith, and that he was waiting for the right opportunity. George told TJ that this lapse in Lloyd George's guard had to be remembered, even in the light of the official hard line. George (the absolutist pacifist) spoke of his sadness when remembering 'the frankness and friendliness of the Sinn Féin leaders', and of hearing of their imprisonment one by one. He went on, 'Perhaps the evil of methods of violence has to be learned by them too, but woe unto us who have provoked them to such things'.

It was quite an initiative for George Davies to recount to Thomas Jones – who had some influence with the Prime Minister – a remark Lloyd George had made in private and in an unguarded moment. It was certainly a comment that TJ could have used to encourage Lloyd George to see, and take, the 'opportunity' as soon as it arose.

However, on New Year's Day 1921, Lloyd George's government instituted a system of 'authorised reprisals' against any Irish people who 'appeared suspicious'. The government's aim was 'pacification'. Amongst other measures, they introduced the death penalty for those harbouring 'rebels'; also, houses were permitted to be blown up if they belonged to someone 'implicated in' acts against the Crown. Realising the futility of his efforts to communicate effectively with Lloyd George, Archbishop Clune gave up his negotiations for peace.

George Davies felt that, in the 'Quakerly' fashion, it would be more fitting to appeal to 'that of God' in the men involved, rather than merely protesting. At a General Committee meeting of the FoR in September 1920, George Davies was deputed by the FoR to go to Downing Street to talk with Lloyd George. The Prime Minister was going into a meeting. George left a note for him, in Welsh. As George left, Thomas Jones said to him: 'It's quite useless. The Prime Minister will agree to no conference except on condition that independence is ruled out.'

(It should be remembered that the third Home Rule Bill for Ireland had been passed by the Commons before the war, but the Lords threw it out; it was never revisited.)

The next Monday, George read in the papers that Lloyd George had invited Éamon de Valera, President of the Provisional Government in Dublin, to meet him in London. There is no evidence that George's note changed Lloyd George's mind, although George may have thought it did. There is no record of what the note said.

On 1 July 1921, George received a letter from TJ, saying:

Dear George
The position changed very quickly after we had met, but you can see how uncertain the issue is. If you or your 'Friends' have any power in Dublin now is the moment to use it. De V. is invited unconditionally and can raise and discuss *any* topic he likes; it will be a calamity if he puts obstacles in the way of a conference.

In his *Life of Thomas Jones CH*, E. L. Ellis wrote:

TJ received useful confidential information from this source [George M. Ll. Davies]. He also used Davies to transmit warnings to Sinn Féin of the dangers of its 'unreasonable' attitude.

It is highly unlikely, however, that the word 'unreasonable' would have been used by George himself. For one thing, he sympathised with Sinn Féin's attitude and their wishes, if not their methods; for another, George could have held that the attitude of Lloyd George, too, was 'unreasonable'. And in the work of reconciliation, words such as 'unreasonable' are seen as words of alienation rather than of peace.

It is clear that George Davies was not acting as a 'spy' for TJ and Lloyd George: he intentionally communicated with TJ and (implicitly) Lloyd George, and with Éamon de Valera, but as a mediator, trusted by both sides. George's unique position of being known personally to the leaders of both sides made his information valid and valuable. His position was, therefore, central – but was the *effect* of his mediation central or peripheral?

There is evidence that TJ had himself been liaising with Irish contacts for some time, and it is difficult to believe that Lloyd George was in ignorance of this, even if TJ, perhaps, kept George Davies in the dark about it. This demonstrates once again how much Lloyd George trusted TJ, a fellow-Welshman: Irishmen would have considered a Celt more trustworthy than many of their English colleagues. TJ had inside knowledge of Ireland: he had lectured there for a while a few years before, and was Professor of Economics at Queen's University, Belfast, in 1909. The valuable insights TJ gained during that year, and the fact that he was a Welshman (not an Englishman), made him invaluable in the negotiations with Sinn Féin at every level. Later, during the Treaty negotiations themselves, Sir Maurice Hankey, the Cabinet Secretary, an Englishman, had suggested that the Prime Minister 'did not want an Anglo-Saxon to run the show!' Lloyd George agreed, and asked Thomas Jones to be Secretary of the Irish Conference.

From an exchange of letters in June 1921, it is clear that both George and TJ felt their 'Welshness' to be important, but they also were in agreement about Ireland, and despaired at Lloyd George's intransigence. George wrote to TJ while Lloyd George was visiting Wales, saying that he was longing for Lloyd George 'to make some announcement of trust and reconciliation and of the better way than force. *That* would be the authentic voice of a child of Lleyn and Eifionnydd.'

TJ replied: 'My dear George, I have your letter and need not say how much I sympathise with your aspirations... We must hope that the atmosphere of North Wales will help the PM in his search for a right solution.'

On the night he received the letter from TJ asking him to go to Dublin (Saturday, 2 July 1921), George wrote back:

> My dear TJ,
> Thank you for your note. Yes, it is disappointing and futile that De V. seems to be manoeuvring for position. On *that* plane it is futile. Only on the human and spiritual plane can any real foundations be laid. I will go across to Dublin tonight. What I can do I can't imagine. What God can do in our weakness – who knows?

George taught little Jane how to answer in Welsh if anyone asked her where her father was: '*Mae e wedi mynd i Iwerddon*' (he has gone to Ireland).

Arriving in Dublin for the second time, George contacted James Douglas, a Quaker. Many of the Quakers in Dublin at the time were at the head of the business community.[4] Because they feared that the Irish economy would be harmed, they were deeply opposed to any form of Home Rule or independence; added to this, they were determined to maintain the Protestant ascendancy. If George Davies hoped the Dublin Quaker Meeting as a whole would be helpful to his efforts while representing the FoR, he was mistaken. But James Douglas, unusually, was both a Quaker and a Sinn Féiner. He had been unhappy with the idea of Home Rule for Ireland until the Easter Rising of 1916, when he suddenly saw the hold Britain had over Ireland by force. Before long he was a Sinn Féin member and later became speaker of the Dáil.

When they met (as George wrote in 'Ireland and Peace

Politics'), Douglas told George that he saw Lloyd George's invitation to Éamon de Valera 'as a ruse to produce a deadlock by inviting de Valera as representative of Southern Ireland and Sir James Craig as representative of Northern Ireland, when partition was the one thing Sinn Féin did not admit'. ('Partition' meant that the north of the island of Ireland would stay British.)

Douglas put George in touch with Erskine Childers, an extreme Sinn Féiner. (George described Childers as 'that tragic and romantic figure, an English aristocrat, distinguished in the war, who had thrown in his lot and his talents with Sinn Féin, only to be executed a year later by the Free State Government'.) Childers agreed with Douglas that the invitation was a trap, but nevertheless contacted de Valera. George wrote to TJ that he had spent a couple of hours with Childers, and that 'They [Sinn Féin] are very anxious for peace, but not for a surrender of principles'.

George went to de Valera's house to wait for him. While waiting, he discovered that Desmond Fitzgerald, whom he had met the year before, was in prison. George also met another IRA leader that he'd met the year before, who told George there was now a price on his head. George wrote at length about his conversation with this person, who introduced himself to George under a name George didn't recognise, but later revealed his real name – which, tantalisingly, George didn't! It could easily have been the charismatic leader of the IRA, Michael Collins (who adopted several false names to protect his identity), but half a dozen of the IRA leaders by then had prices on their heads, varying from £10,000 (Collins) to £3,500 for the less prominent.

De Valera didn't appear that night, and George left the house at 9.30pm because of the curfew. In desperation, George wrote a letter to Éamon de Valera the next day (Monday, 4 July 1921), and went to try to get it to the Irish leader. De Valera was holding peace discussions at the Mansion House with Irish Unionist politicians. The date of these talks – America's

Independence Day – was significant: de Valera, born in New York in 1882, held dual Irish and American citizenship, and flew the American flag 'in appreciation of the sympathy and aid given to our people by their friends in the United States'.[5]

George wrote to de Valera: 'I feel it is vital that this attempt should result in a personal interview between yourself and Mr Lloyd George, at which he will be able to put before you some of the restrictions and difficulties of his own position as a representative man.'

This was a clever move of George's. He had received a letter from a Quaker friend in Ireland who had met de Valera when he was in hiding, and 'Dev' had said to her that he could not meet Lloyd George without discussing Irish independence, because he was a 'representative man'. In using the same expression about Lloyd George, George was appealing to de Valera as a fellow politician, with similar dilemmas to face, and aiming to get de Valera to see his enemy as a human being.

George wrote later that the tension in Dublin was 'indescribable'. When he arrived at the Mansion House to deliver his letter to de Valera, he found a dense crowd outside. He could not get to the entrance, and decided to ask for his letter to be passed forward. He watched it being handed over people's heads until eventually it reached the entrance. His memory of the atmosphere on that day is powerful: it is obvious how important peace was to the Irish crowd:

> The scene was an unforgettable one. In O'Connell Street the sinister lorries of the Black and Tans still raced up and down, but here the Sinn Féin crowds were raising their hats and cheering as Lord Midleton and the other Southern Unionists arrived. While the Conference was sitting groups of people could be seen kneeling in prayer.

George had planned to leave Dublin that night, but late in the afternoon he tried once more to reach de Valera, by telephoning the Mansion House. Erskine Childers answered the phone and cried, 'Come at once, the President has asked for you several times'.

George returned to the Mansion House and Childers introduced him to de Valera, who looked, George wrote, 'very cool in spite of everything'. De Valera listened to George, then repeated that he still thought the invitation was a trap. 'What has England to fear from Ireland?' asked the President.

George reminded de Valera that twenty years before Lloyd George had been a strong Welsh nationalist. De Valera 'asked how he had become what he now was. I could only suggest that having gained power by the language and the methods of antagonism, the Juggernaut he had driven was now out of the control of the driver.'

George's report to TJ appears in TJ's *Whitehall Diary*, Vol. III (this volume deals solely with the Irish situation). George wrote that he spent half an hour trying to persuade de Valera of the sincerity of Lloyd George's offer of talks. The sticking points were the total independence of Ireland, and the matter of a united Ireland, rather than keeping Ulster separate. George said (somewhat naively) that negotiations should be entered on the assumption of the bona fides of the invitation from Lloyd George. The Irishman replied that it was 'always harder for the weaker side to take the risks of trust', and said, 'Taken in once is the other man's shame; taken in twice is your own shame'.

George wrote:

> As we shook hands in parting his strangely passionless face relaxed from its almost fanatical calm, and I saw a certain gentleness in the eyes from which I could partly understand the devotion and affection that this man inspired in so many thousands of his fellow countrymen.

George reported to TJ that he had found profound suspicion on all hands about Lloyd George's invitation.

When George reached London the next day (Tuesday, 5 July 1921), he found that General Smuts of South Africa, an international statesman, had already been sent by Lloyd George to reassure de Valera. That day, a truce was called by de Valera, and agreed by Lloyd George.

Following these meetings, de Valera and Lloyd George had a week of talks in London. At the start of the week, George did something very generous and personal. He sent a letter to TJ saying:

> I wonder if you would hand the enclosed to Mr Lloyd George. It is the book that John Jones used to carry with him in his pocket during his preaching journeys. It is the most intimate and precious relic I have of him. *Rwyf wedi sipian o hon lawer gwaith mewn tywydd garw ac yng ngharchar.* [I have sipped from it many times in rough weather and in prison.] If its associations and its faith can be any help to the P.M. in all the difficulties he will have to face to establish real reconciliation in Ireland – I cannot wish the little book any better destiny.

A reply from TJ dated 22 July 1921 says:

> Dear George
> As promised I handed the precious hymnbook to the PM in the presence of Hamar Greenwood [Irish Chief Secretary to the Government] a few minutes before his first meeting with de Valera. He was obviously very pleased indeed to receive your gift and he has it on the Cabinet table. He told me two nights ago that he had shewn it to de Valera in one of their talks, and had told the President something of John Jones' history.
> I cannot tell you anything about the course of the negotiations at this stage. I have seen a good deal of some members of the Irish deputation during their visit, and I think we have all laboured as hard as we knew how for peace.
> Yours ever, T. J. Jones.

What George Davies wished to achieve by giving Lloyd George his grandfather's book is not on record. True, George and the prime minister had known each other for some years. True, they were both Welshmen. True, Lloyd George greatly admired John Jones Talysarn (a local newspaper reported that, Lloyd George, speaking during the National Eisteddfod in Aberystwyth in 1916, had described John Jones as 'one of the greatest orators in Britain', and he believed the greatest biography ever written was Owen Thomas' *Life of John Jones*). The gift was, therefore, apt, meaningful, and very personal.

In a short television programme, *Pererin Hedd*, made for S4C in 2003 about George Davies' contribution to the Irish settlement, George is represented as saying to TJ that he wants to 'inspire' Lloyd George, but this is not made explicit anywhere in contemporary documents. It may be that George wanted to remind the Prime Minister that peace was an option, or that Lloyd George had once been an avid (Welsh) nationalist himself; maybe it was a straightforward gift to a friend; maybe George thought that the prime minister would be able to focus more effectively on peace with such a gift (George calls it a 'relic') in his hands. Although Lloyd George clearly appreciated the gift, there is no documentary evidence to indicate whether the hymnbook itself influenced him in any way.

George was well placed to have sympathy with many of the Irish negotiators because of their common prison experiences. One of his letters to TJ says:

> I wish the PM could realise something of the nervy attitude of mind that long imprisonment or expectation of arrest gives one. That may explain the mentality of Dev and the Dáil members. They are all strung up for death or victory.

And in September of 1921, during the initial talks, George wrote pleading for TJ to impress on Lloyd George that the Republicans were set to hold out for a Republic ('They are as habituated to the idea of *resistance to the end* as we were in the Great War'), and that he should remember 'the condition of their nerves and passions' – particularly Fitzgerald and Robert Barton, who had been through 'abominable prison treatment'.

As a result of the talks, proposals were made that de Valera rejected, but which he put before the Dáil Eireann, which also rejected them. There was deadlock. However, further talks were held later in 1921, in which Thomas Jones again played an important part, liaising between the Irish delegation and Lloyd George's Cabinet.[6] George Davies wrote a long letter on 15 October 1921 reminding TJ that whatever de Valera claimed as a right, 'he is bound to *allow* as a right to others'. This letter ends, showing the close friendship between the two Welshmen: 'My love and prayers for your success. Affectionately, George.'

In this continued correspondence George clearly wishes to contribute a mediator's insights into the negotiations. Just as he had represented Lloyd George's dilemmas to the Sinn Féiners, he tried to represent the Sinn Féiners' sensitivities and humanity to Lloyd George. There is no record of whether these insights were used or were helpful.

After weeks of negotiations the Dáil Eireann representatives signed the *Articles of Agreement for a Treaty between Great Britain and Ireland, 6 December 1921*. Lloyd George and TJ received many letters of congratulation when the news broke. Lord Esher called TJ 'the PM's good genius'. A letter from Sir Robert Horne to TJ said:

> The country [*sic*] owes you a great debt of gratitude. Next to the Prime Minister you have done more to bring about this settlement than anybody else. Your courage and enthusiasm have been wonderful.

TJ himself had spent many hours alone with members of the Irish delegation. He used much of the information George sent to him, and thanked him after the Treaty was signed: 'You... have helped to keep faith and hope from complete extinction' (16 December 1921). TJ's words indicate how helpful George's involvement was to him personally.

Unfortunately, Éamon de Valera considered that the delegates he had sent to London had sold Ireland short in signing for a Free State with partition, and a civil war raged for just over a year. In August 1922, Michael Collins, by then Commander-in-Chief of the Irish National Army, was assassinated, much to even Lloyd George's deep sorrow, and a lot of the fire went out of the Irish struggle.

George Davies' efforts had not immediately brought peace to Ireland, but from September 1923 onwards the situation improved. Ireland (reluctantly accepting partition) was on its way to being a peaceful Free State, and later a Republic – led for many decades by Éamon de Valera.

In his interventions in Ireland, George proved in a very public way that he was not, as some people believed, a coward who had stayed out of the First World War to save his own skin. He was ready to go into very dangerous and difficult situations in order to attempt reconciliation. His contribution to the Irish settlement was energetic, genuine, and continually statesmanlike.

But was George's intervention the very thing that sorted out the Irish War of Independence and brought peace to Ireland? It is clear that many people think so. Jill Wallis, in her history of the Fellowship of Reconciliation, says that 'while admittedly the time was ripe for de Valera to agree to negotiate with Lloyd George, the skill of George Davies and the efficacy of such personal mediation should not be belittled'. Writing of George in an obituary for *Peace News* (January 1950), Canon Charles Raven was reported to believe 'that George's outstanding public service was perhaps his direct intervention with Lloyd George to try and bring the Black and Tan war to an end'. Gwynfor Evans went further, writing in *Welsh Nation Builders* that 'Canon Raven said it was well known that the barriers that had prevented discussion were broken down by George Davies' efforts'. And in a conversation with me in August 1999, Gwynfor went even further, telling me that George Davies had 'single-handedly' dealt with the Black and Tan war.

In a review in the *Western Mail* in 1971 of Thomas Jones'

Whitehall Diary, Vol. III, T. Mervyn Jones, referring to the Troubles in Northern Ireland at the time, called for 'Welshmen to again play the role of mediators', but added: 'Alas, we cannot now suggest a modern George M. Ll. Davies, that reconciling saint to whose brave and beneficent part 50 years ago the *Diary* makes one reference'.

But it is clear from Éamon de Valera's papers that George Davies' intervention was only one of many efforts to bring peace during 1920 and 1921. De Valera had many visitors from Ireland and Britain throughout those years. It was Sinn Féin policy for other members of the Party not to have unofficial talks about peace with anyone, because a united front was required. It is clear that de Valera sensibly instituted a screening process whereby other members of Sinn Féin saw these potential peace-makers first, to get a good idea of their sincerity. In the dangerous situation in Dublin in those years, it was necessary to employ the most stringent caution.

There are many records of de Valera having meeting after meeting throughout 1921 with people trying to persuade him to meet Lloyd George. But although de Valera believed that seeing 'unofficial intermediaries' would lead nowhere, it was important for him, as president of the provisional government, to hear what they had to say, and then send them all away with the same message: that he was ready to meet Lloyd George for talks, but only if Irish independence was on the table for discussion.

Lloyd George was ready to meet de Valera for talks too... but only if Irish independence was *not* on the table for discussion.

So why did de Valera ask 'several times' to see George Davies? He could have regarded George as just another 'well-meaning but unauthorised person'. Certain factors gave George an advantage.

Firstly, there is the Quaker aspect. De Valera respected Quakers for the work they had done in Ireland during and since the famine of 1845–50. In 1921, George's Quaker friend James Douglas became the leader of the White Cross, the organisation in Ireland seeking to distribute American funds donated to bring relief to those on both sides who had been injured or had lost property. Éamon de Valera supported the White Cross wholeheartedly (as did other prominent Sinn Féin figures, including Michael Collins), and welcomed the presence of Quakers in the organisation. In January 1921 'Dev' wrote to Douglas: 'As a Society, faithful adherence to their principles and ideals have won for them the respect and confidence of all our people.'

George wrote to Thomas Jones: 'In approaching the Sinn Féin leaders it was always made clear that I did so from the Quaker position.'

Apart from the Quaker factor, George's friendships with James Douglas, Erskine Childers, and Desmond Fitzgerald, and quite possibly also his closeness to (and therefore the possibility of his influencing) Thomas Jones and David Lloyd George were also on his side. There is also the fact that George Davies was clearly a Welshman, rather than an Englishman – though conversely, Lloyd George was distrusted among the members of Sinn Féin. George's time in prison, and his undoubted integrity, may also have played a part in warming de Valera to him.

George seemed to believe that General Smuts had been sent to Dublin to see de Valera as a direct result of George's letter to TJ. This is not, however, the case. In March 1921, Col. Maurice Moore of the IRA travelled to London and to South Africa to talk with General Jan Christian Smuts. General Smuts had spoken in the post-war peace conferences in support of the small nations, and Sinn Féin wanted him to put Ireland's case in an imperial meeting in London during the summer. In a full, articulate and itemised report (March–May 1921), Moore told Smuts that, amongst others:

> The English Protestant Bishops and English Catholic Bishops, the heads of all the Non-Conformist Churches, 27 Professors of

the Welsh University, and all leading writers and literary men in England have dissociated themselves from Government policy [on the shooting of Irish prisoners].

According to Maurice Moore's diary, on 29 June 1921 Smuts' Secretary, Lane, arrived in Dublin with a letter from Smuts to de Valera; and on 5 July (the day after the Mansion House meeting and George's conversation with de Valera), Smuts and Dev met for tea.

Clearly, General Smuts' arrival in Dublin had nothing to do with George, and was only part of Smuts' intervention in the Ireland situation.

The fact of George being sent to Ireland by TJ raises another possible question. Was he being used by TJ? There was unanimity among the Sinn Féiners that Lloyd George was not to be trusted. Might it be that George, with his innocence and manifest sincerity, was sent to Dublin as an 'antidote' to Lloyd George's perceived mendacity? There is no solid evidence for this, however, and it must remain as simply a question.

Even after the Irish Civil War, George kept abreast of things in Ireland. He kept in touch with James Douglas and others in Ireland, and particularly with Molly and Erskine Childers. He was very upset about Erskine Childers' death in 1923 at the hands of the Free Staters, and kept cuttings giving details of his trial on 17 November 1922, and his pre-death statement in which he forgave his executioners. Molly Childers wrote to George regularly about the situation in Ireland throughout the Civil War and afterwards, including a moving account of her husband's last hours, writing of Childers' love for both England and Ireland, and saying that he died praying for England to change her attitude to Ireland.

In February 1945, Roy Walker (the Secretary of the Food Relief Campaign of the Peace Pledge Union) wrote to George about two manuscripts George had sent him for his opinion,

Reconciliation in Industry and *Ireland and Peace Politics*. Walker found the latter 'extraordinarily interesting', but comments: 'I did have the impression that you think the personal element almost all-important in the solution of political crises.'

The 'personal element' was indeed all-important to George. Throughout his life, he wanted all possible stones turned in the effort to bring peace to all situations: political, industrial and personal. He saw that too often, big approaches were made, and big policies implemented, without the 'personal element' being brought into play, and that this often missed the point of total reconciliation. He wrote in 'Growing in Pacifism', published in *The Christian Pacifist* in 1939:

> There is a searching word of William Blake: 'He who would do good must do it in minute particulars. General good is the plea of the hypocrite, the flatterer and the scoundrel.' At any rate Christ would seem to have directed His disciples to this 'fishing for men' and to the 'little leaven' of personal rightness and relationship rather than to the big lump of political policy as the distinctive method of the Kingdom of God for the finding and making of peace. And we Pacifists have a lot to learn about that.

George's contribution to the Irish situation in 1921 highlights the Sinn Féiners' distrust of Lloyd George. It also emphasises Welshman Thomas Jones, Lloyd George's trusted confidant, sending Welshman George Davies, TJ's trusted confidant, as intermediary to the Sinn Féiners in Ireland. The trust George gained from them, and the information he was able to share with TJ, was not simply pragmatic and strategic but was personal and insightful.

Did George achieve peace single-handedly? No, but he contributed positively, and risked his life to do so.

10

Westminster

In January 1924, several publications reported that an extraordinary dinner was given at the House of Commons. The dinner was held in honour of nineteen new MPs, four of them Welsh: George Davies, Will John (Rhondda), R. O. Wallhead (Merthyr), and Morgan Jones (Caerphilly). Also present, the *Cambrian News* reported, were 'suffragettes, passive resisters, anti-vaccinationists, two aspects of the Irish political thought, some who had offended against the restrictive legislation of war time, and so many types of Conscientious Objectors'.

The dinner was organised by Mr J. Scott Duckers, 'one of the first [COs] to be arrested under the Military Service Acts and amongst the last to be released'. And George M. Ll. Davies, the new MP for the University of Wales, gave an address, which began:

> Exactly seven years ago today I was on my way to London in [the] charge of a military escort which was taking me to Wormwood Scrubs Prison. This afternoon, I travelled up to take my seat in Parliament.

Every one of the fifty or so guests at this dinner – and the pressmen present – had been imprisoned for religious or political reasons. Stephen Hobhouse, co-editor of *English Prisons To-Day*, was there, as was philosopher Bertrand Russell. Emmanuel Shinwell, James Maxton and David Kirkwood, who had been imprisoned either during the war or soon afterwards, were there, as Independent Labour Party MPs. A toast was proposed to 'the ex-prisoner Members of Parliament.'

Fenner Brockway's autobiography recalled: 'As an ex-prisoner refusing alternative service I was not allowed to vote for five years, but illogically I was allowed to stand for Parliament in 1922'. The same illogicality applied to many of these nineteen MPs.

There were many difficulties for the Conscientious Objectors after the war – not least, the negative reactions of friends, family and colleagues. Some education authorities, for example, refused to employ teachers who had been COs, and former COs were refused reinstatement to their jobs in the Metropolitan Police.

Disenfranchisement was another problem. Parliament had voted in November 1917 not to disenfranchise COs; in a U-turn a few weeks later, this was amended to allow disenfranchisement for five years. Men who had done work of 'national importance' could apply for removal of the penalty, but few men bothered, and many appeared on the electoral register within those five years because officials were not aware of the penalty. So the disenfranchisement – which was an act of discrimination – fizzled out, allowing ex-COs to vote, and to become MPs, as had those at the House of Commons dinner, including George Davies.

One report on the dinner commented that George's letters and articles, published during the war and since, had expressed 'a spirit of love and kindliness that touched the hearts of all by sheer truth and goodness'.

George had no ambition for 'power' when he entered Parliament – conversely, he wished to empower others. His discovery that being looked down on as 'machines' made people revolt had turned him into a socialist. He understood the 'working man' much better than he had before prison. But still he had never joined any political party, though he had the backing of the University of Wales Labour Party.

So how did George get from prison to Parliament in that short time? What did he do between being 'at the bottom of things' (as a prisoner, he said, he'd worked as a stone-breaker, a floor-cleaner, and a dustman) and becoming an MP?

Between the undoubted excitement of his trips to Dublin in 1921, and his first election campaign in November and December 1923, George had continued to live with Leslie and little Jane at Maenan Hall Farm near Llanrwst in the north of Wales. It is not clear how George earned a living for his family. He wrote a good deal (about Ireland, for example). He read and wrote about non-confrontational methods being used at the time in different fields, such as progressive education and even animal training (for example, a book on *The Reforming of Dangerous and Useless Horses*), and was collecting information for use in his later pamphlet *Politics of Grace*, published by the FoR some time after 1925.

George's examination of the influence of politics in general life continued, and he kept his eyes on the situation in Europe and elsewhere. His new-found socialism became clearer in his writings. In 1921 (in *The Welsh Outlook*) he wrote:

> The Class War as expounded by Karl Marx, and other Communist
> sociologists, is not only a theory of politics, but a fact of social
> existence, a vast unsuspected conspiracy in which we have
> all taken our share. It is only when we see blood that we are
> perturbed.

Lloyd George had apparently been taking great pleasure in the 'success' of the 1918–19 blockades of Germany. George declared himself upset by the blockades, and by DLG's attitude: 'Today the desolation we have created in Middle Europe, the shivering women and the emaciated children, is brought home to us in the poignant appeals of the Daily Press,' he wrote. 'The chastisement of our peace is upon them.' His open criticism of the Prime Minister in *The Welsh Outlook* was a bold move: many of its readers were staunch Liberals.

George visited Germany to see for himself. In August 1923,

he published a pamphlet called *Our Responsibility for Europe*. It is clear that this was addressed to church and chapel leaders in Wales. George went much further than before in denouncing Lloyd George for signing the Versailles Treaty, and called the subsequent chaos and poverty 'our especial responsibility as Welshmen and as Christians'. He spoke of the 'misery and despair' that he had seen for himself. George enclosed with this pamphlet first-hand reports of the situation, many from Quakers, who were running relief operations throughout Europe.

George had become closely involved with the Quakers (Society of Friends), through the FoR and the IFoR. He had met them at post-war peace conferences and at reconciliation attempts in Ireland. George read Quaker literature, attended some Quaker meetings, and felt very much aligned with their principles.

During 1922 George considered rejoining the Calvinistic Methodists, but some of his friends, and Leslie, were not happy about it. There were differences between the Quakers and the Calvinistic Methodists, which George would have managed to reconcile for himself, but many Quakers would not have been happy with the Statement of Faith George would have had to sign to join the Calvinists; conversely, many Calvinistic Methodists would not have been happy with the Society of Friends' lack of fixed dogma. At the time, it was not possible to become a full Member of the Society of Friends while being a member of another denomination, though George would have been welcomed as a Quaker 'attender'.

Apart from his writing, researching and public speaking engagements, which included work for the Student Christian Mission, George spent a lot of time in the cottage at Maenan Hall Farm with his little daughter Jane, who recalled her father making up hilarious stories for her about 'Jimmy Squirrel' and 'Sarah Sheep', and teasing Leslie by giving her a perfumed handkerchief for her birthday – Leslie hated perfumed things! Was this George's boyhood practical joker side coming out again? He didn't seem to get jokes right with his womenfolk!

George spoke quite a bit of Welsh with Jane, but found it difficult that Leslie did not understand or speak Welsh herself.

Maenan Hall Farm was more the Davies family's 'home' than anywhere else had been, or ever was to be. According to Jane, Leslie and George were still very much in love, and would go for walks hand in hand. It was hard, though, for Leslie, being married to a man like George – always off preaching or at conferences, always penniless, always ready to put some needy individual before his family. Jane commented that Leslie realised George was a 'one-off', but many people acknowledged that Leslie had a hard life with George. Some had even thought she was stupid to tolerate it. Later, Leslie said to Jane, 'It's all very well *being* a saint, but you can't live *with* one.'

Throughout 1923 George read reports about work being done in various parts of Europe in the relief of famine and poverty, and with refugees. It makes grim reading, and George's gentle heart was torn with sorrow and anger at the plight of his fellow-men.

In February 1923, George received a letter from a German, Prof. Dr Julius Richter, who wrote of the French military occupation of the Ruhr Valley, the coal and steel producing area in the west of Germany. Among those opposing occupation were the German Communists, and a new organisation, the National Socialists, led by one Adolf Hitler. John Maynard Keynes had written accurately of the 'rumblings' in continental Europe, and of the 'fearful convulsions of a dying civilisation';[1] here we see Hitler's Third Reich and the Second World War in embryo.

George was aware of the problems the occupation of the Ruhr could cause. Apart from reading letters and reports, he joined around 200 other members of IFoR in July 1923 in Denmark to discuss the European situation. In his article

'New Lamps for Old', George describes this conference. Many nationalities and religious persuasions were represented, all hoping to find a way to overcome 'social injustice, war and every kind of evil'. There were French and German delegates from the Ruhr ('including Dabringhaus, leader of the Krupps workmen'), a Christian Communist, a Baroness, Catholics, Quakers, and Methodists. They heard about life in Red Russia from Tolstoy's friend (Cherkov) and secretary (Bulgakov), and received reports about the suppressed minorities in Hungary, Poland and Czechoslovakia. There were representatives from the new German Christian youth movements (soon to be taken over by Hitler and turned into the Hitler Youth). 'And underneath our bewildering differences of race, language, creed, caste and colour,' wrote George, 'we touched and found the Universal Heart that makes peace'.

But also in 'New Lamps for Old', George called the Ruhr 'the cauldron of human agonies and terrible outrages of the spirit'. George went on:

A firm friend of France, commissioned by the Quakers to report on the human side of the Ruhr, writes to the *Times* – 'Friends come in to see you and you wonder at their hushed voices, anxious eyes, and trembling lips. At first they talk of the weather, then, very quietly they roll up for you that curtain of tranquillity and you peer into a darkened atmosphere of terror and dismay.'

The heartbreaking reports told of forty suicides a week in Berlin, the deep desperation throughout Germany, and unrest fanned by the Communists. George went on:

The next war is being prepared for. Four million men under arms and three million being trained. Great Britain spends sixty millions more per annum on armaments than in the days of the feverish competition that led to the last war.

The self-righteous attitude of the churches of Britain and

Europe to the situation in Germany caused George to write to the editor of *The Welsh Outlook*:

> And 'the Churches' passed by on the other side, while the chastisement of our peace ground the poor of Austria and Germany to powder, and while our British blockade and subsidised military 'interventions' helped to complete the starvation of Russia... while the Russians and Austrians starved 'the Churches' were busy increasing their endowments and emoluments. Ireland goes through its agony [the Civil War that followed the signing of the Treaty in 1921], the great Saint of India [Gandhi] is imprisoned with 20,000 of his followers, the class war is fought out in the coalfield, the engineering yards, the quarries, and the farms, without any light from 'the Churches' as to the way of peace in politics or industry.

As usual, George, with his internationalist perspective, was able to see the wider picture. Having lost the war, Germany was in desperate trouble. The negative effects of war, the Treaty of Versailles, and imperialism, Communism and capitalism were to be seen all over Europe and beyond.

Since 1919 and the release of the COs from prison, the FoR had been trying to make an impact on as many areas of British life as it could, initiating reconciliation work wherever possible, and becoming involved in education and in combating unemployment. Members also began discussing going into Parliament, and several decided to stand as Labour candidates in the General Election to be held at the end of 1923. George's commitment to making a difference to the world led him to consider entering Parliament himself.

The Liberal Party had been the only party for socialists and nationalists until the Independent Labour Party was founded in 1893. George Davies' prison experience had completed his transformation into an active socialist, but that process of change had begun before prison: in May 1917 he had written to Thomas Jones:

The only untried principles and the only parties in Europe
whose objectives have not been discredited by the War is that of
Socialism. It is without doubt a positive power of the future...
I believe we may well see a spiritual revolution, a renaissance
beyond our dreams, a veritable coming of love on earth.

But as David Pretty pointed out, the labour movement
grew slowly in Wales – partly because the first loyalty of most
workers was to their chapels; many of the chapel leaders
were Liberals, and many were capitalists. By 1914, there were
around 100 branches of the ILP in the industrial south of the
country, and only fourteen in the north.[2] Labour branches
were set up all over Wales soon after the First World War, and
trade unions were started for agricultural workers and others.
Middle-class people were involved too: for example, Caradog
Jones, a schoolteacher, rode his bike round Llŷn establishing
branches of the Labour party and the Workers' Educational
Association.

David Thomas, a pacifist and future CO, son of a stonemason
and smallholder, was significant in the establishment of
the Labour movement in north Wales. He had read the
reformist literature of the time (he described George later as
a 'progressive reformist'), and in 1906 he joined the Fabian
Society and the ILP. Whenever he was not teaching in school,
he was organising or speaking at meetings, or teaching for
the Workers' Education Association. He set up many Labour
branches in north Wales, and was particularly keen to 'root
Labour in the values of Welsh-speaking Wales'. He also liaised
with leaders in the south, with the aim of creating a united
Labour Party in Wales.

David Thomas' main interest was the plight of agricultural
workers. The farmers themselves, by charging extortionate
prices for foodstuffs, were benefiting from the war, but their
workers were very badly paid, and in some cases children were
let off school in their hundreds to do farm work, because it
was cheaper than paying extra men. Some men chose to stick

at farm work rather than join the Army, and had their wages reduced by their masters. The Non-conformists didn't like to criticise the (middle-class) farmers, many of whom were chapel deacons.

Like George, David Thomas undertook 'alternative service' during the war, working on a farm. He gained first-hand experience of the lot of the labourer, which gave him more credibility after the war.

On 24 June 1917, in Magor, Monmouthshire, at an open-air meeting, the agricultural workers organised a revolt. The unrest, and the growth of Labour branches and trade unions, spread throughout Wales. By 1920 there were around 10,000 members in some 300 branches.

Following his release from prison in 1919, George discovered that some farmworkers, unhappy about low pay and long hours, had threatened to set hayricks on fire. George wrote in *Profiadau Pellach* [further experiences], that farmers opposed Unionism for farmworkers, but he now knew from personal experience what life was like on around eight shillings a week. He called in on the Executive Committee of the Workers' Union in Llangefni on Anglesey, and asked if he could talk to them about Christ's way of reconciliation. To his surprise, he wasn't turned out, but was given an attentive hearing, and was told he was welcome to go round the Unions on Anglesey with his message. He added:

> I was often ashamed after that by [farm workers] because of their courtesy and their welcome, and their readiness to believe in the possibility of extending the brotherhood of man towards those [farmers] who had made a big profit in the war because of their [the workers'] labour and their small wages.

After that, George was invited to speak at many agricultural workers' union meetings, and to mediate on several occasions.

In June 1923, George was approached by the Meirioneth

Labour Party to be their candidate in a future election. He replied thanking them, but saying that his views would not permit him to join any political party. He called for a recantation by Labour leaders of their war policy and of their support for the 'merciless Versailles Treaty and its reparations', requesting a campaign against militarism and capitalism, and asking for the Labour Party to become a Christian party. He said that he saw that 'what is morally wrong can never be politically right'. His letter, which has a strong Quaker emphasis, stated:

> I do not know how many workers in Meirioneth share this faith
> – that the way of Christ in politics is the only hope of Society. I do
> not know how fit I should be to represent these truths. I should
> account it neither pleasure nor privilege nor honour to sit in the
> House of Commons (knowing what evils have been sanctioned
> within its walls), but if any fellow-workers really desire me to
> express in that place the truths to which I am bound to bear
> witness in any case and at every opportunity, I should be willing
> to accept nomination as a Christian Labour candidate. While
> in full sympathy with the objects set forth in the Labour Party
> pamphlet (as I am with the *objects* of the Christian Churches), I am
> a member of no party or sect – for at a great cost I purchased this
> freedom – to act without bondage according to my own reason and
> conscience and the light of Christ's teaching.

The Welsh University's Parliamentary seat was created in 1918, under the Representation of the People Act, giving an extra vote to all of its graduates. The University Labour Party was formed in 1922, linking the University's Socialist Societies at Aberystwyth, Bangor, Cardiff and Swansea. University Labour Clubs had been forming throughout Britain since 1918. According to Hilary Marquand, the new 'branch' was treated to 'a most amusing display of hysterics in the Die-hard press.'[3] Linking the four Welsh colleges was felt to be more useful to the Labour Party as a whole. The University Labour Party included a wide range of opinion and thought. The Labour

Movement, Marquand continued, 'must have trained minds at its service. It is the work of the University Labour Movement to provide those minds.'

It is possible that a member of the Meirioneth Labour Party had connections with the Welsh University Labour Party, and had drawn attention to George's stated willingness to accept nomination as an independent Christian Labour candidate. Writing to Judge Bryn Roberts on 13 November 1923, George made very clear his three conditions for accepting the Labour whip, should he be elected: his freedom of 'vote, speech and action' must not be restricted; he was to be allowed 'open collaboration with men of similar sympathies in other parties'; and he must not be forced to vote with Labour if they 'should at any time force through legislation by "duressive majority power".'

These conditions were accepted, and George became the candidate for the Welsh University in the 1923 General Election, as an independent Christian Pacifist, supported by the college Labour Party. The other candidates were the Rev. Professor Joseph Jones (Liberal), and Major Jack Edwards (Independent Liberal). There was no Conservative candidate.

The election had been called by Prime Minister Stanley Baldwin, to be held on 6 December, on the issue of the effect of the occupation of the Ruhr and the general situation in Europe, post-Versailles, on Britain. There was much disagreement about the possible introduction of tariffs to defend domestic trade. While the Liberals supported free trade, the Labour Party manifesto had a Keynesian 'Programme of National Work' as its solution to unemployment and poverty. Its more internationalist approach also called for the League of Nations to be strengthened and enlarged; the revision of the Versailles Treaty; and the resumption of diplomatic relations with Russia. 'This will pave the way for Disarmament, the only security for the nations.' The Labour Party manifesto was the nearest to George's beliefs and principles.

While the candidates for Cardiganshire were busy speaking to their constituents in the county, George M. Ll. Davies, Christian Pacifist candidate for the Welsh University, was issuing his Election Address and holding meetings for his constituents, graduates of the University, scattered throughout Britain: amongst the venues were Aberystwyth, Liverpool, Manchester and London.

George asked Judge Bryn Roberts to send out a statement to the *Liverpool Daily Post*, the *London Daily News*, and *Y Genedl*, requesting publicity, and giving him Judge Roberts' personal recommendation. The statement was to say that George had no personal political ambition, and saw only 'a further opportunity for pleading for principles of reconciliation – the advancement of which is the chief purpose of his life'. George complained that *Y Cymro* and *Y Goleuad*, Welsh weekly newspapers, had described him as 'a Labour Party candidate which is quite incorrect. I have refused from the outset to accept any party bonds... I am out for radical changes by appeals to conscience and consent, which attitude the University Labour people are good enough to support'.

George went on: 'It is the idea of out and out Pacifism, clear, stark, uncompromising that I want to strike into the public mind as far as I can.'

George's 15-page Election Address defined this pacifistic stance. He intended from the start that both the 'Christian' and the 'Pacifist' standpoints would be emphasised: his main objective was, he said, 'Peace and Restoration by the methods of forgiveness, liberation and goodwill'. He said that creating work schemes would help the unemployed, and could be funded by not spending 'vast sums' on 'provocative and illusory armaments for war'. But even more important than that, he wrote, 'is the restoration of European trade and peace through generous and fair settlement and restoration of the impoverished and devastated peoples of Europe'.

The word 'fair' is significant here. George had seen with his own eyes, and had read enough, to know that tariffs can damage either side, and he would not have seen that as contributing to the reconstruction of Europe.

George's Election Address exemplified his capability for lateral thinking, of seeing the 'other' solution to a problem, and of taking up a courageously independent position. This has been confirmed by his later writings, and also by conversations with people who knew George well. In the affairs of others he could usually see through to the foundational situation, rather than becoming deflected by what was being presented as the 'immediate' problem.

Although firmly an internationalist, George also showed himself to be an outspoken Welsh nationalist, in favour of Home Rule at the very least, 'or... even more detailed decentralisation'. He spoke of Ireland and how she had 'demonstrated that mere legal powers of self-determination are quite inadequate without the growth of the practice of positive co-operation'. George went on:

> As a conscientious objector to war, I have myself suffered
> imprisonment, and loss of political rights too long to regard the
> smallness or unpopularity of a minority as any reason for its
> suppression, over-ruling or deprivation.

This is consistent with many things George said about the oppression of Wales in later writings. He ends this section:

> I believe there is a nobler destiny for the youth of Wales – free
> and self-determining – than to be tied to the chariot wheels of
> Big Business, or of British Imperialism, and so live in bondage to
> Bread and Circuses.

George, as well as wishing Wales as a nation to be 'free and self-determining' had the same wish for individuals ('the youth of Wales').

'Rambling Writer' in the *Cambrian News* praised this Address. The writer, who clearly admired George Davies, wrote that George had three principles:

1 What is personally wrong can never be politically right.
2. The supreme example of personal rightness in human affairs is Jesus Christ.
3. It is not sufficient to extol such a standard as a beautiful but impracticable ideal.

'Rambling Writer' described George as 'a remarkable person... transparently sincere, possessing that courage which is said to be held only by fools and angels, and of the type who, in the olden days were martyred for many things – afterwards to be canonised'. The report said that 'George Davies... knows newspaper men, revolutionaries and statesmen', and said that the University candidate wanted to 'find a Christian method and to back away from the mere partisanship that embitters our politics so much'.

George's address showed him to be a radical socialist (though not a member of any party or socialist organisation); a Welsh nationalist (though he never joined the future Plaid Cymru); an internationalist, and an economist. He demonstrated knowledge of agriculture, progressive education, penal reform, Ireland, and the position of women in society. Few matters seemed to have escaped his notice, or his interest. Almost any voter in the University could have found at least one thing to identify with in this address. His writing style was clear, lively and fluent. He juxtaposed phrases powerfully: for example, 'angry mobs or monied minorities'; *thought* out, not *fought* out'; and called for disarmament 'not only with our lips, but in our lives' – a quote from an Anglican prayer.

George spoke for the 'ex-soldiers... [who] walk our streets unhonoured and unemployed'. He spoke of the class war, and of his opposition to state bullying of workers. And he condemned 'extremists of the Right and Left', and called for extremists of the centre to come forward:

> ... men who will completely abandon the methods of mere brute force and coercion, who will live for the righting of human

relationships and human conditions, and will be prepared to suffer violence and coercion rather than condone or inflict it.

This is clearly idealism, but George believed that it was desirable not to lean to one extreme or another but to be a radical thinker of the Centre. He *lived* his idealism. His belief that the personal approach would work in all situations – the path of reconciliation between individuals – never left him, and on many occasions he made it work.

However, George was not averse to firing a broadside when necessary, and he ended his Address with a section on Ireland, appreciating the Republicans' 'sense of moral wrong' at 'being required to swear an allegiance to the British Crown which they neither intend nor respect' – in order for Ireland to be given independent Dominion status!

And there is also a stinging reference to Lloyd George's treatment of the Irish delegation in George's final sentence: 'No Christian Statesman or Cabinet had the moral right to threaten the horrors of war for such fiction even to save their own prestige or that of the nation.'

The election result (one of the last in, presumably because of the widespread 'constituency', on 13 December) was a surprise:

Constituents: 1,922	Turnout 83.1%	Total votes cast: 1,597	
George M. Ll. Davies	Lab [*sic*]	570maj. 10	35.7%
Rev. J. Jones	Lib	560	35.1%
J. Edwards	Ind. Lib.	467	29.2%

Stanley Baldwin's Conservatives lost their overall majority in this December 1923 General Election (the Liberals won 159 seats, Labour 191), and then also lost a vote of confidence in January 1924. King George V then called on Ramsay MacDonald to form a government, supported by the Liberals; MacDonald thus became the first Labour Prime Minister.

Kenneth O. Morgan (historian of politics) sees George's

victory as a political one, 'a public rejection of war and military values by the graduate electors of Wales, as startling in its own way as the Oxford Union "King and Country" debate ten years later', and considers that it showed a move away from commitment to Lloyd George's leadership,[4] and part of a move away from Liberalism to socialism.[5] D. Densil Morgan (historian of religion), on the other hand, says that the election of George Davies, 'the most charismatic (and perhaps most enigmatic) of Welsh pacifists… was seen by many [pacifists] as the ultimate validation of their creed'.[6]

The *Western Mail* reported (14 December 1923) that Labour now had twenty seats in Wales (they presumably included George), having gained two, a clear majority of four over the Welsh Liberals. The column described George thus:

> Not yet forty years of age, Mr Davies is a man of wide culture, and has travelled extensively in Europe in connection with the Fellowship of Reconciliation… He has come into close contact with the various University colleges of Wales through his activities in connection with the Student Christian Mission.

Perhaps it surprised George that he won the election. He had never wanted 'power' for power's sake. In his papers, there are many letters and cards from people in all walks of life and of all political persuasions, congratulating him on his victory. Many were graduates of the University of Wales; many were thrilled by the fact that it was predominantly young people who had voted for George the Christian Pacifist. Many of his friends were thrilled he'd won; many were unhappy with his decision to stand. There is no record of Leslie's response.

Fenner Brockway wrote congratulating George, and asking for an article for *No More War* 'stating what you think out-and-out pacifists should do in Parliament, and what they should advocate in the country. It will be a great help. Please do.'

Bernard Cudbird, a Quaker in Cardiff, wrote: 'What a strange reversal of things in such a comparatively short time – gaol bird

1919 – MP 1923. I wonder whether you will find less liberty in HM Parliament than in HM Prison.'

Dilys Edmunds, an old friend doing missionary work in India, expressed surprise at George's decision to stand: 'The thing I fail to understand is how you, with your scorn of Politics and Parliaments, ever brought yourself to stand. Have you changed your opinion of what they can accomplish?'

Thomas Jones was even less happy, perhaps because he knew George well and was concerned about how he would cope with Parliamentary life, but wished him well.

A letter to the *Western Mail* from 'A Welsh County Councillor' expressed fury that those in the University with 'extreme socialist views' had elected 'one who refused military service'. He called for a reduction in budget to the University, and for an 'unwarped' education for 'Young Wales'. He ended, 'Will not someone... in Wales move in this matter, or must we look for a British Mussolini to arise to do what we are too weak and apathetic to put right?'

Conversely, the editorial in the staunchly Liberal *Cambrian News* was excited about the new MP. Clearly George Davies had impressed many people. He would, the editor said, 'be welcomed by all for his sterling sincerity, though the programme of his party [*sic*] is not generally acceptable'. The Editor went on to say that George had got in by appealing 'to all lovers of fearless straightforward dealing'. The editor went on to say (presciently, as it happens) that George Davies' strong principles would not allow him to stay long in the Commons: 'his is the nature which in days of old braved the stake rather than give way.'

The editor ended:

George Davies is in advance of his age, but age advances. When the general election of 1923 is forgotten, and even the names of great Parliamentarians are mere history, the first Labour MP for the Welsh University will be acknowledged as the man who, preaching a better way and sounding a new note, commenced the blazing of a new trail, the end of which no man can foresee.

George Davies took his place in Parliament on 24 January 1924. That evening, George addressed the dinner in honour of the nineteen new MPs who had been in prison. The *Cambrian News* reported that he had said:

> To be at the bottom of things is to be in the position of power. Once we feel we are looked down upon as machines we revolt... It came to me in prison that fellowship is really life. What we have experienced must make us determined that our whole treatment of the offender must be changed. One thing at least the new Parliament must do, and that is to reform this diabolical mechanism of prison which makes sinful men confirmed criminals.

In spite of his scorn for politics, George Davies had high hopes for his time in the Commons, preaching what he had called 'the Good News of the Politics of Love'. In spite of this faith, George was to find out that being an MP was no easy task.

As Member of Parliament for the Welsh University, George had a widespread audience for his peace message. In January 1924 he wrote four articles for a Welsh newspaper about Christianity and politics. In one of them, he commented astutely that on the continent, 'the very word Christian, as adopted as a political label, almost invariably means "anti-Semite"'.

George also wrote the article for *No More War* (1 February 1924), entitled 'A Pacifist in Parliament: a serious challenge to out-and-outers, both in the country and in the Commons'. On the front of the issue is a character sketch of George Davies, written by 'PB' who had heard George speak at a meeting on Internationalism. The writer describes George's words as slight, conversational and intimate, but:

> ... through them and through his face shone the unique personality about which the most casual acquaintance at once becomes strangely enthusiastic. There is something about him which lifts

you, at any rate for a few minutes, to the full stature of your best self. George Davies is a thorough pacifist in his relations with other people as well as in his convictions... 'We are so angular, we COs,' he will say, 'so pugnacious and cocksure and narrow. I don't wonder we are few.'

PB says George had gone into the campaign 'almost without a thought of winning', but that he valued his election mainly as a tremendous opportunity 'of getting into touch with people who in other circumstances might not be prepared to listen to him'.

In 'A Pacifist in Parliament', George attempted to answer the question, 'What should an out-and-out pacifist do in Parliament and advocate in the country?' George's answer was 'that he should be a peace-maker, not a peace-talker only'. He spoke of the difficulty of being a pacifist, and answered the critics who said there was more 'fist' than 'pax' about pacifists by saying:

> After being repressed and despised for so long as a weak-kneed, meek and cowardly lot, it is hardly to be wondered that some of us rebounded from the 'inferiority complex' and roared as loudly as any other British lion for our class-war or for our 'fight to a finish' on our partisan fields.

As in his Election Address, George asked where were the 'extremists of the Centre' in Parliament, who would:

> ... be in the fight, but not of it; who will keep the peace whatever status or strategy they surrender; who will conquer enemies by conquering the enmity; who will give up everything rather than willingly give up men; who will remedy and report every evil within their power and reach and yet will not resist the evil-doer?

George Davies then set out a six-point programme for a pacifist MP. These included maintaining the freedom to speak and act according to conscience; working to eradicate enmities;

seeking reconciliation 'with any who may be prepared to seek peace by good-will, rights by right means, and settlements by mutual consent'; converting his antagonist to the ways of peace, rather than coercing him.

This article, however, is rather more prescriptive than inspiring, more specifically Christian than broadly tolerant. George made the surprising assumption that all readers of *No More War* – and all 'out-and-out pacifists' – were Christians, or would fully understand and empathise with his Christian language. He called a lot of Parliamentary procedures 'neither good Christianity nor good sense', and went on: 'With all our idealist programme our political *methods* are still pagan and therefore stupid.' He also said that the pacifist in Parliament should keep the faith with 'that of God in every man', and 'to forgive always as God forgives'.

At the end of the article George again spoke of 'Christian polity and Christian methods' as the ideal way to live. He continued: 'Somewhere in a coalition between a Socialised Christianity and a Christianised Socialism I see the beginnings of a new Heaven and a new Earth in religion and politics.'

George wrote as if Christianity was the only way, or as if Christian language could express all their (different) standpoints. In fact, George would have known that many members of War Resisters International were humanists, atheists, Marxists – anything but Christians. George seemed also to assume that Christian Pacifism was the only pacifism. A 'Programme for a Pacifist MP' could have been all-embracing, to include people such as James Maxton MP (a humanist) and George Lansbury MP (a Communist), both of whom had been at Scott Duckers' dinner in the House of Commons only a short time before, and both of whom George must have known personally. However, the majority of his non-Christian colleagues would have understood and respected George's language, agreeing with the principles and practice without agreeing with the religious content. It was the language of the day.

But it is always noticeable that when George sounds most determinedly Christian, prescriptive, and somewhat pompous, as in these articles, rather than dynamic, inspired and inspiring, it is indicative of a period of mental illness. George's tendency towards depression and breakdowns followed him through his life. Even this early in his Parliamentary career, George had been drawn into a situation that triggered stress reactions and a consequent mental collapse.

On 29 January 1924, only a few days after taking his seat in the Commons, George wrote to his friend Judge Bryn Roberts, in Wales. He was clearly agitated. He explained that his Election Agent had disclosed that he had 'made some small disbursements not shown' in the Returns. George 'immediately asked for an explanation and said the Return must be amended'. The agent, and Ellis Davis MP, a solicitor from Cardiff, 'rather pooh-poohed the difficulty'.

The deeply honest George Davies and his brother Stanley, however, believed that the matter was serious and that it should be dealt with, 'even if I am unseated and suffer the discredit that is associated with being unseated under the Corrupt Practices Act'. George worried more about the effect on his Agent, 'a gentlemanly young fellow with a rather flippant view of legal formularies', whom George, the former bank manager, had warned repeatedly of the need to be 'precise and exact in his returns'. George and the agent were meeting a solicitor on the coming Friday, 'and unless new light comes will instruct him to take the necessary steps to open the Return and to appeal for Relief of the Court'.

George seemed to accept the possibility of losing his seat, almost sounding as though he would welcome returning quietly to Wales. His letter to the judge ends with his apology to his supporters, 'but perhaps it will work out in some better way'.

Clearly George's predicament was discussed in many quarters, and caused consternation. The anthropologist and geographer Herbert Fleure, then Gregynog Professor of

Geography at Aberystwyth, wrote to the judge asking if 'persons whose names are known' could be called upon to write to George's electors 'just to say that we who have gone into the whole matter carefully feel moved to express our admiration of his conduct in this (and in as many other matters, one might add)'. On 21 February, Fleure wrote again saying that the University Vice-Chancellor had 'a warm personal feeling for our friend' and was 'most concerned to see that George's good name is thoroughly upheld'. In March 1924, Harry Darbishire, an FoR member, wrote a very warm and sympathetic letter to George, offering help 'in the difficulties', and saying that he would 'see the Public Prosecutor or do anything else if I can be of use'.

Much later, in 1927, George Davies wrote to Percy Bartlett, then General Secretary of the Fellowship of Reconciliation, describing the 1924 situation with his Election Agent. George wrote, 'It was an agony of perplexity and of darkness'.

Even later, in 1929, George wrote to the Elected Moderator of the General Assembly of the Calvinistic Methodists:

> I... was obliged to face the possible infliction of heavy legal penalties upon a thoughtless friend for a moral debt of a hundred pence. Ultimately the legal authorities of the State decided to take no action but the strain of having to assent to Law while pleading grace convinced me that the august and respectable sanctions of coercive Law were essentially a secular method and an essential denial in practice of the grace of God.

In the same letter he commented, 'My freedom of fellowship with men of all Parties remains a very happy memory of the House of Commons'.

It is good to find that George had this 'very happy memory'; nowhere else in any writing about him is this revealed. Only the fact that he had a breakdown is ever mentioned; clichés used are that George 'overworked', or was 'not fitted for the rough-and-tumble of political controversy'.

However, the truth is that the breakdown, far from being caused by George's weakness of mind, was caused at least in part by his perhaps slightly over-zealous stance on principle over a relatively small amount of money – around 8s 3d.

George's daughter Jane remembered him returning to Maenan Hall Farm around this time, in a bad state. Jane was just over eight at the time. She found it very difficult to see her dear father so unhappy:

> I remember him wandering around the place groaning, and pulling threads out of his white bathrobe... And then he got very obsessed by someone that had hanged themselves on the back of their door. Leslie was very nervous because he was sort of contemplating the back of the door, if you like.

When going through Jane's effects after her death in 2005, her daughter Nancy White discovered an old and large white bathrobe, very much the worse for wear, and not knowing its history, threw it away. Only when I sent her the transcript of my interview with her mother did she realise what it was. Nancy and I wondered why Leslie had kept it.

On 10 April 1924 Leslie wrote from Maenan to Judge Bryn Roberts, informing him that the Public Prosecutor had said that he 'will not sanction any prosecution' and that the incident was closed. He had arrived at his decision after consultation with the Attorney General. There was to be an official announcement in the *Daily Herald* saying that George would keep his seat. 'All the officials with whom I have been in communication have been so kind about it all. George is still very depressed – about his own soul now. He is obviously relieved at the clearing of the political atmosphere – and this will help his recovery.' On the back of the letter the judge wrote his sympathetic reply, saying the Agent had received the treatment he deserved.

Besides all this stress, George had to contend with all the usual calls on an MP's time and attention. Some people made demands on his attachments to the Peace Movement, and others on his alliance with the Labour Party. For example, he was asked to speak to an ILP meeting in Cardiff. The ILP in Swansea also wanted George to speak, because of the rising threat of 'a bastard Welsh Nationalism which we ought to counteract'. (It should be noted that Plaid Cymru, the Welsh Nationalist Party, was formed soon after this, in 1925.)

George was used to living in London – he had done so in 1914 and 1915. But now he was spending long periods away from his wife and daughter, and away from his beloved Wales. As a University MP, he had no geographical 'constituency' to return to. These, on top of his parliamentary duties, added to the pressures in his life.

Before taking his seat in Parliament, George had been trying to get some of his essays published. George had been consistently critical – on many occasions angrily so – of the churches and their lack of leadership towards peace. For instance, in his essay 'In Forma Pauperis', George pointed out that faith in the churches had decreased because they had 'darkened their windows and hid their light from men'. George commented that the three men who had resigned from the government over the declaration of war (Viscount Morley, Sir Charles Trevelyan and John Burns) were all agnostics; he also said that other 'men of the world' had 'advocated forgiveness, consideration, compassion and "letting the oppressed go free"', while the churches had 'exchanged the protection of Mammon for the previous protection of Mars' and 'acquiesce in a world of vanquished and victors in field, factory and mine [and had] become partisans in ecclesiastical and class struggles'.

This was one of George's strengths: while he was a man of peace, an active peace-maker, and one who could make an individual of any background feel immediately special and valued, he was ready to confront anyone he felt deserved it in the interests of peace, whether an individual (such as Lloyd George) or fellow pacifists, organisations such as churches, or 'experts' such as educationalists. It is a testament to his love of people that few bore him any ill-will. His criticism of Lloyd George during the First World War and afterwards was sometimes harsh, but later George was several times a guest of Lloyd George at his house in Churt, Dorset.

George's generosity in 'In Forma Pauperis' towards Morley, Trevelyan and Burns shows that he could respect non-Christians who had similar values to his own, even when they did not have the same god. This made his occasional lack of inclusivity, for example in the 'No More War' article, all the more surprising – except that it occurs almost every time he feels depressed, as if he is withdrawing inside his own faith as behind thick curtains.

Twenty-two of George's articles were eventually published as a collection in 1946, under the title *Essays Towards Peace*.

The problems of Ireland were the subject of George Davies MP's long and articulate maiden speech to the Commons on 1 October 1924, which appears to be the only time he took part in a debate (his breakdown had taken several months out of his ten-month term in Parliament). The subject under discussion was a rewording of a clause in the Irish Free State Bill concerning the border between the Free State and Northern Ireland.

George said, 'It seems to me that the question of putting pledge against pledge does not lead us in this House to any solution', and urged the House to realise that 700 years of coercion had failed to bring peace to Ireland. He, though having no sympathy with republicanism, sought to represent the feelings of the Republican movement in Ireland, especially after his experiences there. He suggested that Westminster had 'relied far too much on our powers of coercion... and too little upon our powers of conciliation and friendship'.

George also spoke of the attitude of Westminster towards the Republicans and their refusal to pledge allegiance to the king. He noted that the recent settlement in South Africa permitted citizens to declare 'recognition of' the king, rather than 'allegiance to' the king: why, then, not in Ireland too? (This is hardly a 'dead' issue; in 1997 the democratically elected Sinn Féin MPs Gerry Adams and Martin McGuinness were refused Parliamentary privileges because they could not swear allegiance to the Queen of England. Republicans cannot swear allegiance to the Queen. They are Republicans!)

Following a vote of no confidence, Prime Minister Ramsay MacDonald was forced to call another General Election, to be held on 29 October 1924. Following the 1923 election, the University of Wales Liberal Graduates' Association had worked hard to avoid another split vote. For a while it looked like another three-cornered fight, with Major Jack Edwards again considering standing (presumably as an Independent Liberal again). The feeling was, said the *Western Mail*, that the Liberals would win the seat back from George, on the basis that 'at this election, the graduates would be less likely to vote for "freak" views on matters which require practical political treatment'. In the event, however, only George and the new Liberal candidate, Captain Ernest Evans, contested the seat. Captain Evans had been MP for Cardiganshire until 1923, and was perhaps considered a 'safe pair of hands' by the University Liberal Graduates' Association, although it seems unlikely that his past record would have influenced such a scattered 'constituency'.

The two University candidates once again travelled far and wide to meet their 'constituents'. Both candidates spoke at a meeting in Aberystwyth. Ernest Evans received a warm welcome at Caxton Hall, Westminster, London; a motion pledging support to him was moved by a representative of Bangor College, seconded by Swansea College and supported by Cardiff College.

There is nothing to suggest that George actively wished to contest this General Election. His campaign seems to have been very low-key, with none of the excitement of the year before.

There is no indication that he wanted to win; indeed, after his previous term at Westminster it would not be surprising if he had hoped to lose. There are no letters in his archive about the fact that he lost. (Had there been a third candidate George might well have held his seat.) The result was:

Constituents: 2,252	Turnout 79.0%		Total votes cast: 1,778
E. Evans	Lib	1,057 maj. 336	59.4%
George M. Ll. Davies	Lab	721	40.6%

The ten-month existence of 'George M. Ll. Davies MP' was over, and it was time for him to look for his next role.

11

Welsh Schoolboys' Camp Movement

ONE OF GEORGE'S projects, and a further manifestation of his desire to promote co-operation through action, was the Welsh Schoolboys' Camp Movement (WSCM), which was founded in 1921. (There was a similar organisation for girls.)

(The WSCM is not to be confused with *Urdd Gobaith Cymru* – the Welsh League of Youth – founded in 1922 to give young people a social life solely in Welsh, and to 'protect and promote' the language. George became a supporter, and according to Gwennant Davies in *The Story of the Urdd, 1922–1972*, he was very popular with the *Urdd*'s members.)

George was one of the founders of the WSCM, and his involvement with the movement went on almost till his death in 1949. According to T. I. Ellis, a Welsh classicist, another of the founders, there was 'a desire to extend to boys in Welsh Intermediate Schools the benefits which could be gained through living together in simplicity and naturalness under holiday conditions'. T. I. Ellis was the posthumous son of T. E. Ellis, Liberal MP and Welsh nationalist, who died in April 1899. TI was born in November 1899; he was a member of the SCM, and the Secretary of its Welsh Council from 1923–4.

The inspiration for the WSCM, said Ellis, was the Student Christian Movement (SCM) Summer Conferences, as well as 'the change occasioned by the war'. Following the First World

War there was a general feeling throughout Britain that some of the youth movements, such as the Boys' Brigade and the Boy Scouts, were too militaristic in ethos.

After the First World War there was a revulsion against anything military. The slaughter in the trenches had its effect on the organisations that parents wanted their children to join. There was also a relaxation in attitudes to authority. Thus, in the 1920s, there was room for movements that followed a non-militarist – or even anti-militarist – approach, as an alternative to the mainstream organisations. These movements shunned awards, badges and uniforms. Out of this new ideology came the Welsh Schoolboys' Camp Movement. A committee was formed, and they decided: 'that the work [of the WSCM] must of necessity be [run] by Welsh men and women.'

The first Welsh Schoolboys' Camp was held on 6–15 August 1921 at Builth Wells. It was open to boys aged thirteen to sixteen years old. Though the Camps were non-military in ethos, they used military terminology: there was an Adjutant, and other 'officers'. The Chaplain was George (as yet unordained), who was also on the General Committee. *Urdd Gobaith Cymru* also used military ranks for their 'officers'; it seemed quite acceptable. (Incidentally, the *Urdd* held their first camp in 1928, at a cost of 10/- per person or 1/- per day.)

In 1922, there were two camps in August, this time in the Edw Valley in Radnorshire. The charge was £2 per boy per camp. With many working-class men earning only around £1 a week at the time, this put the camps firmly in the middle-class bracket. One Committee member, Ken Rees, wrote to T. I. Ellis worrying that the boys might feel hungry because the cost of food was reduced to 12/- per head, whereas in 1921 it had been £1.

On the application form for the 1922 camps, George Davies was again named as Chaplain. Most of the officers have the names of their University colleges after their name, but George, not having attended any university, had simply 'Gregynog'.

It is clear, though, that all the officers were from the middle classes.

A booklet celebrating the 1921 camp and preparing for the 1922 camps is entitled *Mudiad Gwersyll i Fechgyn Cymru: The Welsh Schoolboys' Camp Movement*, with the Welsh-language name above, and in larger type than, the English. In an article in the booklet, the writer (unattributed, but very likely George) answered the question, 'What's the good of [camp]?' by saying that 'One of the discoveries human beings have made about themselves is that there is a great hunger somewhere in every heart for freedom, simplicity and fellowship'. He suggested that people were always trying to get one of the three at the expense of the other two. 'Well now, Camp is a place in which the three – simplicity, freedom and fellowship – can be learned and enjoyed together.' The writer extolled the virtues of the camping life: the outings, the open air, and the comradeship, from the first reveille (military terminology again):

> ... there are things that can only be done *together* – making the fire and cooking the porridge, serving out the rations, carrying water and firewood, tidying up the tents for inspection [military again], to say nothing of the football and cricket matches and the bathing parties and the 'sing-song' at night perhaps round the glowing embers of the Camp fire. And last but not least is that gathering together at the close of the day to thank God for everything that brings us nearer together in the spirit and purpose of the Prince of all true comradeship and loyalty.

The writer went on to say that 'a Something' has brought them together, and 'a Someone', 'whose longing to make friends of all of us is strangely felt in our hearts. And after the camps, on the way home, *something* remains, and warms the hearts through many a wintry lonely day, and gives us hope of the better and happier Wales for which we are to labour in the Spirit of Camp'.

The Welsh Schoolboys' Camps, then, according to this

writer, were for the benefit of individual boys, the group as a whole, and Wales.

This article is reproduced in Welsh opposite the English in the booklet *Mudiad Gwersyll i Fechgyn Cymru: The Welsh Schoolboys' Camp Movement*. By 1931, though, the English language was printed above the Welsh on the cover of the booklet. For some reason, and to the Committee's regret, the Movement never became popular in the north of Wales, where the Welsh language was stronger; it is likely that the *Urdd* had a stronger influence there.

In an article for *The Welsh Outlook* in 1928, one of the Movement's officers, Phil H. Burton, a schoolteacher from south Wales (who later adopted the future film star Richard Burton), explained the working of the camps, which were 'designed to help develop the personality of the secondary school boys of Wales'. Each camp consisted of fifty campers. The number included 'officers', regarded as 'merely older campers, and are generally ministers of religion, university lecturers, assistant-masters, and university students'. Each unit consisted of four or five boys and an officer. All kinds of outdoor activities were enjoyed, and each day opened and closed with a short service, with an address given by someone 'who is sufficiently near to boyhood in age or spirit to have something of vital interest to say to boys'. By the time this article was published there were five ten-day camps each year.

One of the people judged sufficiently near to boyhood at least in spirit (he was forty-one in 1921, when the camps began) was George. Leslie also attended occasionally; in September 1928 Phil Burton received a letter from her saying how she had enjoyed a visit to the cinema with some of the campers, and how well-behaved they had been.

One of the boys who attended several camps was Iorwerth John from Cardiff, who had been a pupil of T. I. Ellis, and who later became a Conscientious Objector in the Second World War:

Those camps were very unusual. Boys I knew in school who perhaps never went to any place of worship would happily have a Morning Chapel and an Evening Chapel, and the Evening Chapel very often had a little talk... and when George came it was wonderful... he was a tremendous influence on me.

From the late 1920s, German boys joined the Welsh camps. George wrote to T. I. Ellis late in 1929 saying he was keen to get 'internationalism' into the camps, but he was concerned about unwelcome influences from the new regimes in Europe:

The name 'Christian' means so little on the Continent. 'Christian Socialist', for example, is short for Anti-Semite. And French Protestants are often *plus royaliste que le roi* in their narrow nationalism.

And in another letter, he wrote: 'We must be careful not to get Fascisti or Nationalisti boys. I saw an Italian youth who had been at the Aber International show – a perfect bounder who wanted to break every Socialist's head.' Whilst George was passionate about Wales and about self-determination for her, his nationalism was never of the aggressive right-wing sort that was in the ascendancy in Italy and fast growing in Germany.

In 1931 the WSCM ran four camps and a trip to Switzerland. George was by then President of the Movement. The cost of the camps in Wales was 36/- per camper, and it was suggested that boys bring no more than 10/- pocket money – around half a week's wages for many working-class parents at that time. The cost of the Swiss trip was £10 for three weeks. Costs were kept down as far as possible: in 1936 a poster for a camp in the Rheidol Valley near Aberystwyth announced that the price would be reduced to 25/-. Again, very few working-class families would have been able to afford to send their sons to this camp.

In 1937 an appeal for funds was sent out to 'old campers',

saying that the Movement was not as well off as it had been seven or eight years before, and that the 1936 camp had made a loss of £12 9s 4d.

In 1939 a camp was being arranged in Germany for twenty-four campers and twelve officers of the WSCM, from 29 July to 11 August. The cost was to be £10 10s. In February of that year, A. E. Stokes, the Hon. Secretary of the Movement, received a letter from Hans Meyer of Wernigerode, where the camp was to be held, suggesting that tents could be borrowed from the Hitler Youth of Wernigerode:

> Herr Schmidt as gym master has a responsible position in the Hitler Youth. He will kindly help us at any case. You know that every German boy has to join the Hitler Youth, you will find practically outside the organisation there are no small societies, clubs, etc. outside the Hitler Youth.

It seems incongruous that a non-military camp movement from Wales might have to prevail upon the Hitler Youth for its tents. There is no record of George's feelings on the matter, though he was still one of the (seven) Vice-Presidents at the time. Herr Meyer went on to suggest that funds saved by borrowing the tents could be used to bring boys whose parents were 'unemployed or in economic distress', or (poignantly, with hindsight) 'to pay the camp fees for one of our boys whose means do not allow to come to your country next year'.

On 25 March 1939, Tom Ellis wrote to Stokes: 'I wonder how this international situation will affect us. I hope it won't do us any harm, but fear it will keep down numbers.' By 19 May, Stokes was pessimistic: 'I suppose that we shall have to cancel the German camp, unless things become definitely easier.'

The camp was cancelled. War with Germany was declared on 3 September 1939.

The issue of sexual behaviour in the camps is not mentioned explicitly in any of the letters in George's papers, nor in T. I.

Ellis', but there is mention of an incident in 1930 in which a letter from George caused great offence to Ellis – although mistakenly.

After one of the camps at Afon-wen in July of that year, George had heard a critical comment from someone not directly involved with the camps, and George, wishing to show himself a good friend to Ellis, had written to him about it, but in what George himself later admitted was 'a gauche and clumsy way'. Ellis misunderstood George's letter, took umbrage, and felt alienated from George. Phil Burton had a long talk with George that day, as he had told Ellis he would, and clearly managed to get the two others to meet.

A week later George wrote to Ellis, saying how pleased he was that they had had a chance to meet, and that if they had met earlier:

> ... it would have dissipated... fantastic imaginations that homosexuality was hinted at. I was rather horrified and flabbergasted that such an idea could possibly have been read into my letters... the nature of the complaint... was simply that a number of the older boys felt themselves to have been dropped by you and were sore in consequence. I suppose all people are sensitive when a friendship even *seems* to cool off, and boys, particularly when they have been made a lot of, are especially so.

Judging by their letters, George, T. I. Ellis and Phil Burton were all active, enthusiastic leaders, with the boys' well-being and education very much at heart. But all three were very intense and emotionally expressive personalities, needing close friendships. It would have been easy for that intensity, in the heat of camps full of pubertal and adolescent boys, to be misunderstood.

For a time after July 1926, George was an elected member of the Executive Committee of the Welsh National Council of the League of Nations Union. The Vice-President was George's old friend David Davies, who had campaigned hard to get a Welsh arm of the LNU – in truth a 'defencist' movement rather than a 'pacifist' one.

Also in July 1926, IFoR held a peace conference in Oberammergau in Bavaria. According to the essay 'Peace by Reconciliation' in *Pilgrimage of Peace*, George went, ever-interested in the international situation, and unusually, Leslie went with him. Around 200 other people attended. One of the items on the agenda was the experience of those who had opposed war in various nations, many of whom had been punished for their beliefs. Not all countries had had rights of Conscientious Objection. There were possibilities of official alternatives to military service – for example, in Switzerland, where a volunteer 'Service Civil' had been formed by George's old friend Pierre Cérésole (1879–1945), also one of the founder members in 1919 of the International Fellowship of Reconciliation. He became a pacifist in about 1912, and refused to pay military taxes or serve in the Swiss army. He was frequently imprisoned. Cérésole was to be important to George's future work in south Wales.

Some Scandinavian countries had by 1926 recognised some kind of alternative National Service. The IFoR accepted that state disarmament was a forlorn hope, and that opposition to any future war had to come from small groups, or individuals. Some countries were trying to secure disarmament: Denmark, in April of that year, had even debated a Bill to abolish their navy and army, on the principle that, since Denmark was 'undefendable', it was a waste of time and money, 'and of capable young men's time', to try to defend her. The Conference also discussed the increasing unrest throughout Europe, much of it caused by the rise of the Fascist movement.

While involved as a volunteer with the Welsh Schoolboys' Camps, the peace movement, and his writing, the former MP George Davies was still looking for a job that would both support his family and satisfy him. Early in 1926 he was invited to become the minister in the English Presbyterian Church in Tywyn, and also of a small Welsh-language Calvinist Methodist chapel in Cwm Maethlon, a lovely valley a few miles inland.

12

Tywyn

TYPICALLY, IT TOOK George Davies several months to make up his mind to take on the stipendiary pastorship at Tywyn. He felt he needed to write to the appointing Pastoral Committee to lay down exactly where he stood on a number of matters; he had also told them that he was closely aligned with the Quakers, though not an official member, and shared with them 'the need for freedom of the individual conscience in all things and also the equality and priesthood of all believers'.

George didn't make it easy for the committee members to accept him, but apparently they felt he was needed in Tywyn. At the beginning of March 1926, he wrote to the church saying that he would come to Tywyn. He pointed out that he was not yet ordained (that eventually took place at a meeting in Rhosllannerchrugog in November 1926), and that he had some speaking engagements in Wales and Austria, which would occupy him until the end of August. The Davies family eventually moved into the manse in the late summer of 1926.

(At the time, many prospective Calvinistic Methodist ministers did their 'training' by undertaking a requisite number of preaching engagements within a set period; they were expected to know the Bible extremely well.)

The manse was far from luxurious. Leslie reported to her father than it had three outside walls and was very damp; the ceilings were 'looking very uncomfortable' and having to be repaired. Leslie's tone in the letter was cheerful and brisk; she said that George had gone away for a fortnight and she and Jane were taking picnics on to the beach every day and enjoying the sunshine. But Leslie was making the best of what already appeared to her as a rather bad job – for her, for Jane, and for George himself.

The position of a chapel minister in the 1920s was perceived as one of status and some power. However, there were expectations, with implications for George and Leslie. The minister, according to David Jenkins, 'was, or ought to be, above party, with the role of an "institutionalised outsider", free of the connections that would make his standpoint suspect'.[1] Ministers were expected to have no family ties in the area (it was virtually unknown for a chapel to appoint a minister from the locality), to make no connections with any families other than those in his chapel, and to show no favouritism therein. A minister and his wife and family, therefore, were largely thrown in on themselves.

A minister, thus coming in as an outsider, wrote Jenkins, 'enters the highest status of the group as a virtual stranger'.[2] His induction to the chapel had to be carried out 'in an impressive manner in keeping with the high regard in which this office was held'. He was 'one of the few persons in the district addressed with the title "Mr"'. He was expected to devote 'all his energy to the formal and informal work of the chapel at the expense of outside interests'.

George, of course, had many 'outside interests', and perhaps they kept him stimulated while he was in Tywyn. He quickly realised that moving to Tywyn was a mistake (though he loved going to preach in the Welsh-speaking chapel in Cwm Maethlon), but the commitment was not one he could easily get out of.

He explained to his old friend Thomas Jones in a letter early in 1927 that he had gone to Tywyn to 'promote the "personal" rather than the "mass-results" ethic'. He had hoped, he wrote, to have been invited to a miners' chapel in Rhosllannerchrugog, near Wrexham, not only because he loved the miners and their company, but because he would have been able to implement the 'social gospel' there. But they didn't ask him. 'I long to be among those fellows,' George wrote, 'although Leslie not understanding Welsh and Jane needing to be educated makes a complication'. It is likely that he is saying here that the stipend at Tywyn was higher than he would have received at Rhos, thus helping to pay for Jane's private schooling, but also he appears to be resenting Leslie, who had not learned Welsh even after some ten years living in Wales. Jane could, presumably, have gone to local schools, but it seems Leslie did not want that.

During 1926 Leslie wrote to her mother: 'Now that George is going to be at home much more, it is imperative that Jane should go to [boarding] school.' This is a puzzling statement. Did Leslie find George's depressions easier to cope with when Jane was off the scene? Jane told me she loved being with her father but didn't see much of him, to her great sadness, after she was eight years old. Did Leslie perhaps see Jane as competition for George's time and affections? No one will ever know – certainly Jane had no idea why she was sent away from this time.

Although Jane went to Sunday school at George's church, there is no record of Leslie attending any of George's services. As a Quaker attender (and a member from 1928), she would not feel a need to do so, because no pressure is ever put on Quakers to be at even their own meetings. Quite probably it didn't bother George either (he surely had never expected Leslie to become the conventional 'minister's wife'), but one wonders what the people of Tywyn thought about the new minister's wife not attending his services. It is likely that remarks were made to George, and quite probably behind his back.

Even though he spoke Welsh, George, from Liverpool and the very north of Wales, was more of an 'outsider' than most of the ministers of the area would have been, and Leslie, an upper middle-class Englishwoman, particularly so. Leslie could have been seen as a supportive and 'good' minister's wife if she had learned Welsh and thrown herself into chapel affairs, but she would have felt it very unnatural – and as one who was considering becoming a Quaker, quite unnecessary.

It is difficult to find any literature which speaks directly about the duties of a minister's wife in the first half of the twentieth century. The novel *Tywyll Heno* ('dark tonight') by the eminent Welsh writer Kate Roberts, is about a minister's wife in the 1960s whose depressive illness is not helped by the expectations of her (very kind) husband and his congregation. A conversation with Dr Meredydd Evans indicated that things had been the same in the late 1920s, when he was growing up in Tanygrisiau, near Blaenau Ffestiniog. Then, men training in Bangor for the chapel ministry in Wales met young women training to be teachers, the ideal wives for ministers: educated, articulate, respectable. Chapel-goers expected 'two for the price of one', he said: the minister's wife was *expected* to do things: Sunday school, work with the young people, and visiting in the area, if nothing else, but preferably also to be involved with the Missionary Society and the Temperance Society. Merêd remembered one minister in the village whose wife had decided to be 'deliberately independent', and attend only Sunday services, nothing else. This was quite a shock to the villagers.

From 1926, Leslie, a former teacher, was 'the minister's wife' in Tywyn; but if the English Presbyterian Chapel congregation had expected 'two for the price of one' when they 'called' George to be their minister, they must have been disappointed.

Money was tight for the couple. Leslie wrote to her mother: 'We are so much poorer than we've ever been now that we live "respectable" and have into the bargain to "support" the cause – *all* the minor causes.'

Sometime in 1926 Jane started at a private boarding school, possibly in Liverpool. In 1927 she moved to Sidcot, the Quaker school near Bristol, as a boarder. It seems Leslie made the decisions about Jane's schooling, and tried to pay for this schooling herself; an aunt of Leslie's had given a small sum of money to Jane, but Leslie would not use Jane's money to help out. 'I don't feel justified in using *her* capital for a process that *I* ought to pay for.' The emphases are Leslie's, and it is interesting that she uses 'I' here, rather than 'we'. It could be that as a socialist George disapproved of private schools (he certainly criticised state schools), and handed responsibility to Leslie, who wanted Jane to go to a 'good' school; perhaps he had washed his hands of the decision. Perhaps, too, it was not acceptable for the children of a local minister to attend a local school. For whatever reason, Jane was sent from Tywyn during term-times. Certainly George is well-remembered for loving the company of children, but because of his busy life his own daughter never experienced much of that company, even in the holidays. She told me that an emotional gap grew between her and her father from about this time.

Leslie had to work hard at turning George out 'respectable' by, for example, reworking his gloves to save buying new ones. She made all Jane's school clothes. She was a naturally practical, industrious and capable person. By October 1927 she had also become involved in starting a branch of the Women's Institute in Tywyn, which proved to be hard work. She found herself 'lost in a maze of Joneses', all of whom knew much more about Leslie than she about them. She reported brightly to her mother that 'The Towyn sensation is that R. J. Williams the stationer is engaged to be married – after a week's acquaintance'. Once again one gets the impression that Leslie is making the best of a bad job. She continued to support George, but found it hard:

> George, though plump and able-bodied, is feeling very depressed, and I try to get him out into the air. Otherwise he spends *all* day in his study – window tight shut, smoking horrible tobacco and typing, which is very bad for his nerves.

Leslie's letters to her mother indicate that she and George were growing apart. In Wales, decades later, people still suggest disapprovingly that George 'left his wife and child' after their time in Tywyn, but Leslie quite clearly did not like living in Wales, and wanted more from George in terms of time, company and support than he was able to give. George spent long periods away from home at conferences or on preaching engagements; when he was in Tywyn he was working, and doing a lot of writing, in Welsh and in English. On Sundays, when he wasn't preaching in Tywyn, he was walking the four miles or so to the chapel in Cwm Maethlon and back, and preaching in Welsh to the congregation he loved there. The 'office hours' life Leslie had foreseen in 1911, when she fell in love with George Davies the middle-class bank manager, had disappeared, and she was left to her own lonely resources.

There were others who wanted George's presence in their projects. Mrs Lindsay (wife of A. D. Lindsay, Master of Balliol College, Oxford, and influential Socialist thinker), and Henry Gillett (social reformer), of the Oxford Quaker Meeting, wrote in November 1926 to ask him to go and work with them. The letter acknowledged that George had just started at Tywyn, but offered him work in Oxford 'if at any future time you feel called to something different'.

TJ expressed relief that George hadn't gone to Oxford: 'I am biased, as I want you to be near [Coleg] Harlech.' In a letter to TJ at the end of January 1927, George admitted that he had lingered over the Oxford proposition, partly because they would be good people to work with, but also because he had gone to Tywyn hoping to find a 'group of "seekers" weighed down with any sense of their own and the world's need', but so far, he wrote, he hadn't found a single one. His words about Tywyn were harsh:

> The Chapels are full and their feuds notorious... We are all
> conformist and conventional with secret cabals of dissent.
> There is no industrial problem because there is no industry. The
> young escape from Towyn as from a prison. The old keep shops

or let lodgings in the summer and worship the easy affluence
and assurance of the Birmingham bourgeois who come. The
County School has 400 pupils who pass exams and miss life most
conspicuously... when they leave school they turn with relief to
dances, whist drives and Jazz as being so much more interesting
than education. At the Seiat [fellowship meeting] we have
Gladstonian prayers but no *cri de cœur*, no confessions made, no
problems asked.

He ends, with perhaps a touch of sarcasm:

But for the present I must try... And after all there are very gallant
individual lives here, and much bravery in Boarding Houses with
plush antimacassars. And if the ministry of reconciliation and of
education is a reality it has somehow got to touch unromantic
uneventful lives like theirs. I find I have a great deal to learn.

There is much evidence that George was unhappy. But
somehow, he survived the physical and mental claustrophobia
of Tywyn. He and the family were there from August 1926
until January 1932 (apart from a year spent in Birmingham,
at Woodbrooke College). Both Leslie and George disliked the
town, as is evident from a comment in one of Frank's letters to
George in December 1926, and from remarks made by Leslie
in her letters to her parents.

George, who was so comfortable and fulfilled among
internationalists, idealists, thinkers and reformers, farm
workers and coal miners, was in a stagnant backwater. He
struggled to make the 'social gospel' work in Tywyn, but
apparently failed. He felt his failure very keenly.

There were some lighter-hearted times for George, however. Two
articles written by Enid Williams (for an unknown publication)
portray George as a friend to many, especially children. In one,
she writes of the annual 'Sunday School treat', when they would
travel on the narrow-gauge Talyllyn railway to Dôl-goch, for
sports and a picnic. George (the children called him 'Georgie

Giraffe') would join the children, 'elegant and beaming'. In her
other article, Enid Williams describes George as:

> ... tall, erect, grey-haired, sensitive mobile mouth, and direct,
> kindly grey eyes. He dressed in the most unclerical of garbs, a
> tweed knickerbocker suit with thick socks, Panama hat in summer,
> felt trilby in winter, an immaculate white shirt, and smart bow tie.
> He never wore a dog collar or clerical grey.

On the Sunday school treat journeys, the children climbed
into the trucks at the back of the train. George Davies always
sat with the children, joining in with their songs and choruses.
'He was ever watchful that no one was left out in the cold,' Enid
Williams wrote. She went on to describe the isolated farmhouse
about two miles outside Tywyn, where her best friends lived.
They would all climb a big tree outside the farmhouse and
sing. If George, on his parochial rounds, heard them, he would
climb up the tree too and join in!

But there was another side to George. One night, soon after
Enid's father had died, she and her mother stood heartbrokenly
looking at their home, empty of their furniture, which had that
day been sold. There was a knock at the door and George was
there offering company and comfort. 'I never saw him again,'
she ends the article, 'but life has always been that much sweeter
for having known him'.

In 1928 George wrote at length and with passion to his brother
Stanley, talking of his dilemmas about his future. Clearly he
was already thinking about moving on from Tywyn. He had
received several offers, added to the earlier request from
the Oxford Quakers. In December 1929 the Fellowship of
Reconciliation had asked him to be a 'servant... at the service of
individual members'. The Colleges at Selly Oak, Birmingham,
had also asked him to be a 'sort of Quaker pastor' there. And TJ
had asked him to be Warden at Coleg Harlech. But George was
reluctant to take up any of these offers because he was, as he

wrote to his brother Stanley, 'committed to a religious outlook to be worked out in action'. He wanted to get involved in action in the 'distressed areas' of Wales – it was not enough for George to be simply a preacher. He had seen the real spiritual need of the people of Tywyn, but they clearly did not see it themselves: they were not 'seekers', and George could not open them up to seeking. The Quaker ethos was becoming increasingly important to George. One of their precepts in *Quaker Faith and Practice* is:

> Do not be content to accept things as they are, but keep an alert and questioning mind. Seek to discover the causes of social unrest, injustice and fear... work for an order of society which will allow men and women to develop their capacities.

George was not 'content to accept things as they are', and worked hard to change the 'order of society', in spite of living and working in conditions which were completely opposite to his own hopes and dreams. But the people of Tywyn wished to keep things as they were. That he could not develop the capacities of those people was an enormous disappointment. He learned a hard lesson in Tywyn. It was 'about the last place on God's earth that I wished to go to; it had a particularly distasteful feel to me from the outset', he wrote, but George and Leslie needed 'a home and... some kind of life together after ten years wandering and living in nine different houses'. And the Tywyn Presbyterians had said there was need of George's message.

But George found that his initial instincts about Tywyn had been correct. He wrote to Stan:

> It was as dead as ditchwater; stodgy and petty to the last degree; dominated by the crude domination of the local potentate [Haydn Jones, thirty-five years the MP] and underneath, torn by fear, servility and hidden revolt... [At the local Secondary School] I am looked upon as an interfering crank because I speak against the crudest cramming and flogging here, though

I do it with all the tact I can... The stunting of these children by fear and cramming haunts me. And so does the evil domination of this town and the bitter revolt that it engenders and the smouldering feud for years.

George complained to Stanley that in Tywyn 'a very fine teacher [was] ostracised for protesting against personal violence to other children'. Events such as this upset and angered George – it was another rejection of the practical peace-making in which he believed so strongly. He wrote often about education, promoting, as usual, progressive, peaceful and co-operative methods of running a school.

In 1928, George told Stanley: 'Sometimes I feel that civilisation as we have known it is going to break up in our generation.' He was writing after seeing, at a cinema in London, 'a rather terrible Russian film which is the first to be admitted of its kind'. From George's description it is clear that the film is Sergei Eisenstein's *October 1917: Ten Days that Shook the World*, made between April and October 1927. This was Eisenstein's third film, a propagandist representation of the Russian Revolution.

What Eisenstein had realised was that a single film could arouse a larger number of people in a relatively short space of time than radio and the press, and could appeal to the emotions of the audience, rather than to its intelligence.[3] Certainly George experienced this, sitting in a London audience: 'The theatre was packed to the roof and watched the film in a tense silence.' His description of the film (now available on DVD), with all its sharp contrasts and symbolism, its montages and violence, is very accurate, and the representation of the Revolution obviously affected him deeply.

Eisenstein used a heavy press machine as a metaphor for the factories' crushing oppression of the workers – in the 1920s, the machine was a god; most Soviet films had an allegorical machine. The film is full of negative stereotypes of capitalists living off the fat of the land and off the honest toil of the heroic workers.

George tells Stan that *October 1917* 'is a wonderful piece of art and of propaganda in its contrasts'. Eisenstein portrayed very clearly the causes of the Revolution: the poverty of peasants and workers, the war, 'the yelling patriotism of the Stock Exchange against a background of the mud and maiming and misery of the peasant soldiers'.

The film seemed to be some kind of catalyst for George. He had been struggling to find some meaningful way to live. Parliament had not given him that meaning, nor had Tywyn. George found it heartbreaking that the Revolution had created for the Russian workers 'the oppression of their peers instead of the oppression of their Masters'. He told Stanley how he longed for the church to do more, voluntarily, to ease poverty. He also said, significantly, that he had become aware of 'the danger of power'.

George had already rejected capitalism and the class-war elements of socialism; *October 1917* turned him against Communism as manifested in Russia. He felt that in order to tackle poverty it was essential to find a 'concentration of compassion, realism, humanity and divinity'.

Over the years, George had many arguments with his brother Glyn about Communism. Glyn held 'Uncle Joe' (Stalin) as a hero. Elin, Glyn's youngest daughter, joined the Communist party, and when she went to Oxford to study Zoology in 1932, she became a keen member of the October Club. George knew what was happening in Russia, and state socialism did not chime well with his belief in fostering 'webs of good neighbourliness'; Glyn did not believe Stalin was a tyrant, and neither did Elin. Glyn 'thought Uncle Joe could do no wrong and Uncle George was up the pole', wrote Gwion to Jane, 'but they were very close really, for all their disagreements'. At the end of Glyn's life, Elin kept from him *The New York Times* transcript of the speech in which Khrushchev had denounced Stalin; Elin said, 'Father died with his illusions'.

In 1993 Gwion wrote, 'Both Elin and I, being sadder and wiser, now see a lot more sense in what Uncle George believed in than we did when we were young'. They were both baffled and despairing about events in the then Yugoslavia, 'where the good neighbourliness of small communities, on which Uncle George was so keen, has curdled into viscious hatreds... What a mess so-called Socialism got into in the USSR and the Eastern European countries it took over. What went wrong with that dream, that inspired millions the world over? I don't know.'

In April 1930, George became a Town Councillor in Tywyn. Though Leslie wasn't sure he was 'the right man for the job', she reported to her mother that many local people were very pleased: George was looked on as 'a deliverer by all the folk whom Haydn [Jones] threatens or oppresses', and it seems his election had enraged Haydn Jones' 'satellites' and thrilled the 'anti-Haydns'. This made things difficult for George, who was 'always out for reconciliation'.

For Tywyn and its neighbour Bryn-crug, it was an eventful time. Discussions about public health had apparently been going on for over ten years. At last mains water was being brought in, and there were proposals for bringing in electricity. In his notes for an address for Health Week, George said how difficult it had been for people to 'interfere' and try to improve things elsewhere:

> A friend of mine who did interfere with 106 houses which had only 3 taps and were filthy slums found himself attacked for his theology very soon. Are there insanitary conditions in Towyn? The water of Towyn is too hot for me to touch upon but the revelations as to Bryn Crug were a scandal.

George complained that he met very few townspeople walking in the lovely countryside that lies around the town, and made several only slightly veiled references to the lack of fresh air in Tywyn houses. He pointed out that:

213

... in recent years the consumption on drink and cigarettes has reached as much as £469 on drink and £440 on cigarettes in a year, i.e. nearly 30/- a week for every family in the land. And that in hard times. (I confess I've turned to Herb Tobacco with an ounce of mixture a month.)

The water scheme was making progress, but on 20 December 1930 a correspondent for the *Cambrian News* considered that Tywyn seemed to have less of 'that spirit of hostile criticism which has cursed the town during the past few years', and suggests that: 'the transparent honesty of men like the Rev. George Davies is proving to the critics that there are those who are prepared to serve the ratepayers without fear, favour, or affection.'

But in spite of his successes, George wrote to Stanley, 'I pine for the kind of simple affectionate folk that we know in Enlli and Lleyn', and Frank wrote to George saying he hoped the family was 'as happy as one can hope for in a place like Towyn'.

George had met the same 'simple affectionate folk' in prison, and on the stone-breaking teams. He had been disappointed when the miners in Rhosllannerchrugog had not invited him to be their minister. Obviously, notwithstanding the beautiful countryside, and the welcome of the local children, 'stodgy and petty' Tywyn was somewhere George did not relish staying.

There were also reasons outside Tywyn for George's unhappiness. In 1926 the General Strike had deeply affected the mining communities of south Wales; involved with the miners was George's friend, Tom Nefyn Williams (known simply as 'Tom Nefyn'), a minister in Tymbl, an anthracite-mining town near Llanelli. Two results of George's friendship with Tom Nefyn were that his future relationship with the Calvinistic Methodists would be irreparably damaged, and that his future work would be decided.

13

George, Gandhi, and the 'Social Gospel'

INDUSTRIAL DISPUTES AFFECTED Wales badly in the 1920s. The General Strike, and the ensuing lock-out, caused appalling turmoil and long-term hardship. George Davies was in Tywyn during that time, and distant from the industrial problems, but he was emotionally involved: he felt he could have helped with reconciliation. Another complication was his friendship with Tom Nefyn.

In an article, 'Tom Nefyn', written in 1928 for *The Welsh Outlook*, George quoted Professor Miall Edwards' words: 'the age is ripe for a courageous movement towards a positive restatement of the doctrines of the Christian faith.' Tom Nefyn turned out to be in the vanguard of this movement.

Tom 'Nefyn' Williams (1895–1958), minister of Ebeneser Calvinistic Methodist Chapel in Tymbl, south Wales, had been born near Nefyn in Llŷn, and is remembered to this day, particularly in Welsh-speaking communities, as 'Tom Nefyn', a charismatic and complex man, a powerful preacher, and something of an enigma.[1] Chapel ministers were expected to be non-political and uncontentious. Tom Nefyn challenged this by bringing political ideas into the chapel, and inviting comments from his congregation after his sermons. In December 1925, when 164 miners were arrested after a labour dispute and treated harshly by the courts, the congregation at Tymbl – in a political move that was bound to attract the attention of the

Presbytery (the ruling elders of the chapel) – passed a vote of condemnation of the sentences.

It was Tom Nefyn who, in 1926, had sent a report to the coal owners about the miners' housing in Tymbl ('106 houses which had only 3 taps and were filthy slums', as George wrote in 1930), and as a result the houses were improved. During the General Strike and after, Tom Nefyn organised collections of money for the strikers, and donated his stipend.

But Tom Nefyn's 'interference' on behalf of the health of his community began to alienate some of the chapel members, who believed that chapels should concentrate on the 'Biblical gospel' – evangelical and spiritual activity – rather than supporting striking miners and a secular socialism (or, they feared, Communism). But Tom Nefyn believed strongly in the 'social gospel', and continued to do all he could to alleviate suffering in the area. Ebeneser chapel in Tymbl was a microcosm of what was happening elsewhere in Wales.

George, a fellow Calvinist Methodist minister, waded straight into the controversy by allying himself with Tom Nefyn. The two men became firm friends. George, especially following his experiences in prison, felt strongly that the churches should be working harder to relieve poverty and distress. George protested long and hard about Tom Nefyn's treatment by the Methodist authorities. After many months of wrangling, discussions, and allegedly unfair meetings, Tom Nefyn was called before the Calvinistic Methodists' ruling body in London on 26 October 1927, and was eventually suspended from ministry in the Calvinistic Methodist denomination.

It has to be questioned whether George, well-known for his reconciliation in many fields, was swept into the conflict by Tom Nefyn's own 'agenda'. By being more objective he could perhaps have brought his usual quiet good sense to bear on both Tom Nefyn and the Methodist authorities. George, though, was still trying to make sense of his role in Tywyn, and was not in a good mental state himself.

George's brother Stanley wrote to him suggesting 'a rest week every month – your work would be the better for it, and poor old Leslie would have a little of you for herself'. Stan also considered that Tom Nefyn could easily 'slide into bitterness'; he had read articles in *Y Cymro* [The Welshman] by Tom, but 'it is not all said in the spirit of constructive charity'.

In his thesis, Gethin Evans describes Tom Nefyn as 'a tortured, sensitive soul, restless if not insecure, [in] turmoil'; D. Densil Morgan calls him 'intellectually unstable and spiritually restless'.[2] Much of this also applies to George – especially following prison and the Commons, and during his difficult time in Tywyn. The two men were kindred spirits, then, although George was by nature a reconciler rather than a campaigner. However, George, it seemed, used up a huge amount of time and energy campaigning for Tom's reinstatement, maybe being too sympathetic, instead of trying to reconcile the individuals involved, which could have been a better deployment of his strengths.

Tom went to the Woodbrooke Settlement in Birmingham for a break. Fearon Halliday, the psychotherapist who had been best man at George and Leslie's wedding, and who was at the time working at Woodbrooke, wrote wisely to George:

> I fear that you may be hurt by troubling too much about what cannot be lightly healed... the fact is that we are only responsible for what we can help, and we should not take too much to heart what we and others cannot help.

George's eventual resignation from the Calvinistic Methodist church was largely because of the denomination's treatment of Tom Nefyn Williams and its attitude to the social gospel.

In 1929 the Elected Moderator of the General Assembly of the church received a long statement from George in which he said that he had explained to the congregations at Tywyn and Cwm Maethlon that he saw 'the church as a society of friends rather than a congregation of hearers'. But the way the Tom Nefyn situation had been dealt with:

> ... point[s] to a bondage to the legal and secular mind and method rather than that freedom of ministry which follows an erring sheep into the wilderness and which welcomes the flock to come in and out of the fold to find pasture.

George pointed out that he had appealed to Tom Nefyn to keep the doors open in case one of the church leaders wished to attempt reconciliation, but none had. George ended his 1929 statement to the Moderator of the General Assembly:

> I have no wish to embarrass or force myself on an unwilling minority. So often have I heard it argued, 'If Tom Nefyn doesn't agree with the Corph's decision why doesn't he simply retire.' I do not agree with the Corph's decision, so I simply retire.

['Corph', from the Welsh *Yr Hen Gorff*, relates to the Connexion or Calvinistic Methodist denomination.]

George was about to finish his rather unhappy spell as a minister. In fact, he carried on in the post until late in 1931 – but with a year's break from September 1930 until July 1931.

The nine-day General Strike of May 1926 was both the culmination and the beginning of long-term unrest in the industrial areas of Britain. Since before the First World War, there had been a struggle between the coal-owners, the government, and the miners about the long-term future (and profitability) of the coalfields. Because of the high proportion of miners in the population of the 90-mile length of the south Wales coalfields, from Pontypool in the east to St Brides Bay in the west, the whole area was badly affected.

Following the Versailles Treaty of 1919, Germany was exporting large quantities of free coal to France and Italy – replacing coal that had, prior to the First World War, been bought from south Wales. France was producing more coal (particularly in the areas she had seized from Germany). Italy, who had been buying Welsh coal for her state railways, was taking less Welsh coal, and closing her office in Cardiff. Most of the newer naval boats and passenger liners were powered by oil rather than coal. The USA, with the improved times and ranges of large post-war vessels, was exporting coal to Mediterranean ports formerly served by merchant ships from Cardiff and Penarth. Demand for Welsh steel was also falling, and in the whole of Britain only half the blast furnaces were working: unemployment was rising in those industries as well as in the coalfield. Coal-owners (as well as miners) were suffering from the reduction in demand for Welsh coal, and were considering reducing miners' wages and hours.

The South Wales Miners' Federation – known as 'the Fed' – was in financial difficulties, having used up much of its strike fund during the industrial conflicts between 1921 and 1925. Many miners had been locked out of pits by the owners since 1925, with no pay, after refusing to accept wage reductions of 10 to 25 per cent. On 1 May 1926, the TUC decided to support the locked-out miners, and called a General Strike. In the biggest, most important industrial conflict in Britain's history, 1¾ million other workers went on strike in support of a million miners, starting at one minute to midnight on 3 May. Opinions were divided: the government of the day thought the strike was 'a Communist plot'; the TUC considered it 'an attempt to defend wages'; and the Communist Party of Great Britain took it as 'a revolutionary opportunity'.

Early in May 1926, Councils of Action were set up. In Bedlinog, for example, 'Miners' Lodges, women, the Post Office, woodworkers, NUR, NUT, unemployed, Dowlais Co-op Society and employees, the Labour Party, the Communist Party, and religious bodies'[3] worked together to tackle poverty and malnutrition. Miners' committees negotiated with the local Co-ops so that credit could be extended during a prolonged dispute. All this was needed: not only was the Fed short of funds for hardship cases, but Poor Law relief was arbitrary and subjectively administered, and as the months of lock-out continued, the situation became alarming. Local Boards of Poor Law Guardians had received a directive on 5 May by the Minister of Health (Neville Chamberlain) instructing them not to give relief to strikers. Relief could be given to families. A man considered 'so reduced by want as to be unable to work' could receive temporary relief, but when his physical condition improved he was liable to be prosecuted under the Vagrancy Act if he wasn't in work.

The status of single miners was difficult to determine: some were supporting a widowed mother; many lived alone in situations of great hardship. In south Wales, fewer than 2,000 single miners received Poor Law relief.

A few weeks after this, however, the slow drift back to work was more or less complete. Eventually a new agreement, including lower pay and longer days, was signed on 13 December 1926. But according to Hywel Francis and Dai Smith, victimisation and exploitation were rife in the coalfields. Production was intensified, and pits employed young and inexperienced miners, rather than their fathers, who had been militant strikers. Safety was sacrificed: an explosion in Ebbw Vale on St David's Day 1927 killed fifty-two miners.

So it was into an environment of anger, exploitation, bitterness and poverty that the Quakers came in 1926, to set up their Educational Settlement in the Rhondda Valleys. George Davies eventually joined Maes-yr-haf in 1933, determined to play whatever part he could in improving the quality of life for the unemployed miners of south Wales.

During 1926 and 1927, when Leslie reported to her mother that George was spending 'all day in his study [in Tywyn] typing, which is very bad for his nerves' (and perhaps for Leslie's), he was writing what he intended to be a published book, 'Christian Reconciliation in Industry'; the incomplete 83-page typescript (among his papers) is dated 1927. It was never published, and is certainly not one of his better offerings. From the text, his unsettled state of mind is obvious: the typescript is undisciplined, with long rambling sentences. The tone is typical of George in a depression. It is ponderous, and without the incisiveness and sparkle which makes so much of his writing lively and arresting. However, with robust editing it might have become a seminal text about reconciliation in industrial conflicts. Even as it stands, 'Christian Reconciliation in Industry' is a telling document of George's beliefs in those times of unrest in society. He rejects capitalism, rejects Communism, rejects the class war, and proposes his own alternatives.

Much of George's depression sprang from the fact that because of the artificiality (as he saw it) of his work in Tywyn, he had been isolated from the reality of the industrial turmoil of 1926. His non-party socialism began shortly before he went into prison in 1917, and was confirmed by the time he came out. Although he had tried to return to middle-class respectability (working with David Davies at Gregynog, becoming an MP, becoming a church minister), he was finding it increasingly difficult to suppress his socialist beliefs. Having gone to Tywyn, he was clearly also becoming less and less patient with middle-class values, and felt more and more that he wanted to live with working men, and particularly miners. Their plight during 1926 would have been particularly disturbing and frustrating for him to watch from afar.

The document was written as a response to the Strike and lock-out. It is unapologetically pro-Christian. Although it has a lot to contribute to those individuals and organisations who wish to examine radical ways of bringing reconciliation into situations where perhaps all else has failed, it reads unevenly: the tone tends towards pomposity and a lack of acceptance of any other point of view. George believed firmly that only *Christian* reconciliation had all the answers to the problems of social conflict, and this belief is expressed strongly, even amongst the plodding and the waffling of the text.

George suggested throughout that the main problem in

the industries of Britain was 'class propaganda' – from both sides – and those who tried to break down this 'insuperable' barrier were punished or pilloried by their peers. During the 1921 strike, for example, a Nottinghamshire coal owner had offered hospitality to two miners' leaders; 'suspicions were aroused', and the coal owners and the miners' leaders objected. During the same strike, George was informed confidentially by a coal-owner that his Company had prepared a profit-sharing scheme; a few weeks afterwards a leading official of the Miners' Federation told George he was personally willing to accept such a scheme. 'But neither could publicly declare their private views without accusation of disloyalty, or of blacklegging, from their fellow-owners or fellow-miners.'

The Parliamentary Labour Party congratulated the miners and their wives for their 'magnificent stand against the united forces of the coal owners and the government', and assured the Miners' Federation of the full support of the Party. This was a clear commitment of one Party to one side only, rather than on working with both sides to solve the dispute.

On the same day, it was announced that a Miners' Lodge in Northumberland was to be disenfranchised from the Miners' Federation because the majority of the members of the Lodge had decided to restart work (pending a general settlement). The colliery was owned by the Co-operative Wholesale Society, and the shareholders and management were workers themselves. The decision was therefore a local and mutually favourable one, but the disenfranchisement was upheld.

So, according to George, 'the fight went on, in futility, between the fighting forces. As in war, so in industrial strife, the fate of millions may be allowed to depend upon the gladatorial combats of the fighting leaders on either side.' The Roman Third Republic's 'gladatorial combats' were exhibitions of prowess for entertainment, exclusively male, and often fights to the death. George was defining what he saw as structural faults and sources of despair in industrial relations, just as he had done in community relations in Tywyn, settlement relations in the centre for young people at Riverside (Melton Mowbray), and in the prison system.

George then moved on to discuss the existing British system of running industry, and looked at the 'new coercion' in Mussolini's Italy and Stalin's Russia. None of those systems, he suggested, did anything to reduce the 'mentality of war in political fields'. George called for co-operative ways of running industries, such as that which had 'brought peace and prosperity to rural Denmark'. However, he pointed out that men needed to be prepared to learn exactly how to live and work in this way while setting up such a new system, before that new system could become successful.

George, experienced mediator and reconciler, commented: 'How far a Christian employer or shareholder or worker is right in involving himself in an Association in which he commits himself to a "united front" of antagonism, needs the gravest thought.'

In the remainder of 'Christian Reconciliation in Industry', George pointed out that there were some 'pioneer experiments' in industry (such as Cadbury's in Birmingham and Rowntree in York, both Quaker companies) which, he claimed, were 'bringing new and constructive possibilities to light for co-operation and harmony in industry'. He also gave case histories of situations in which personal contacts between individual employers and workers had led to a constructive and long-term solution of a dispute.

George's document is long, somewhat self-indulgent, and undisciplined. There is no evidence that this version was offered for publication. A letter from Ted Rees, Treasurer of the Welsh Schoolboys' Camps, 28 February 1927, commented frankly that it did not read well: 'It seems to us to be rather like a running commentary of facts than a development of a thesis... I can see your mind and personality at the back of every page of it, but I wonder whether John Citizen will be quite clear, save for certain passages, as to what you are really driving at.'

Indeed, anyone familiar with George's best lyrical and shiningly-clear prose would experience pain and distress on reading this work. It is clear that George's mind was clouded and confused at the time.

The final few pages of the existing typescript (which ends mid-sentence on page 83) are about the 'Power and Place of the Individual in Reconciliation'. This is what became known as George's 'personal gospel', the place of individual initiative. As exemplars George names 'Woolman and Sturge for negro emancipation... Wilberforce for child labour... Howard and Elizabeth Fry for prisoners... Emily Hobhouse for Boer women and children, of Quaker Relief Workers in Europe'. Of these, the majority were Quakers, and all were part of a tradition of middle-class philanthropy, the rationale of which George did not question, and of which he clearly felt himself a part. And it was the already-strong influence of Quakers that was going to take George on to the next stage of his life.

In July 1930, in the midst of his deliberations about what to do after Tywyn, George received a letter from H. G. Wood, from the Woodbrooke Quaker Educational Settlement in Selly Oak, Birmingham, offering him a one-year residential Research Fellowship: 'If you wish to work out more fully some of the questions of industrial peace, we should be glad to consider if we could help you.'

George responded at once. Herbert Wood wrote to him again on 1 August offering him a Fellowship from September 1930 to study his chosen topic: 'Techniques of reconciliation'. The Fellowship was worth £250 for the year; Fellows were to pay for residence at £20 a term. Herbert Wood advised George to consider whether he wished to 'break off' as minister to do a year's research that might have no bearing on his return to Tywyn. George had resigned as a Calvinistic Methodist minister, but he seems (from a letter Leslie wrote to her mother dated 17 July 1931) to have returned to the pastorships (or at least to the Manse) for a while after his

Woodbrooke year, though it is not recorded how or why this happened.

Although Leslie Davies had become a member of the Society of Friends in 1928, there is no evidence that George ever did. At that time the Quakers did not allow 'dual membership', and George, though no longer a Calvinist Methodist minister, was still a member of the denomination. He may, too, have stayed out of Quaker membership to allow himself to be able to preach in chapels in Wales.

Being at Woodbrooke would allow George to spend time debating topics that were important to him. Daily fellowship with the resident community and fellow-students of all ages would challenge and inspire him after the dulling years in Tywyn. George wanted Leslie to go with him (Jane was away at school in term-times). They continued to pay rent for the Tywyn Manse 'to save storing our furniture', and for 'somewhere to go to for all the holidays – and a retreat in case of emergency', as Leslie wrote to her parents late in August. She felt excited and positive about going to Woodbrooke with George: 'We know all the lecturers and officials there, so it will be a removal to a friendly circle – as well as an uncommonly intelligent one.'

There is little evidence of how George spent his time at Woodbrooke, apart from writing about 'Techniques of reconciliation', and researching 'the importance of process as against product' in the industrial field. The Bengali polymath Rabindranath Tagore (the first European to win the Nobel Prize in Literature in 1913) visited Woodbrooke in 1930, and he and George met there. The two men had previously exchanged essays, with Edward Thompson acting as go-between, and admired each other's writing.

George's life had been full of tensions. Perhaps 1914 to 1916 was his most carefree time, in spite of the war and the prospect of prison. Since his release in 1919 he had tried to find his feet, and somehow failed. Woodbrooke was a kind of 'retreat' for him, where he could stand aside from conflict with rules and authorities, and from trying to be acceptable in other people's eyes. He was fifty years old in April 1930. Prison had aged him, but he still wanted to be useful. Being at Woodbrooke, living with the Quakers for a whole year, gave George a different focus and a new clarity. He needed to find somewhere he could do practical work, and preach his gospel of reconciliation, for the rest of his life. Woodbrooke gave him the key to that.

On 17 July 1931, Leslie wrote to her mother that she and George had returned to Tywyn 'for good', and were having ten days' holiday. Woodbrooke had been, she said, 'very strenuous and very absorbing and full of noise of all kinds – and all very interesting and remarkable'. George, Leslie wrote, was due to take up the ministerial reins again at the end of September, when their 'year off' was officially over, but in the meantime he was going down to south Wales for a fortnight, while Leslie stayed in the Manse and 'scraped the mould off everything'.

The Quakers had begun their 'social work' in various areas of south Wales in 1926. They were undertaking projects George wanted to be involved with, and specifically helping unemployed miners and their families. George's signature first appears in the visitors' book for Maes-yr-haf, in Trealaw in the Rhondda, on 21 and 22 January 1928, but this might not have been his first visit.

On 16 October 1931, Leslie wrote to tell her mother that George had met Mahatma Gandhi, who was staying at the Kingsley Hall Settlement in London. Muriel Lester, who ran the Settlement, had invited George (who had laid 'the brick of politics' when the Hall had a new building in 1927).

Gandhi, representing the Indian Congress, was due to take part in the second Round Table Conference about Indian independence. Around 19 or 20 September 1931, Muriel Lester arranged for some of her friends to meet Gandhi. This might have been the occasion when he and George met and walked in the early morning.

George and Gandhi had both been imprisoned for their

principles, were both peace-makers, and had the same policy of personal contact as a means of avoiding or reducing conflict. George wrote later in *Peace News* (17 October 1947) that when they met, unsurprisingly they talked about non-violent resistance. They discussed Lloyd George's advocation of the Education Act of 1902, and of 'the conscientious objectors to compulsory religious education of the Anglican kind... Mr Gandhi at once said that he would be particularly glad to meet Mr Lloyd George'.

George sent a telegram to Lloyd George, who invited Gandhi to Churt. Gandhi and Lloyd George talked for three hours. Afterwards, Lloyd George thanked George for setting up the meeting, and saying that Gandhi (DLG called him 'a saint and a shrewd politician') had clarified many things. Lloyd George left for India that same week, and the conversation was essential to his understanding of the situation there.

One of George's 'networks' involved the Quakers, who had helped the members of Ebeneser chapel in Tymbl, and had befriended Tom Nefyn; another network involved Thomas Jones (TJ) and his educational project, Coleg Harlech. These networks would intertwine in the years to follow, and give George a direction for the remaining two decades of his life.

In the seventeenth century, there had been a large and strong group of Quakers in Wales (for example in the Dolgellau area), but many had left for Pennsylvania, with William Penn. In 1927 a minute from the Quakers at Woodbrooke stated that they wanted to present their message afresh in Wales, and that 'arising out of a conversation with George M. Ll. Davies, the way seems open for Friends to arrange a lecture school on Quakerism at Harlech next Easter'.

Since 1926, through George, Tom Nefyn and the whole Tymbl affair, the Quakers had learned much about life in a mining town, and had intensified their contact with the Valleys. Gethin Evans attributes the whole of the Quakers' interest in Tymbl to George, 'who was not even a member of the Society of Friends... Davies' contact was with the more prominent leaders of the Society [Henry Gillett, Joan M. Fry, etc.] and not with the members of South Wales Monthly Meeting, so that the interest was directed from England.'

The Maes-yr-haf Quaker Settlement (and Kingsley Hall, where Gandhi had stayed), were part of the wider Settlement Movement that had begun in the late nineteenth century in London. Some settlements were educational, some social, some agricultural/horticultural, and some combined these functions. Most involved students from universities spending time living and working in disadvantaged areas – indeed, this residential aspect led to the name 'settlement'.

The first social settlement, in the east end of London, was Toynbee Hall, established in 1884. By 1898 there were twenty-four settlements in London and ten elsewhere in England and Scotland. There was a strong emphasis at that time on the Settlement workers' 'special obligation to assume the responsibilities of leadership with the communities they were reshaping'.[4] Scott Lidgett, of the Bermondsey House Settlement, wrote that when a community was denied the presence of 'the educated, the prosperous, and the leisured' – i.e. the Settlement workers – it too often passed into the hands of 'men with lower aims, or at least less competent' – meaning, presumably, the local people. This seems to take the 'responsibilities of leadership' to a highly paternalistic degree.

The Society of Friends' settlements were ostensibly providing adult education, but not simply in the basic skills of reading, writing and arithmetic. It was felt that because people were drifting from chapels and churches, settlements should provide a kind of spiritual fellowship, as well as education in international relations, economics, literature, etc. A decline in attendance at classes run by the National Council of Labour Colleges was being ascribed to the activities of the Quakers, and there were claims – happy from the churches and unhappy from the socialists – that people were being turned away from thoughts of revolution.

By the summer of 1934, ninety-three towns and villages in south Wales had social schemes of one kind or another, supervised by 193 different 'communities'. By 1937 there were nine full settlements in the eastern part of the coalfield.[5]

Writing to her mother in August 1931, Leslie said that George had gone to south Wales for a fortnight, prior to resuming his ministry in Tywyn. The likelihood is that he was visiting a Quaker, Peter Scott, in Brynmawr, a small town on the eastern side of the south Wales coalfield, where 60 per cent of miners were unemployed. Scott saw himself as being in charge of rebuilding the community of Brynmawr, or 'Saving Brynmawr', as one leaflet put it. Scott had written to George suggesting that George could contribute significantly to the group that was already working at Brynmawr. 'One of our failings,' he wrote, 'is that we have no Welsh person with us and in the relationship between the group and the town this does count'. The cultural differences between the predominantly working-class and Welsh-speaking citizens of Brynmawr, and the team of middle-class English incomers, would have been difficult to reconcile. Scott went on to say that George Davies (not only Welsh, but Welsh-speaking) would be invaluable with 'helping in personal relationships and on the more spiritual side there is unlimited scope'.

As far as Leslie knew, after he had visited Brynmawr, George would return to work in Tywyn. There is no information on her reaction when George first mentioned going to live in Brynmawr. But in mid December 1931, Peter Scott wrote again, looking forward to having George with them for 'the next two months' if not longer.

On Christmas Day 1931, Leslie Davies wrote to her parents thanking them for their presents. She went on to say that as George was going to live in south Wales, she was going to move to 'a hideous villa' in Somerset, near Jane's (Quaker) school, Sidcot, and she and Jane would go there in time to unpack before school started. 'All this I have decided and arranged during the last ten days… I shall hate to leave the mountains; but life just now doesn't leave me much choice – and there will be compensations in English educated company down there.'

It is difficult to see from this letter what the true situation was between George and Leslie. Was it simply to get Jane into Sidcot School as a day girl rather than a boarder that Leslie decided to move over the border, instead of living in Brynmawr with George? Were there no facilities for married couples at Brynmawr? Or had Leslie had enough of feeling out of her depth in Tywyn, and couldn't face it again in south Wales? Had Woodbrooke perhaps reminded her how she missed her middle-class educated English background?

Perhaps this is what a friend of George's meant when writing to him in November 1931 about his difficulty with his 'vocation': 'My instinct is that you should follow your deepest instinct and guidance and your CALLS from men in their NEED. Surely if this stares you in the face you could take it and not feel selfish?' Had George confided that he felt 'selfish' going to south Wales without Leslie? Or had she called him 'selfish'?

The situation is even less clear when it is realised that after being in Brynmawr for some months during 1931, George returned to the still-rented Manse in Tywyn before going on to his next project; and that, in a list of volunteers who took part in work in Brynmawr and Rhosllanerchrugog during 1931 and 1932, George's address is given as Craigside, Sidcot, Somerset – Leslie's home.

Unitarian minister Emyr Evans, who lived in Cheltenham, met George in 1942 at a *Heddychwyr Cymru* conference held at Tretower. He and George spent time together walking and talking. Emyr's view was that it was impossible for George to give Leslie and Jane what they needed whilst 'personalising' at the same time.

Certainly Leslie and George didn't 'leave each other', as rumours have claimed: they were clearly very fond of each other, as Jane described to me later. Leslie's letters to her mother a while later speak happily of George's fortnight-long

holidays from south Wales, and the fact that Leslie could give him some peace and quiet when he was in Somerset. Jane said that Leslie tried to get George out of his 'Welsh aura' for a time, because George was always busy with his Welsh friends, and Leslie knew that quietness would benefit him. She was concerned about his growing deafness, but pleased that he was generally 'much hardier and healthier'.

There is also, among George's papers, a letter from the Peace Pledge Union (PPU) to George, and on the back Leslie wrote some words of a novel, suggesting that not only George, but Leslie, had a vocation to pursue. Who knows what that was, except that Nancy told me she had discovered a novel Leslie had written, but this disappeared after Jane died!

According to Jane, Leslie knew George was a one-off, and took the consequences. Perhaps being on her own suited the independent Leslie better than trying to be with George all the time, and certainly living in England suited her far better than living in Wales.

For George, the task in Brynmawr was challenging. Unemployment was at a desperate level in the town. Shopkeepers were suffering badly from lack of custom; chapels could not pay their ministers, and community life was at a standstill. The town that had relied on coal and iron for its livelihood urgently needed to diversify. The independent-minded citizens would pay their rent rather than pay for food; some grocers were owed £5,000 by 1930. Poverty and malnutrition were endemic. As the 'QuakerWiki' website reports, the Quakers in Worthing had a solution:

> Children were taken to Worthing to nourish them and take care of them – not that their own families wanted this to happen, but more facilities could be offered away from home at that particular time. Children were taken from their loving families in Brynmawr and temporarily housed into loving homes of Worthing families, and each child was given a glass of hot Horlicks Malted Milk and

some biscuits every morning throughout the winter. A few of the more delicate children were put under the tender loving care of 'Dr Worthing' for six weeks.

Presumably the idea that Horlicks and biscuits could have been supplied in Brynmawr, rather than taking possibly monoglot Welsh-speaking children to the south of England for their health, did not occur to the middle-class Worthing Quakers; ironic, in the light of the fact that one of the proposals for Brynmawr was to turn it into a health resort.

The idea of the 'Brynmawr Experiment', as it came to be known, was well-meaning. An article entitled 'Reconstruction in the Coalfields: an experiment in South Wales' in *The Social Service Review* reported in 1930 that the town was studied 'from every angle, historical, social and physical' by, among others, 'various departments of Aberystwyth University'. After that, it was felt that the work should be done within the community.

Two schemes were mooted: the first, because of the healthy climate and beautiful surroundings of Brynmawr, was that the town was a possible health resort; the second (perhaps more realistic from the start) was the establishment of small industries in Brynmawr, and agricultural developments elsewhere in the valley. A meeting was held at which the town decided to turn its back on the coalfield as the major source of employment; Brynmawr and Clydach Valley Industries Ltd (BCVI) was formed.

A leaflet, *Help a Welsh Mining Town Help Itself*: *appeal for 'Donations or Shares' for Brynmawr and Clydach Valley Industries Ltd* was produced; apart from Peter Scott (who was English but lived in Brynmawr), and Peter Freeman (MP for Brecon and Radnor), all the signatories (including the Duke of Beaufort, the landowner) were from England; all were upper or middle class.

Coincidentally, the only boot-making factory in south Wales, which had recently closed, was in Brynmawr. BCVI Ltd took it over, and the factory made a profit within five months.

Another successful enterprise was furniture-making, under the guidance of Paul Matt, whose father Karl Matt, an experienced cabinet-maker, had arrived in London from Hamburg in 1899, and produced furniture to Charles Rennie Mackintosh's designs. Paul Matt joined the Brynmawr group in 1929. He set up a furniture workshop and trained unemployed miners to make fine furniture, selling to big department stores such as Morgan's in Cardiff, and Lewis' in Birmingham and Manchester.[6] Gwendoline and Margaret Davies bought some for Gregynog. Paul Matt made two large chairs and various other items of furniture for George in around 1933, staining them green because George often wrote with green ink. The chairs were extant in 2001 when I visited Jane Tilley, George's daughter, but, having been well-used, were in a fragile condition and did not last much longer.

George arrived in Brynmawr in January 1931 for an initial two months; clearly he decided to stay on, because in April of that year, when the International Voluntary Service decided to join the scheme too, he was still there.

The IVS included the Swiss organisation Service Civil, the International Student Service, and various other individual volunteers. In 1931, a core group of about eleven went to Brynmawr. They stayed for three months (July to September), supported at various times by around sixty-five other volunteers from Britain and overseas, to help build open-air swimming pools, make a public garden, and work on a youth hostel. The swimming pools necessitated clearing a vast area of coal-waste, and conducting water down from the hill. One corner of the children's pool had to be dug out of solid rock. The daily routine was demanding: breakfast 6.30am, work began 7.00am, tea break 9.30–10.00am, meal break 12.15–1.15pm, afternoon work 1.15–5.30pm.

In September, George wrote to Pierre Cérésole (founder of Service Civil) appreciating the way Service Civil's 'gesture of peace and international fellowship' had impressed many in Wales.

But all was not well in Brynmawr. A report was written about the camp by an anonymous local person. The camp, said the writer, was an example of 'the best and most joyous work', developing both efficiency and personality. It had shown 'intellectual workers how very much they have to learn from manual workers'. Brynmawr no longer felt it had been forgotten, and had linked with other communities.

However, the report writer felt that the 'ideal from without' had been imposed, rather than the 'helping of development from within'. The Camp had been separate from the town, which had prevented the students and townspeople from really getting to know each other. The Camp was run, apparently, on 'too military lines'.

More importantly, the Press, though it had been useful in publicising the work in Brynmawr, was in danger of 'making the Camp feel heroic and superior, and induc[ing] a slightly patronising attitude to the people of the place. We have been too concerned with letting the public know what the Camp and the Service have been doing, and have rather left the Brynmawr people out.'

The writer said that Service Civil, in coming to the Camp, had been working out its own agenda, 'as an alternative to military service, and eventually to war'. The people of the town, however, had had a different aim, that of 'solving the problems caused by fear and hatred between classes, political parties and nations' – the same problems that cause war. In Brynmawr, the 'intelligentsia', as they saw Service Civil, was working along their own lines without co-operation with the townspeople, and that any co-operation was very difficult because of 'deep-rooted differences of tradition and education'. The town had hoped the Camp would help bridge the gap, but it had not done so, being separate from the town, and not sharing 'a common experience under conditions of complete equality'; further, they should have gone to Brynmawr having been invited by the people of the town – only then would they have been truly welcome.

This report is surprising if one reads only the publications of Peter Scott and other Quakers, who quite clearly believed that they had been welcome in the town; indeed, they were welcomed by some. But there was opposition: the trades unions and Labour Party members in the area were angry about the proposal to use volunteer labour, which was undermining their campaigns for better pay. It seems that George's inclusion in the working parties did not have the effect Peter Scott had hoped. Scott's idea had been to 'heal deep wounds from the past', but in spite of his best intentions this had not happened. Peter Scott had not understood (and maybe had not tried to understand) what the project would mean to the local people.

After finishing their work at Brynmawr, George and the Service Civil volunteers moved on to Rhosllannerchrugog, near Wrexham in north-east Wales.

A leaflet prepared by the International Voluntary Service in 1933 gives a brief account of the work in Brynmawr in 1931, and then a fuller one about Rhosllannerchrugog in 1932. The townspeople had organised the work at Rhos, and because of the example of Brynmawr they had contacted the international volunteers. Eighteen acres of land known as Ponciau Banks (sometimes 'Ponkey Banks') in the middle of the town were to be transformed into a recreation area. Eighty-five volunteers were involved throughout the summer, working alongside local people. But this time things had been organised differently. It had been accepted, the leaflet said, that the Brynmawr camp system had not broken down 'class and international barriers'. In Rhos, therefore, the volunteers were billeted with the townspeople, in return for a small weekly payment (£92 15s 7d was paid in total), rather than living in a separate 'camp'. The Rhos Miners' Institute provided two large rooms as a refectory; food was cooked by local people. Contacts between the volunteers and the people of Rhos were much closer than they were at Brynmawr.

The directors of the Rhos Miners' Institute had purchased Ponciau Banks for £460: almost 17 acres of former coal workings, which afforded wonderful views into Shropshire and Staffordshire. The land was to be levelled, and transformed into gardens, lawns and greens for the recreation and enjoyment of Rhos people, with a bandstand, sports pitches, rock gardens and terraced walks. Students came from Britain and Europe to work for three weeks in teams of forty. 'To achieve so much will require complete co-operation within and much help from without, but one feels confident it will be forthcoming if the Rhos Miners' Institute Committee and its officials are supported now.'

The *Rhos Herald* – in one of its many informative, entertaining and enthusiastic reports of the 'Beautifying of Ponkey Banks' – reported in April that at a Public Meeting in the Miners' Institute, Miss Kitty Lewis, representing the international volunteers, and Mr George M. Ll. Davies of the FoR (and also a member of the Committee) had explained what was planned. Mr Davies, 'who is nothing if not a visionary', had visited Ponciau Banks and had subsequently opened the eyes of the Institute Committee to the possibilities, and they had bought the land. George said to the meeting that he had developed 'quite a sentiment' for Ponciau Banks; he felt that peace and understanding was not going to come from mass movements, but 'if only a hundred men, or one village, got down to it and demonstrated what could be done by harmonious co-operative efforts, the world would stand amazed'. Many local dignitaries were at the meeting, and were clearly excited about the project, which needed, George said, the hard work of *all* classes of the community, not just miners and trade unionists.

On 19 July the *Daily Express* ran the headline 'Turning a Coal Dump into a Park':

A coal dump in North Wales is being transformed into a beautiful park by the strangest band of labourers that ever tilled the soil of this country. They are camped around Rhos, a mining centre, near [Wrexham], and from dawn to sunset they can be seen at work – miners, college professors, students, and businessmen from all over Europe – all shovelling.

The reporter spoke to one Spanish student who had walked to Paris, flown to London, and was working hard in Wales. Two Swiss watchmakers had cycled from Switzerland to join the group; they planned to go to Derby after the Ponciau Banks work was done, to help flood victims rebuild their homes. (This report also said that the Duchess of Beaufort had that same week officially opened the swimming pools at Brynmawr.)

The *Rhos Herald* spoke on 30 July 1932 of the works and their progress, the drainage problems of the site, the autumn plantings of some areas, and some of the people working on the project. Some of the volunteers were apparently still awaited: two Germans had hired a small boat to take them down the Rhine; it had capsized. The two managed to swim to the bank and were trudging through France. Others were hard at work: 'The colour-washing carried out so artistically by Mr G. Davies and his lieutenant Miss Norway has attracted considerable attention during the past week... All are unanimous in their praise.' 'Miss Norway' was the nickname of Inge Christensen from Stavanger in Norway. She and George became great friends, and the correspondence continued until the end of the war, with a break in Inge's letters between 1942 and 1945 due to the Nazi occupation of Norway. According to the *Manchester Guardian* (9 August), Inge's pink, blue and white colour-washing of cottages was viewed a little suspiciously at first (she had also colour-washed houses in Brynmawr), but by August 1932 people were going out of their way to see these houses. All kinds of people, the paper reported, were helping with the work in the town: ministers, teachers, tradesmen, children. The *Daily Herald* sent out its radio van to entertain the workers with a programme of music.

The whole impression that is conveyed by these press reports is one of joy, enjoyment, excitement. Clearly George had enjoyed the experience: the Ponciau Banks cuttings among his papers (tied together with ribbon) far outnumber the Brynmawr ones. The 'Rhosites' had entered into the work alongside the students. They had got to know one another through living together, and there was clearly lasting enthusiasm in the town. George, according to the *Rhos Herald* of 6 August, had left Rhos earlier that week to attend various conferences and to pay his annual visit to the islanders of Bardsey:

> He will be greatly missed from the Banks, for his winsome personality was always an inspiration. On Tuesday evening he gave the students a brief account of his romantic life, particularly his pilgrimage of peace. Mr Davies... has frequently stated that there is something in the communal life of Rhos which is absolutely unique. He left with a heavy heart.

In September 1932 the *Wrexham Evening Leader* reported that some international volunteers were still at work, but the people of Rhos were carrying on with the work. The gardens, tennis courts, children's playgrounds were clearly defined, as was the site for the bandstand. Work on the Banks has continued over the decades. In June 2009, after a successful bid to the Heritage Lottery Fund, Ponciau Banks Park officially reopened after extensive refurbishment works.

In February 1935, George received a letter from Inge in Stavanger, Norway. She sent news of many of the volunteers who had kept in touch with one another, such as Hanns Huber, who had attained his doctorate, and, Inge said, was 'doing important work for the government. A strong Nazi.' Sadly, the Nazi regime had broken the engagement between Hanns and Magnhild Steversen, who had become sub-editor of a newspaper in a small town near Oslo. Otto Weis had had his health broken by the Nazis, who regularly searched his house because of his involvement with the SCVI. Joe Rastis, from Lithuania, a friend of Pulgis, had had to spend a year in national service, but was 'free now', and wanting to study literature; but 'as he is no nationalist, odds are against him'. Inge asked if George had heard from Victor, who was from London, who had written to her for a while, and had said he had 'turned out a bass singer. Since then I had no news. It must not be nice for a coloured man in England. Life is often so cruel.'

It is moving to think of these young people and how complex their lives were becoming in the second half of the 1930s, after the freedom, joy, and international co-operation of their weeks in Rhos. George had loved working with them, and sharing their lives. It must have grieved him to see how difficult things were becoming for them, due to the international situation. Inge Christensen continued to write to him when she could, until after the Second World War, and their friendship was clearly equitable and happy. George's letters to Inge lack the unfortunate lugubriousness of his letters to his daughter Jane.

George built on the best of Brynmawr in helping to set up the Rhos project. His contribution was helped both by his position as a peace-maker, and his commitment to Wales and the Welsh language. In a way, too, he had a foot in both middle-class and working-class 'camps'. His eloquence and charisma very likely led to the extension of the 'quarter-hour' breaks at Rhos, and his joy and fun would have leavened both the Ponciau Bank project and the Brynmawr Experiment.

14

The Rhondda

IN 1933 GEORGE Davies, aged fifty-three, began work at the Maes-yr-haf Quaker Settlement, in Trealaw in the Rhondda valleys. The Quakers had also bought a large disused malthouse in Wick, on the south Wales coast, not far from Llantwit Major, and about twenty-five miles from Maes-yr-haf; George volunteered to become the Malthouse's warden. The Malthouse, and Maes-yr-haf, were to take up most of his time for the next fourteen years.

Hugh Doncaster wrote this description of George in the Rhondda at this time:

How do I picture him? Indoors it is simply his head that stands out. A noble striking head, with a great expanse of forehead rising into the dome of his skull, bald on top, and with grey-white hair on either side. His finely chiselled features were entirely his own; he would never be confused with anyone and never forgotten. His face had the grave wisdom of an elder statesman, illumined by the intense caringness of a pastor and the serenity of a saint. But it was not in his features, striking as they were, but in his eyes that the real George lived and loved: blue eyes, quick to light up with humour and to shine with sympathy.

If one first saw his head, one hardly noticed the bow tie and stiff collar below, a strange incongruity that in him ceased to be strange or incongruous, but somehow belonged and essentially were a part of him.

Outside I think of his tall slim erect body, covered by another characteristic garment of his, a heavy cape mantel which swung around him in the wind. On his head was an old trilby hat. Like his other clothes, age gave these sanctity.

And there he goes striding down the hill to Dinas trailing
clouds of children to his glory. As many as can have grabbed a
hand or a bit of the old cape; others are dancing round him like
dogs round their master at the beginning of a walk; one is diving
into one of his pockets for the sweets he always kept for them;
and he is supremely happy, as childlike in his delights as they.
As he goes, more and more children spy him and run to attach
themselves to the joyful party. About his clothes there is something
a little theatrical and yet not the least trace of the ludicrous; about
his love for the children and theirs for him there is nothing but the
most genuine reality.

Even before the General Strike in May 1926, the Society of
Friends (Quakers) had had 'concerns' about conditions in
the south Wales coalfields. At the Quaker Yearly Meeting in
Manchester in 1926, there was 'prolonged consideration' of the
situation in south Wales, and the conclusion was drawn that
'whatever the rights or wrongs of the case, the human tragedy
remained'. Emma Noble, wife of William, from the Oxford
Friends' Meeting, spoke with Henry and Lucy Gillett, and they
said she should go to see for herself.

Emma Noble first went to the coalfields for a week. In
June 1926 she wrote that there was a 'deep need for material
help and loving sympathy'. But far from finding a chaotic and
disorganised community that needed 'reshaping', she found
'calmness and order. A good fellowship prevails. The men are
organising concerts and sports and in several towns I saw
groups of people painting and decorating their chapels, glad
they have such useful work to occupy their time.'

Emma told the Oxford Quaker Meeting in June 1926 that
there was a 'strong spirit of independence'. Very few mothers
were claiming free meals for primary school children, and
even fewer were claiming for children at secondary school. The
women regarded parish relief with 'intense distaste'. Men were
'struggling to hide their poverty' and were determined to hold
out for a fair and just settlement. Emma sympathised with the
families' self-respect, and that she hoped that Friends would

give help 'in such a manner that no man, woman or child shall feel demeaned by accepting it'.

Soon after that one-week visit, Emma returned to the Rhondda and moved in as a lodger with a family in Tonypandy. The Friends' Crisis Committee began sending gifts for distribution to the people of the Rhondda.

By November 1926 there were fifty-two boot-repairing centres in the Rhondda, with 520 unemployed miners working in them. During one week 3,053 pairs of children's boots had been repaired. There were also twenty women's sewing groups, unpicking, cutting up, repairing and/or remaking clothes from bales sent in by the Quakers.

The Quakers decided to send Emma and William Noble to the Rhondda. The couple had first met when Emma was a cook at the house of a Navy Commander; William (b. 1885) was a marine engineer. They were wealthy, but believed, with most Quakers, that 'Wealth is a trust that carries with it obligations'.

The Maes-yr-Haf Settlement Annual Report 1927–28 says that on 13 April 1927 the Quakers bought a large house, Maes-yr-haf, in Trealaw, for £1,700. A committee was formed for its management – but based in Oxford, 'for convenience'.

At the start, there was no intention for Maes-yr-haf to become a 'centre of relief', but donations arrived, there was huge need in the area, and operations commenced almost immediately. Before long there were Sunday groups and adult schools in the area. There were classes in Welsh on Welsh life, history and literature. Groups read plays and did country dancing, and boys had instruction in handicrafts. Two graduates arrived from Oxford to conduct classes during the winter of 1927–28 for no salary, just board and lodging. Mr Brooke took 'Problems of Philosophy', 'Social Ideals from 1600–1928', and 'A Survey of Political Thought'; Miss Emmott took 'Moral Philosophy' and 'Plato's Republic'. This Oxford-style curriculum did not go unchallenged, however: according to Alun Burge (in 'A "Subtle Danger": the voluntary sector and coalfield society in South

Wales 1926–1939', published in *Llafur*), 'The unemployed men, schooled in the Marxist independent working-class education tradition of Dietzgen's philosophy, made clear their objections, and the young graduates were obliged to redraft their course content'.

'The greatest need [the Quakers] found,' George had written in 'Christian Reconciliation in Industry', 'was not even food or clothing, but insight, understanding and spiritual vision for those who will be in darkness and despondency for many a long day in the coalfields'. He added, typically, that it was also necessary to understand the managers and directors of mines who had been on 'the other side', but 'who in many cases have maintained friendship and fellowship with the men'.

There was also a need to understand the Welsh people who had been the original inhabitants of the area, and still made up the majority.

What surprised some of the incoming Settlement workers from English universities was how well-read these unemployed and poverty-stricken Welsh miners were. State-run primary education had begun in Wales, as in England, in 1870, but became compulsory only in 1880, and free from 1891. But for Non-conformist Welsh-speakers there had also been, from early in the nineteenth century, the adult Sunday schools; later, miners and coal-owners had contributed to the establishment of Miners' Institutes. Education has always been held in great regard in Wales, and self-education was commonplace. In 1925–6, 2,800 adult students attended university tutorial classes, and 300 students chose one-year courses.

The Miners' Institutes became a welcome retreat after a hard shift. Miners wanted to read, but not always Marxist propaganda. The socialists wanted miners to read in order to equip them for revolution, but the *Glamorgan Free Press*, 5 March 1909, suggested that the adult education world wanted miners to read 'for a purpose', rather than 'trying to spot the winner of the Grand National', or enjoying '*Famous Fights, Trials of Famous Criminals,* or *Detective Stories'*.

Chris Baggs, in his essay 'How Well Read Was My Valley?', shows that the miners did 'read for a purpose': escapism! Fiction, which was, between 1900 and 1930, around 45 per cent of the average Institute library's book stock, was by far the most popular genre. Many preferred novels by writers such as Zane Grey, D. H. Lawrence, and Émile Zola, perhaps because of their robustly masculine heroes, rather than more 'edifying' works by Charles Dickens, Walter Scott, and William Thackeray suggested by the newspapers and Workers' Educational Association (WEA) lecturers.

Some of the Settlement workers, then, coming from their privileged situations into the Rhondda valleys – full of filth, poverty and unemployment – were surprised at the miners' eclecticism. Miners had had access to, and had utilised, a rich treasure-house of books of various kinds.

The miners' wives, too, had been taking part in WEA classes in some places. Most Institutes forbade 'lending on' (that is, miners borrowing books for their wives to read) but the existence of the rule proves it happened, and certainly female authors were very popular with the male borrowers! Not all Institutes barred women: Ferndale had women library assistants, and Bargoed had a ladies' reading room.[1] The people of the Rhondda, then, were already experts in self-education, and the Settlement workers found they had to tread sensitively to avoid patronising the miners and their families.

It seems that most of the Quakers believed (perhaps naively) that they had no ulterior motive in going to the coalfields.

UNEMPLOYED
MEN'S CAMP

THE MALTHOUSE
WICK -

COWBRIDGE
GLAM.

But William Noble himself acknowledged one: 'If Maes-yr-haf can continue to work through this strong sense of communal loyalty,' he wrote, 're-animating it and creating new values and standards within it, then the contribution of the Settlement will prove to have been of real worth to the locality'.

But did the Rhondda need 'new values and standards'? And if so, were they the 'new values and standards' William Noble wished to create – or might they perhaps have come from the Welsh mining community itself, without Noble's contribution?

The Maes-yr-haf Annual Report of 1927–28 comments that local authorities in the Rhondda had come to the end of their financial resources, and the area needed help from outside, but an atmosphere of trust had to be created before that would be accepted.

The visitors' book for 1928 shows that, in January, one of the visitors was 'George M. Ll. Davies, Towyn'. A week or so later A. D. Lindsay (Master of Balliol) visited; then Lucy Cadbury and Rowntree Gillett. The Cadburys and Gilletts were long-established (and wealthy) English Quaker families. Many of them were old friends of George.

The annual report for 1928–29 showed a deficit of £43 16s 3d; that for 1929–30 reported a balance in hand of £25 3s 9d. By then there were seventeen educational classes of various types, and a full-time tutor-organiser. A small commercial hand-weaving and hand-embroidery industry had evolved. Clubs for unemployed single men had started: this was very important for the morale of men who were facing great hardship, not receiving any parish relief. By then, the Maes-yr-haf library contained over 1,200 volumes; more were requested, especially on modern science and modern economics. There was a possibility of starting other settlements.

By 1936, the annual report was pessimistic. The situation in the rest of Britain had changed, and 'the cloud of unemployment' seemed to be clearing from many places. Enquirers were finding it 'rather irksome' to be told that things in the Rhondda were as bad as ever: 'Their concern tends to become increasingly perfunctory.' At this time, the management committee included the Lindsays, the Nobles, Henry and Lucy Gillett, and Rowntree Gillet. Apart from the Nobles, they all lived in England. There were fifteen named staff members. Maes-yr-haf continued as a Settlement throughout the Second World War, although the Malthouse changed its use several times during the war years. George Davies was involved in one way or another from 1933 until 1947.

After joining the Quaker Settlement, George's first task was to get the Malthouse up and running as a holiday camp for unemployed single miners (who rarely received Poor Relief). The building was in a bad state. From May to September 1933 unemployed men went to the Malthouse to live and to work. The campers included, George wrote, 'all sorts and conditions of unemployed miners, old soldiers, young toughs, Communists, Chapel Deacons, men from Somerset, Gloucester, North Wales, etc'. Everyone co-operated happily: 'Duties as orderlies, cooks, gardeners, wall-builders, painters etc were quickly apportioned and readily, if roughly, done with great good humour. The afternoons and evenings were spent on the shore or in rambles along an interesting cliff and coastline.'

From the start the Malthouse, with George as its warden, had a positive effect on all who stayed there. One camper said that George's name was 'revered in one's memory for all time by all who took part in those camps'.

Over the winter of 1933–34 campers and volunteers moved in, prepared to face the cold in order to have fellowship with other men and work to prepare the Malthouse for future visitors. Apart from maintenance jobs such as outside drainage and garden work, they learned carpentry and toy-making from volunteers. By Christmas 1935 central heating had been installed. George appeared to be there most of the time; he listed his own duties as 'cooking, cleaning, gardening, carpentering, clerking, singing, entertaining, encouraging, comforting, helping'. Frank wrote in January 1935 asking, 'How often do you get home?' He suggested that George would have 'lonely moments... at the Brewery [sic]'. But that same month, in a broadcast to listeners in the Unemployed Men's Centres in Britain, in an appeal for 'togetherness' and brotherhood, George spoke of the weeks in the Malthouse with the unemployed men there, where:

> ... it was a comfort to be with one person who cared, one person who had struggled and suffered as you had, one person who felt as you had felt – perplexed, despondent, indignant at times, and yet who minded deeply about doing the one bit that was clear and right in a world where so much was dark and wrong.

The miners cared for the warden as much as he cared for them. Their acceptance and love meant a great deal to him. On New Year's Day 1934, he wrote to T. I. Ellis:

> These colliers with whom I have lived intimately, roughs and toughs as they seem, have a grace of generosity and forgivingness... Under their rough language and ways there are qualities of innocence and tenderness that are amazing.

And in his farewell message to the Peace Pledge Union in June 1949, George said that the Malthouse had been 'one of the happiest and most friendly communities I had met, and vastly more congenial than living in the comfortable suburbs I had known in Liverpool and London, where men "kept themselves to themselves"'.

But there were challenges to face in the Rhondda. In November 1939 George, in a report to the Maes-yr-haf Committee, wrote of 'the sense of political resentment and class suspicion against "concentration camps" that had made discipline and a programme of voluntary work difficult at times'. Clearly local people, seeing punitive camps being set up in Germany and elsewhere, were concerned that similar things might happen in Wales. But, George wrote, 'as the world without grew darker, the fellowship and frankness grew warmer, and the feeling of mutual dependence deeper'.

The Malthouse was a huge success with the miners. During 1935, 746 men and seventy-two boys stayed there in weekly groups throughout the summer. It was being transformed by successive campers into a beautiful and convenient holiday centre. The kitchen and sanitary arrangements had been improved, and a field provided for growing the Malthouse's vegetables. Visitors from outside Wales often stayed at the Malthouse, which increased 'respect and affection for men whose lives are so poor in money and so rich in sympathy, humour and courage'. A visitor (one Athelstan Whaley of Wokingham) commented with surprise that the men 'were an absolute treat... so completely different to the average unemployed man in England... where their policy seems to be "We are as good as you", and they take all but give nothing'.

In 1934, perhaps as a report for Maes-yr-haf, George wrote that living with an entirely unselected group of unemployed men, and for only four months in the case of ten of them, has revealed to him that though they seemed rough, uncouth and revolutionary, 'the finer qualities of generosity, cheerfulness, humour and kindness are very near the surface'; they were 'free from servility' but 'susceptible to leadership in a shared service for one another'; that they were at their best in entertaining others, such as the children from the Cardiff slums, showing 'efficiency, zest, tenderness and kindness'; and that communal living was a possibility.

George himself had discovered the worth of the working man during his years in prison, of course; this report seems intended to convince the middle-class Quakers in the Settlement.

In September 1939, George reported (from Leslie's home in Somerset) that he had just finished twelve camps at the Malthouse, which had housed over 1,000 men over the summer. Thereafter, the military took it over; later, women and children were evacuated there from London. In 1941 eighteen mothers and thirty-six children were living there, still under the supervision of the Maes-yr-haf staff, including George. Gwynfor Evans (later to be Plaid Cymru's first MP, and at the time a Conscientious Objector) told me he went there to help George, and had peeled hundreds of potatoes.

Most of what is written about George's time in the Rhondda is full of praise for him, and even hagiographic, especially from the pens of various unemployed miners who had stayed at the Malthouse. It is difficult to find any record of any negative impressions. A Dr Thomas, however, in a taped interview from 1961, took a different view:

> And [the local people] *hated* Maes-yr-Haf, and they *hated* the people who ran it. There was old George M Llewellyn [*sic*] Davies – now [sarcastically] I wouldn't say anything derogatory against George, but he stood there in his cape in the garden but he was obviously never a gardener, never a workman, never one of *them*. But he was the great George M Llewellyn [*sic*] Davies, orator, preacher, whatnot, who'd come there to work amongst them by the grace of God and by the grace of his own lowering himself to do it. If he'd *looked* like one of them at any time he could have got away with it, but he just didn't because he didn't ring true to them.

Clearly Dr Thomas had no idea that George had spent many months doing farm work and 'hard labour' during the First World War, or that he had always loved gardening. And clearly, too, Dr Thomas had never heard the Malthouse residents saying that George was 'one of us, just one of us', as many of them did. E. C. Phillips, a Peace Pledge Union member from Maesteg, wrote to a newspaper after George's death saying that he was to be seen 'not at the head of the board, but intermingling with all, a constant influence, a peculiar grace'. And author Arnold Bender (later Benn), a Jew who fled Germany in 1933, stayed at the Malthouse for the first time in 1934 (his novel *The Farm by the Lake* won a $5,000 prize for the best refugee story). In 1948 Bender wrote in *Peace News* of George's 'healing and beneficent influence' which 'brought out the good qualities of the men within its walls', and 'showed up the best that was in everybody'.

At the end of one particular week in 1937 a tribute to the Malthouse, and its Warden, was paid at a concert, in a long poem written by a camper (according to an undated press cutting). Part of it reads:

> The Warden, resourceful, versatile,
> His charm and smile angelic,
> A brother in the Christian sense,
> Deserves our panegyric;
> His fine endeavour – words of grace,
> Good advice he gives;
> No sycophancies are my words,
> George Davies speaks and lives.
> His morning prayer inspires us,
> Takes one to mountain height,
> Encourages and stimulates,
> Yea, sets the soul alight,
> There's something more than daily bread,
> Far greater wealth than gold,
> Thus do we soar in ecstasy,
> Like eagles ever bold.

But though he loved looking after others, George did not appear to be looking after himself. In October 1936, he received two very appreciative letters that appear to have been written after a committee meeting. Clearly George was discussed, and it appears he had been unwell – perhaps one of his depressions – and needed encouragement. Rowntree Gillett wrote that the Committee felt they hadn't backed George up enough in his work at the Malthouse, and appreciated George's 'influence on the Settlement – on the Staff and in the Clubs... You do definitely *mediate Christ* to us all. I do hope you are somewhat rested. Can we do anything to help you with getting a real change?'

The other letter was from Henry Gillett, who had been asked by the Committee to write to George 'to thank you for your help and the important contribution you make in the work.'

These efforts at encouraging George would probably have been appreciated, but if he was ill with depression they wouldn't have been enough to raise him out of it.

In January 1937, George spoke at the wedding of John Cripps (son of the Labour politician Stafford Cripps) and his new wife Ursula, who had been involved at Maes-yr-haf. Ursula wrote to thank him for speaking at the wedding. In March 1937, she wrote again, clearly anxious about George's health:

> I am glad you are going up North this weekend. You sound as
> if you badly need a rest… I can tell you have been doing *far too*
> *much* and not taking care of yourself at all. I can't bear to think of
> you getting chills and feeling so miserable and I vividly imagine
> you have been going out late on the coldest nights when nothing
> in the world could protect you from the wild weather and you
> ought to have gone to bed. You really do need looking after, dear
> George, and I am relieved to think your brother will have you in
> his clutches this weekend…
>
> You mustn't feel sad, dear George, though I know how the
> terror and cruelty and denial of love in things must overwhelm
> you. But you and your Wales and the people we all love so
> specially in Wales are always making us realise the true real values
> of friendship and sincerity of love. I believe it gives you such
> sensitiveness that the evils hurt you all the more and the suffering
> is more vivid to you. And people like myself whom you have
> helped… want so much for you to have too all the rest and peace
> and happiness you give.
>
> I **do** hope it will come for you.

The 'sadness' Ursula Cripps mentions sounds like George's depression 'overwhelming' him again. Interestingly, there is no mention of Leslie in Ursula Cripps' letter, and George is going north to be with Stan, not to Somerset to be with his wife. It could, of course, be that Leslie had had enough of 'looking after' George – she had seen him through several breakdowns and perhaps her patience had worn thin.

A year later, in June 1938, George wrote to Thomas Jones (TJ) saying that he was again on 'sick-leave, or rather, rest-leave… as I had got pretty tired after six years in the Valleys'. Curiously, he was once again staying at Stanley's home rather than with Leslie in Somerset – was this another breakdown?

Barrie and Sheila Naylor, wardens at Maes-yr-haf after the Nobles, knew George Davies for twelve years. They remembered him living in a hut in the garden, and washing his own tweed suits. They told me that the Davies sisters (Daisy and Gwen) once visited Maes-yr-haf and found him sitting in his hut with his feet in a box of hay to keep them warm. 'But that was George. Not orthodox. So we played up to him quite a lot.' Perhaps the middle-class English Quakers at Maes-yr-haf found George's 'eccentricities' uncomfortable to live with. Barrie reported that he and George 'got on fine', although George was 'very Welsh' and Barrie was 'very English'. They said George used to walk for miles in all weathers in the Rhondda valleys to visit people and preach in services, usually followed by 'a cloud of kids'. He was friendly with everyone, they said, but spent a lot of time talking with Emma more than anyone else.

Jane visited him at the Malthouse a few times. She remembered George going into the main room with her and calling out: '*Cwm Rhondda*, bois bach!', and 'the singing rose out of the stones of the building'.

George's niece Elin also visited Wick, and was amazed at the relationship between him and the miners: 'There was *no* barrier. He was one of them. A *complete* rapport between him and the other men.'

In spite of living and working closely with George, Barrie and Sheila had no idea till his death that he had had depression all his life, though they remembered 'a very bad patch' around the time of a severe illness, possibly pneumonia.

George was burning himself out.

Although George was committed almost full-time to Maes-yr-haf and the Malthouse from 1933, he was still deeply involved with the peace movement. With Hitler and Mussolini rolling out their Fascism throughout Europe, British pacifists were watching the situation carefully, with a view to avoiding, somehow, another devastating war.

Three articles in Box 2791 in George's archive show that George was well in touch with the situation. An article from the *Manchester Guardian*, 18 October 1932, entitled: 'Ten Years of Fascism: A National Rebirth,' from 'Our Rome Correspondent', lays out the achievements of 'Signor Mussolini' since 1922, including implementing modern farming methods (so that Italy did not need to import food), afforestation, irrigation, and re-equipping of harbours. 'Il Duce' had breathed a new spirit of 'burning patriotism' into his countrymen, and an 'ethical and psychological transformation' in 'very large sections of the Italian nation both at home and abroad'. The correspondent is subtly critical of Mussolini's regime, however.

The second article (unattributed, 8 December 1934) was also published in the *Guardian*. This may have been written by a first-language German speaker, and talks Hitler's 'purge of Jews and so-called Marxists': 'German politics, science, art, letters, and music were impoverished by the elimination of a whole multitude of famous names'.

The third article, from W. G. J. Knop, which appeared in *The Spectator* in April 1938, was entitled 'Five Years of Persecution', and speaks graphically of the depletion of numbers of German Jews. No one reading it would be under any illusions about what was happening: the situation of the Jews was hopeless, and thousands of them had emigrated since 1932. The article refers to the difficulty of emigrating, both because of Nazi bureaucracy and because other countries had stringent rules for accepting Jews.

How, then, could people in Britain say they did not know?

In February 1933, the Oxford Union Society debated the motion 'That this House will in no circumstances fight for its King and Country'. The press picked up the story and ran with it into the international news. The motion, proposed by Professor Cyril Joad, was passed by 275 votes to 153.

In 1934–35 the League of Nations Union (LNU) held a 'Peace Ballot' on 'the use of military measures to stop a peace breaker'. Although the campaign instructions had been 'pointedly biased', fewer Welsh voters wanted military sanctions compared with those in England, Scotland or Northern Ireland. The leader of the campaign in Wales was David Davies, George's old friend. In 1933 he was told anxiously by the Rev. Gwilym Davies (no relation to either David Davies or George Davies) that there was a 'decided drift towards out and out pacifism in the big religious denominations of Wales'. This would mean a move away from the LNU (which was a defencist rather than pacifist movement).[2]

On 16 October 1934, Dick Sheppard, vicar of St Martin-in-the-Fields in London, wrote to the press, aiming to find out 'how strong the will to peace has grown' in Britain. He requested any men who could say once and for all that they have 'done with wars of any kind' to send him a postcard saying that they supported the declaration:

We renounce war
and never again, directly or indirectly,
will we support or sanction another.

Sheppard expected very little response; he received over 100,000 postcards in two days![3]

In 1935, he called a public meeting in the Albert Hall, which was packed. Soon afterwards groups were formed for running the Peace Pledge Union (PPU), as it became. George was an early member. In March 1937 the No More War Movement, formed after the First World War, merged with the PPU. Their joint aim was to prevent another war.

Dick Sheppard died suddenly in October 1937. The PPU carried on, though missing his charismatic leadership. At the end of 1938 war looked inevitable. Anyone who spoke against war was accused of being 'pro-Nazi'. The Munich crisis had frightened people. Recruitment for the Air Raid Wardens' Service began in April 1937. As Sybil Morrison wrote, the PPU, 'a movement... based on human values and human behaviour, now had to exist and work in a community whose motives were based on values concerned with hatred and violence and fear'.

In the face of accusations of pro-Hitlerism from a population scared by stories of what was happening to the Jews, and what the Gestapo were doing, members of the PPU took in Jewish refugees – the British government would let them in only if there was a guaranteed home waiting for them, with guaranteed payment for maintenance and education for children up to the age of eighteen.

When conscription was introduced in May 1939, many of the young men who had signed Dick Sheppard's pledge in 1934 were forced to reconsider. The Central Board for Conscientious Objectors (CBCO) was formed, linking the existing organisations, 'pacifists, socialists, anti-conscriptionists' (including the PPU and FoR),[4] and providing a specialised service for members who came within the scope of the conscription laws.

Women, too, were given the right of Conscientious Objection when conscription was extended to them in 1942, but they were particularly frustrated by the attitude of tribunals, most of whom were all-male. Women, Ifanwy Williams told me, wanted to be treated the same as men – they were ready for prison. But they were disappointed. Tribunals were inclined either to pat the woman on the head and send her off to be 'useful', or ridicule her.

The PPU was active in Wales, with Gwynfor Evans, the future Plaid Cymru leader, a driving force. In June 1937, however, there was a call for a pacifist organisation with more of a Welsh standpoint. The decision to establish a Welsh and Welsh-speaking wing of the PPU, *Heddychwyr Cymru* ('Welsh Pacifists') was taken in April 1938; the first President was

George.[5] Gwynfor and George were old friends. A few years after the founding of *Heddychwyr Cymru*, George addressed the gathering when Gwynfor married Rhiannon, the daughter of George's old friend Dan Thomas, whom George had befriended in the bank in Liverpool when Dan was fourteen.

Heddychwyr Cymru grew rapidly during 1938 and 1939. When Chamberlain returned from Munich with his 'piece of paper', the Movement supported the policy of negotiating with Hitler, as did many others in Wales (even flying the swastika over Cardiff City Hall!). Surprisingly, very few members resigned from *Heddychwyr Cymru* because of this policy: Gwynfor Evans said at the time that he believed that Hitler's policies were caused by the Versailles Treaty, and that Britain should meet Hitler half-way. The PPU in England insisted that 'the war could and should be stopped and a peace negotiated'.

There is no record of George's response to this emphasis on appeasement, although for many years, as we have seen, he had known about, and written about, the German Fascists' attitude to the Jews, and it would have been surprising if he had simply agreed that 'negotiating' would have made a difference.

In 1999 I asked several Second World War COs what they had known about Hitler's concentration camps. They all found it a very difficult question to answer. Gwynfor Evans answered that he had known very little:

> I did see a reference in the middle of the war to persecution of the Jews, but I didn't know much about what was happening. Oh, but Nazism in general, you mean, of course. Oh, well, I knew about that. One of the things that George M. Ll. Davies did was to go to Germany after the First War, when there was terrible famine there, and he prophesied that terrible things would happen if this was allowed to continue. It was one of the causes of the rise of Nazism.

I find it surprising that Gwynfor, involved in politics before the war, had so little idea of what was happening – especially when his friend George Davies had known about anti-Semitism in Germany from the 1920s.

Iorwerth John clearly suffered when he found out about the concentration camps, and still found the matter 'awfully difficult' in 1999. His ideas on how he would have dealt with Hitler were indeterminate.

Islwyn Lake told me he found out about the camps only after the war, and found it 'very, very disturbing'. He went on: 'One naturally thought how one would have felt about making the pacifist stand if one had known all the details beforehand. This is one of the most difficult things for pacifists, when they face all the cruelty and visciousness which is in the world.'

Erastus Jones knew before the war about the Third Reich, but considered (correctly, unfortunately) that it was not the Third Reich's anti-Semitism that had caused Britain to go to war, but 'the pride of nations'.

In George's circle, not only were PPU members welcoming Jews into their homes, but Quakers too were guaranteeing accommodation for Jewish refugees. Some turned up at Maes-yr-haf – like author Arnold Bender, who stayed several times at the Malthouse and formed a lasting friendship with George. The Jewish writer Lily Tobias might have had Bender in mind when she wrote to George in December 1934, asking for the name of 'the German friend you mentioned' so that they could welcome him to their home. 'There are so many lonely refugees,' she wrote, saying that she'd been in Palestine, 'the place where refugees lose their loneliness and find healing'.

So with this very personal evidence before them of the Fascists' persecution of Jews, it is puzzling that the PPU was so keen for negotiation with, and appeasement of, Hitler.

In 1936 George received proofs of a pamphlet. He crossed out the original title, 'England gone atheist' and replaced it with 'Wales at War'. This is the strongest pro-Wales statement from George. He says that Wales had succeeded Ireland in being 'the most distressful country that ever yet was seen'. Prophetically, he wrote:

In north and west Wales, where Welsh is spoken generally, and where men's occupations are mainly rural, the same migration goes on remorselessly, as shown in census after census. And the depletion of the countryside with its social and cultural peasant tradition is made up in part by the doubtful advantages of alien immigration into suburbanised sea-coast towns like Rhyl, Llandudno and Colwyn Bay, whose populations know as much of the native Welsh tradition as the 'English garrison' knew of the ferment of feelings in Ireland.

George wrote too of the events in Llŷn in 1936, when three Welsh nationalists set fire to the Bombing School that was, in spite of protests from all over Wales, being imposed on the nation, on a culturally sensitive site, 'while proposals to set up Bombing Schools at Abbotsbury in Dorset and at Holy Island in Northumberland were promptly withdrawn after letters to *The Times* had pleaded for immunity for the swans and ducks which bred in these places'. (George spoke at a rally to protest against the Bombing School in May 1936; on 8 September, George's friend D. J. Williams was one of 'The Three' who lit fires on the aerodrome as a protest.[6]) George said that to the 'English government... Wales is a region on the map and [they] know nothing at all of the culture and language of Wales, but will desecrate our sanctuaries like a dog raising its leg at the altar'.

As Gwynfor Evans told me, George never joined Plaid Cymru, but this writing seems very close to Welsh nationalism. However, the next year, in notes for a talk, George seemed to backtrack. He wrote about the Spanish Civil War, of Guernica, of poison gas attacks in Ethiopia (1936), and bombing on the North West Frontier (1936–7). He asked his audience to think what was right for each of them to do, rather than waiting for governments to tell them. About Spain, he said: 'All foreigners should withdraw from a civil war.'

He also asked, 'What do we think of the Nationalism which says that what is wrong for another country is right for our own?' Later he referred to the 'new Nationalism'. Clearly he meant Fascism, and it seems, too, that he considered organised Welsh nationalism a potentially similar danger. Around this time George wrote to a friend, Iorwerth Peate, who considered George to be a Welsh nationalist:

> I appreciate the culture and the old language of Wales as much as anyone, but if Welsh nationalism wants to throw bones of contention at the strange *Internationale* of the Rhondda, God help us.[7]

Certainly the then President of Plaid Cymru, Saunders Lewis, was no pacifist, and had been criticised for not condemning Franco for his actions in Spain.[8] Ironically, in 1938, George's friend Gwynfor Evans, a staunch Welsh nationalist, was instrumental in turning 'Plaid Cymru, the Welsh Nationalist Party', into a 'pacifist party'. Gwynfor Evans had been campaigning for this since 1934, and in August 1938 he wrote in the PPU newsletter, *Peace News*, of his belief that English pacifists would support Plaid Cymru in the struggle 'for the recognition of the rights of Welsh nationality'.

In spite of failing physical health and continual bouts of depression later in his life, George's thinking was clear. He still wrote articles and read widely. In July 1940, he wrote in *Peace News* that he had recently read two books by the Russian philosopher Nikolai Berdyaev, *Solitude and Society* and *The Fate of Man in the Modern World*. Both these books had appeared in English for the first time in 1938.

George was called to broadcast at times – partly because of his pleasant speaking voice, according to Barrie and Sheila Naylor. He was also involved in the local Citizens Advice Bureau, and wrote to his daughter Jane Hedd Davies on 26 November 1945, before her marriage to Peter Tilley, remarking about the young couples he met in the Citizens Advice Bureau each week who needed some kind of marriage guidance counselling.

260

By this time he had relinquished the idealism of a global peace, but spoke often of the need for all people to be 'little islands of peace', 'little islands of gracious and right relationships in a sea of individualisms and nationalisms', and 'little nets of loyalties to persons'.

George Davies continued to undertake speaking engagements in his later years. In the Rhondda, for example, lived Egyptologists Professor J. Gwyn Griffiths and his Jewish wife Käthe, known as Kate, who had fled from Nazi Germany in 1936. George addressed a meeting of *Cymdeithas y Cymod* (the Welsh version of Fellowship of Reconciliation), which took place at the Griffiths' home in June 1942. In 1969, responding to the first volume of a biography of George by E. H. Griffiths (no relation), Kate Bosse Griffiths wrote (in Welsh) of her memories of the meeting to the *Swansea Evening Post*. She remembered that George had spoken of the importance of 'personal contact', but also of 'his belief in devolution as a means to win true democracy'. He also appreciated the nation's liking of being '*agos-atoch*' – that is, her 'human, homely spirit'.

George had always loved Wales, but his love seemed to grow through his life, and to grow teeth too. Elsewhere, in a symposium, George said, 'There is something in the Celtic tradition of community life, in the clan with its affinities and affections, that no efficiency of imperialism or legalism has ever been able entirely to conquer'.

But towards the end of George's life, even his beloved Llŷn seemed to be unravelling. George would have been downhearted when in November 1944 Glyn wrote to him:

Porthdinllaen is a strange place to me. I went over the headland and simply could not find the old familiar places. The ramparts have been levelled to the ground by golf vandals... The place stank of English visitors. I didn't want to see it again... And Lleyn was certainly a wash-out in culture of any kind – I mean Pen Lleyn. It was philistine in the main. And it is not surprising. Aberdaron has become like New Brighton.

15

After 1945

Spring came and passed almost unnoticed.
In this our time of trouble even her radiance and
laughing grace seemed somehow to jar.
The green of the larches, the blue mist of the wild hyacinths,
the lambs in the meadows – for all this we are out of tune.

George M. Ll. Davies

IN JANUARY 1946, George was still working at Maes-yr-haf,
but troubled by sight and hearing problems (there was talk
of a cataract operation in 1942), digestive troubles, and his
recurrent depression; in September 1941 he had undergone two
operations for prostate problems (George's brother Glyn had
referred to this, with empathy, in a letter in July of that year).
George was sad that his daughter was marrying an Englishman,
and feared he and Wales would lose her; on 6 December 1941
Stanley wrote to say he completely understood:

> I do hope you are feeling more reconciled about Jane. I can
> imagine what it is to you to feel that she is likely to sever more or
> less finally all her Welsh links and affections. Gwen has drifted
> away from them woefully... what a tremendous lot there was in
> the old lady's idea of a marriage of helpful contacts.

But Stan and George were wrong about their daughters. Jane
never lost her love for Wales, and passed it on to her daughter
Nancy; Gwen married John Robson from Huddersfield, who
initiated the Allotment Scheme in the Rhondda, and they lived

in Glyndyfrdwy for many years. Unfortunately, George's letters to Jane were rather 'preachy' and heavy – he calls the one congratulating her and Peter on their engagement a 'homily'. In another, he warns them not to marry soon (though they had known each other 'so long'); 'Unless our temperaments and ways and purposes are intimately known before marriage', he wrote, 'it is easy for subtle discords and alienations to destroy the deeper happiness of real companionship... Love itself can become an *égoïsme à deux*, absorbing for a time and then disintegrating as the strains of living come upon you.'

Is this, perhaps, autobiographical?

This letter is less of a sermon, and seems to speak out of George's heart, but it's full of anxiety for the 30-year-old Jane, rather than trust in her adult choice of partner. He signs his letters 'D.D.D.' – Dearest Darling Daddy, which is how Jane's letters to him began when she was little and away at school.

Early in the 1940s George went to Woodbrooke again to give a talk: 'An Interpreter of Wales'. Again his anger at the way Wales had been treated historically became obvious. He considered it was 'not altogether a disadvantage to belong to a defeated race, like the Jews or the Welsh, and that one's national hymn is not 'Deutschland über Alles' or 'Britannia Rule the Waves'. He spoke of the conquering and controlling of Wales by Henry VIII, and the insensitivity of nineteenth-century English commentators. He quoted Judge Bryn Roberts' words to an Englishman who had considered monoglot Welshmen 'ignorant', and who was astonished to hear that many had had a classical education, through their adult Sunday schools. As he had done in 'Extremists' some years before, George demonstrated his deep love of Wales, and his considerable anger at her fate.

In the same talk George spoke of a farm kitchen he had visited:

> ... where no-one came but he was welcome, no-one went away
> but that it seemed they loved him, where the old parents, the sons

and daughters and friends and farm servants share in the common meal, in harp music and ancient dance and in family prayers. The English visitors and the Italian farm workers shared the charm of this old Welsh peasant hospitality, while outside the roar of the mountain stream, the distant bleat of sheep, and the stars shining above the rocky crest of the mountain gave the background of an old world yet in existence to redress the balance of the 'Brave New World' of modern industrialism.

This was the old farmhouse at Pant-y-Neuadd, Parc, near Bala. George had made friends with one of the daughters of the house, Meinir, and stayed with the family regularly. When he was at home in Dolwyddelan, Meinir would pick him up and drive him to meetings. Perhaps while George was living at Dolwyddelan with Leslie (after retiring from Maes-yr-haf) he missed the warm fellowship of the Rhondda, and found it at Parc. The people there were, after all, the type of people he loved best – those who related to the land, and to Wales, and to God, equally.

George loved being at the farm. Meinir told me the kitchen table was always surrounded by people. The 'Italian farm workers' were prisoners-of-war – there was a German too. The harp music was from Meinir, who had learned to play against her father's wishes; he had then travelled to Liverpool and bought her a harp. The 'ancient dancing' was by Hywel Wood, one of the famous Wood family of Welsh Romanies, who had worked on the farm for forty years.

In 1942 Hywel wanted to go to the fair in Bala, but he was worried that his friends would want him to get drunk with them; Hywel didn't want to get drunk. George said he would meet Hywel every half an hour on the corner of a different street, and then Hywel and George would go home together. Meinir translated this letter that George wrote to Hywel some days after the fair:

In the quiet meeting of the Quakers came warm clear remembrance of you. I saw the rocky tops of Arenig and the plain moors, and I heard the sound of the river and the murmur of the trees. I felt how lovely it would be wandering with Hywel up the river and see where the silvery trout shelter, and hear from afar the cry of the curlew and see the delight and beauty of the world that our Father designed for his children, if only they would be friends together... How proud I was that you came through Bala fair more than a conqueror because you carried the day without hurting anyone, or lost your testimony, and who knows that others like me were proud of you. Warm love to you all. Your friend, George M. Ll. Davies.

One of George's letters to Meinir – undated, of course – is full of joy of meeting her and the family and having fellowship around that kitchen table. But there is also a troubling use of the past tense: 'Somehow all of you became my friends... The fire in my heart is still warm and grateful to God and you for all you gave me. Warm love, George M. Ll. D.'

Meinir recalled that one day she had gone to the Davies' house to pick George up to drive him somewhere; Leslie opened the door, and Meinir seized the chance to speak of her concerns about George's health. Leslie snapped, 'George is all right – and you leave him to *me*'. Meinir was still taken aback by Leslie's tone fifty years later when she told me about it. Was Leslie jealous? Meinir and George could, of course, converse in Welsh, and Leslie had excluded herself from those conversations by not learning Welsh. But perhaps, deeper than that, was the genetic bond of those born into a particular culture. Leslie had always preferred England, and English company. George had always preferred Wales, and Welsh company.

Could it be significant that in 1944, speaking in Tonypandy, George referred to marriage as 'the highest and hardest of sacraments, the tragedy of our time'?

In September 1946, George moved to Dolwyddelan with Leslie. He had written to Maude from Brynmawr: 'I'm afraid sometimes that the mountains mean too much to me for my peace of mind,' but wanted to be back in the land of his forebears.

Late in 1946 George was invited to become Chairman of the PPU. On the front cover of the PPU journal of December 1946 is a note by 'One of his friends in Wales' (from its tone and content, possibly Gwynfor Evans) who gives a somewhat conflated version of George's life: 'When he resigned his position in the bank he was content to spend most of his leisure serving the poor and unemployed in the south Wales valleys where he is revered and loved by all.'

Speaking to *Heddychwyr Cymru* in Aberdare in January 1946, George spoke of his 'sense of deflation – the election over for five years, and the atomic bomb and the fear of Russia and the miseries of Middle Europe... we learn that we cannot project our ideals and wishes like a lantern on a screen'.

In 1948, George contributed two articles to *Peace News* about small communities – one of them described life in Dolwyddelan during the hard winter of 1947. The village was marooned for weeks, but 'this had the effect of increasing our sympathy if it lessened our mobility'. He spoke of visiting the village school 'to tell yarns to the children, to see a Gipsy labourer do a step dance or tell stories of tickling trout or catching a fox, to a roomful of eager children'. It seems as though George enjoyed being back in his mother's home village. More than likely the 'Gipsy labourer' was George's old friend Hywel Wood.

Stanley was still very concerned about George's health, and wrote to him in November 1948 pleading with him to take things easy. But even with Leslie looking after George in Dolwyddelan, Stan reminds George that 'your homes at Tynyfron and here are always waiting for you' – does this suggest that Stan considered that Leslie wasn't giving George what he needed at that time?

One wonders how Leslie felt about leaving her home in Somerset after sixteen years, and moving back to Wales, and a predominantly Welsh-speaking part of Wales at that, to look after her ailing husband. When they went to live in Dolwyddelan in September 1946, Leslie and George had (according to a solicitor's letter to Maude, Leslie's sister) rented a cottage, Tynybryn, for 'three years certain and thereafter from year to year'.

A little after those 'three years certain', George Davies was dead.

In June 1949, George wrote a farewell message in *Peace Matters*, the journal of the Peace Pledge Union. He was about to retire as National Chairman (to be succeeded by Vera Brittain). His article for the journal looks back at his life and some of the ways his prejudices about people had been overturned when he got to know them better.

To the AGM he wrote:

> I am very much better, but still a bit wobbly on my legs and uncertain if I can get to the AGM. In any case I am very conscious that Anno Domini, the long journey to London, and my long illness have combined to make me a broken reed as Chairman.

The nature of his 'long illness' is not recorded, but we know that his sight and hearing were failing, and his general health was not good. He also had cerebral arteriosclerosis, which might have been caused, or exacerbated, by electric shock treatment at some stage; a letter to the *British Medical Journal* in 1954 stated that 'in a case of cerebral arteriosclerosis (which may remain latent till a sudden stress arises) one must curb one's natural enthusiasm for ECT till all the pros and cons have been discussed'. George had electric shock treatment in about 1912, when it was experimental, and Electro-convulsive Therapy (ECT) in Denbigh Hospital in 1949.

He was also depressed again.

Early in January 1949, George went to the private Quaker mental hospital, The Retreat, in York, where he had electric shock treatment. In February 1949, he was admitted to Denbigh Hospital (a psychiatric hospital) as a voluntary patient. On the admission form, in Leslie's handwriting, is the statement, 'The Patient has always been highly strung' – a term 'of its time', but somewhat dismissive of George with his long history of breakdowns and depression.

George was in the hospital until 2 April 1949, and clearly felt much better afterwards. He enjoyed meeting old friends at the National Eisteddfod in Dolgellau. In October, however, Leslie wrote to Dr Williams at Denbigh Hospital asking if George could be readmitted. Leslie's letter says that George's 'mental health has been deteriorating during the past three weeks'.

An undated letter from George told Dr Williams that he had been feeling very well until a few days before, but asked to see the doctor 'tomorrow' and perhaps be readmitted, because he was feeling 'nervy and despondent... In the last few days my mind has again been so introspective and restless that the night-watches have become unbearable.'

George was admitted to Denbigh Hospital on 17 October 1949. His condition, according to the letter Dr Williams wrote to the Secretary of the Board of Control late in December, was 'recurrent depression with cerebral ateriosclerosis. He was not considered to be suicidal... after three weeks treatment in bed with sedation he was allowed up and given ground parole, and his clothes were returned to him'. At the inquest into George's death, Dr Williams said that George had seemed mildly depressed, and had 'ideas of guilt, believing that his motives were unworthy'. Dr Williams had decided to treat George at the reception hospital, Gwynfryn, which was more relaxed than the main hospital. He said that George was a man who could not tolerate being 'hemmed in', and undue restrictions were thought to be harmful to his mental state.

Leslie wrote to Dr Williams on 7 December asking if George could return home for a few days to have his eyes attended to. 'I should not have suggested this if you had not said that you did not feel that you could do very much for him, owing to the condition of his arteries.' Dr Williams had no objection. It is not recorded whether George did leave the hospital.

The Deputy Charge Nurse on George's ward was Goronwy Davies. He was well into his 80s when I talked on the phone with him in 2003, but remembered George clearly. As on most nights when 'Gronwy' was on duty, he and George would sit and talk – largely about Tywyn and the area, because Gronwy was from nearby Abergynolwyn. According to Gronwy, George had given no clue at all about committing suicide. He was not considered a risk. He would spend hours walking on his own around the extensive grounds of the hospital – still wearing his long black cape. Gronwy was unsure why George had admitted himself to hospital. He did not appear to be having a breakdown at the time, or even to be particularly unwell on the face of it. Gronwy remembered him as a very peaceful man, 'a real gentleman', with a gentle sense of humour. They always conversed in Welsh.

On the evening of Thursday, 15 December 1949, George had his usual medication to help him sleep, and then went to Gronwy for more in the early hours of the morning. After a chat, George went back to his room, a side room with two doors to the verandah, one glass and one wooden. At around 6.30am on 16 December, Gronwy saw George cross from his room to the toilet; he seemed 'quite composed' and said he had slept a little. At 7.30am, Gronwy went to check George, as routine, and found him standing, as he thought, against the door. Then he noticed that George's dressing gown sash was knotted around George's neck, and the ends were over the door. Gronwy and another nurse tried artificial respiration but it was too late. The poor state of George's arteries probably quickened his demise.

Gronwy puzzled over George's death, wondering why George killed himself in his room like that, rather than outside in the grounds, where he had access to trees, and also to a lake. Gronwy said that George didn't like being a burden to people (he always apologised, for example, for asking Gronwy for more medication), and concluded George had wanted a member of staff (and maybe, particularly, Gronwy himself) to find him, rather than some local person walking in the grounds, or perhaps a child. George's suicide might not have been premeditated; it's possible that he decided to do it knowing Gronwy was there and would find him.

Jane's son, Philip, was just a month old when one morning Jane was overcome with deep misery – soon after, she heard that had been the morning that George died.

The Times of 23 December 1949 reported, under the headline 'Former M.P. Found Hanged', that the Coroner recorded the cause of death as 'shock due to hanging when not in a normal state of mind'.

Leslie suggested that George had made a 'suicidal gesture' but had not meant to kill himself. Dr Williams thought what Leslie had suggested was probably true. The Home Office pathologist Dr Grace disagreed. Questions were asked about the patient being allowed to keep his dressing gown sash; the answer was that he was not considered a suicide risk. Leslie, when asked to comment, insisted her husband had not meant to kill himself. 'He wanted to be found like that because he was of a dramatic nature, and that did away with any attempt of suicide.' She also said that she had herself sent the dressing gown to her husband ten days before the finding of the body.

According to Gronwy, and much to his puzzlement, Leslie then said: 'There is no fault to be found with Gronwy Davies or the hospital – if there is any fault with anyone, it is with me.' Gronwy never knew what she'd meant by that; he had never spoken of it with anyone before he told me.

In spite of Leslie's wishes, the Deputy Coroner said he could find no evidence that the hanging was accidental. He said:

> Except for depression, Mr Davies knew quite well what he was doing, and if I accept the suggestion which has been made it could apply to everyone who killed themselves... I find that Mr Davies

took his life by hanging himself at a time when his mind was not in a normal state.

It is understandable that Leslie would not want a 'suicide' verdict, at a time when there was a stigma attached to suicide. There is considerable evidence, though, that Leslie hid the truth from the inquest – and from herself. For example, she said that George 'had no suicidal tendencies', but it must be remembered that in 1923 George had become obsessed by the suicide of a neighbouring farmer who had hanged himself from a door; as Jane said: 'And Leslie was very nervous because he was sort of contemplating the back of the door, if you like.' This obsession seems to have been lifelong, hence Leslie removing hooks from doors in all the houses they'd lived in.

Leslie Davies did not tell her daughter how George had died; she died without ever discussing it with Jane. Jane eventually found out from her aunts.

The value of George's estate, when released in May 1950, was £628 1s.

George's funeral was held in Dolwyddelan. The slate quarry workers in Blaenau Ffestiniog donated his headstone. The chapel was packed. Jane remembered that the farmer and his wife from Maenan, where George and Leslie had lived for some years, were there; Jane was amazed to see Lloyd 'with tears streaming down his face'. There was a trolley in the chapel for carrying coffins up the steep lane to the graveyard, but 'He wasn't put on the trolley at all. He was carried. By his friends. They insisted. Right the way up, he was carried.'

The obituaries were sad and warm. Stuart Morris in the *Peace Pledge Journal* spoke of the debt they owed to George. Under his three-year leadership, the National Council meetings became more than business meetings, and were extended to allow the members to get to know one another as 'real friends'. George's sphere, the article said, 'was the individual'.

Peace News' long obituary was written by Corder Catchpool, a former CO who had been a fellow-prisoner with George in Wormwood Scrubs. He called George 'One of the loveliest human souls ever to live on this earth', and went on:

> He was by temperament poet and artist, but a genius for friendship was his supreme quality... All his gifts... were dedicated to peace-making by personal contacts... He could not understand why anyone should care about him; or did he ever suspect that it was because he cared so much about them?

After PPU Council meetings, George would often stay with the Catchpools in Hampstead: 'How I hate committees!' he would say as he arrived on the doorstep, 'The family's the thing'. George was always closer to his brothers than to his wife. Gwion, George's nephew and Glyn's son, told me that one morning in December 1949, Glyn was sitting in a chair that had belonged to 'Mater'. It had suddenly 'burst', and Glyn found himself sitting on the floor surrounded by fragments of chair. He later found that that was the time George had died.

At a memorial meeting for George in the Friends' Meeting House, Euston, on 4 January 1950, Stuart Morris, General Secretary of the PPU, spoke of George's charm and gentleness, and the choice he made: not for Westminster, but for Wales. George's old friend Canon Raven said: 'There are few people whom we meet in life who have that peculiar quality of saintliness, and I myself could not rank George Davies lower than saint.'

In a television programme in 1978, O. Emlyn Edwards of Tan-y-castell, Dolwyddelan – John Jones Talysarn's former home – said:

> The man who committed that tragic act was not the real George Davies... he always had a word of greeting for the villagers of Dolwyddelan. One of his greatest delights was to visit the local school and talk with the children. He had a great physical

presence, being over 6' tall, and he had a deep humility and gentleness which seemed to create a special atmosphere about him, as if it were a halo.

Afterword

MANY PEOPLE HAVE told me their 'reasons' for George's suicide. The Second World War; Hiroshima; Belsen; the Cold War – all been given as 'definites'. Some say 'he was a depressive', but many with depression don't kill themselves, and many kill themselves who have never (to anyone's knowledge) had depression.

George was not well physically or mentally. Things were not harmonious between him and Leslie, and hadn't been for years. He felt distant from Jane. What he said to Meinir about 'starting at home' is surely significant. He had always feared not doing enough good to be remembered, and Dr Williams' words at the inquest about George believing 'his motives were unworthy' are puzzling: what motives, and unworthy of what, or of whom? Had he and Leslie 'had words'? We'll never know.

Recent research says most older suicides seem to be a response to a total life situation more than to a single event. I believe this is true in George's case. Dr Meredydd Evans said there were 'many disappointments' when people heard about George's death; Gwladys Japheth and Elin Williams thought they could have done more for him. But as Merêd said, 'George was very tired. He'd had enough.' I tend to see that as the main reason. But does anyone ever really know why someone takes their own life? I think not. Maybe after all those years of trying to make peace for, and with, others, George was simply trying to find his own peace.

Jane's daughter Nancy said that from her understanding, as a young person Leslie was very gentle:

... but as time and hardship took its toll there was no choice but that she toughen up. My mother found her pretty hard going at times, and I remember that she could be disapproving from a mighty height. The whole body language as the back straightened and the haughty/withdrawn mask slid into place and her folded hands rested on the edge of the table or in her lap...

Nancy and her brother did not much enjoy going to stay with Leslie when they were children. Nancy stayed with her when she was eleven and pronounced it 'awful'. The family hated having her living with them; she was such a martinet, Nancy said. Only five years after Leslie died did Jane begin to miss her and understand her.

Suicide leaves deep sorrow and bitterness in many people. George would have regretted that. Leslie was certainly bitter in her later years. And after her father's death (and to some extent before it) George's daughter, Jane, never felt she 'fitted in' anywhere. After George died Jane went into a two-year depression, the double grieving of love and abandonment that is not uncommon in the survivors of suicide. Jane never mentioned George's suicide to Nancy when she was growing up – she found out when she was in her late teens. The only time Jane spoke to Nancy about it was when she was in her 70s, and said how rejected she had felt at the time. That was all.

But as the obituaries and funeral addresses show, George left much more than sorrow. His main legacy was love, mixed with admiration, affection and inspiration. His love of laughter and practical jokes tend to be submerged under the television version of George, the black-suited, dog-collared, sober-faced 'Parch' – who, according to his daughter, never existed!

George's friend Hugh Doncaster wrote:

> If a saint is one who makes it easier to know God, George was one of the greatest of saints. Few men can have had more spiritual sons than he, and no greater privilege could I have had than to be one of that large family. He opened the door of life for me, showed me The Man in every man, beneath their various coverings.

Merêd Evans said: 'George was a naturally good person – he simply *oozed* goodness. Not because he "should", but more as a well overflowing than a determination to do good. As if it wasn't difficult for him to be good.'

Having read the book, Nancy wrote: 'One is struck by how often the word 'friend' comes up. It really was one of his gifts.'

George gave so much to so many, and he is still remembered as a saint in Wales. If a 'saint' is created by public veneration, and the recognition of goodness, then George M. Ll. Davies should be recognised as a Non-conformist saint (in all senses of the word).

At the beginning of this book, I mentioned having dreams about George. One, in February 2009, was so amazingly clear and unusual that I wrote it down. I hardly ever have dreams I remember. In brief:

I was at a chapel event on a northern Welsh grey, wet day in the 1950s. Suddenly people saw George come in, and rushed to find a chair for him. 'Poor old thing,' one said, 'I thought he was dead.'

The gloom lifted from the meeting. I was trying to find a chance to go and talk to him, tell him that I was writing about him, that I'd talked to his friends, that I loved him. But when I found a way through to him, he'd gone.

Then he and I were sitting together in the half-dark. He was very, very frail and old. He took my hand.

'You will tell them, won't you?'

'Tell them what, George?'

'You will tell them about me?'

'Yes,' I promised, 'I'll tell them.'

And he faded from my sight.

Notes

2: The Liverpool Welsh Community

1   R. H. Humphreys, 'The Welsh in Liverpool', in *Liverpool Family Historian* (ed. Dr R. A. Yorke), quarterly journal of the Liverpool and District Family History Society, Vol. 7, September 1985, No. 3.

2   J. R. Jones, *The Welsh Builder on Merseyside* (Liverpool, 1946), p. 162.

3   J. A. Picton, *Memorials of Liverpool, Historical and Topographical* (London, 1875), p. 353.

4   Julie Light, '… of inestimable value to the town and district'?: A study of the urban middle class in south Wales with particular reference to Pontypool, Bridgend and Penarth, *c.*1850–1890 (unpublished PhD,

5   Gareth Miles in J. Mervyn Jones and D. Ben Rees, *The Liverpool Welsh and their Religion* (Liverpool, 1984), p. 23.

6   F. M. L. Thompson, *The Rise of Suburbia* (Leicester, 1982), p. 3.

3: Growing up in Liverpool

1   F. M. L. Thompson (1982), p. 3.

2   Eric Hobsbawm, *Industry and Empire: the birth of the Industrial Revolution* (New York, 1999), pp. 161–2.

3   Alun R. Jones and Gwyn Thomas, *Presenting Saunders Lewis* (Cardiff, 1983), p. 17.

4: Rise and Fall

1   *Regulations for the Territorial Force and for County Associations 1908* (reprinted by The Naval and Military Press Ltd, Uckfield), Part I, Section 3, Clause 76.

5: The Coming of War

1   Jill Wallis, *Valiant for Peace: a History of the Fellowship of Reconciliation, 1914 to 1989* (London 1991).

2   Mass-Observation File Report FR 312, 'Report on Conscientious Objectors', Mass-Observation Archive, University of Sussex, July 1940, pp. 24–41.

6: The Peaceful Route to Prison

1 Fenner Brockway, *Towards Tomorrow* (London, 1977).
2 W. David Wills, *Homer Lane, a biography* (London, 1964).
3 Maurice Bridgeland, *Pioneer Work with Maladjusted Children* (Staples, 1971), section on Russell Hoare, Superintendent of Syonsby House, Riverside Village, Melton Mowbray.
4 E. H. Griffiths, *Heddychwr Mawr Cymru* (Caernarfon, 1967).
5 Ibid.
6 Kenneth O. Morgan, *Rebirth of a Nation* (Oxford, 1981), p. 164. (Morgan refers to George M. Ll. Davies as a 'symbol of hope for the dissenting minority', but calls him a 'minister', which, at that stage, he was not, officially.)
7 Lois S. Bibbings, *Telling Tales about Men: conceptions of Conscientous Objectors to Military Service during the First World War* (Manchester, 2009).

7: Prison

1 Stephen Hobhouse and Fenner Brockway, *English Prisons To-day* (London, 1921), throughout.
2 Fenner Brockway, *Towards Tomorrow*, p. 61.
3 Stephen Hobhouse, *An English Prison from Within* (London, 1919).
4 Horace Shipp quoted in George M. Ll. Davies, *Joseph Rowntree Gillett* (London, 1932), p. 36.
5 Simon Brooks, 'Cof am Fath Arall o Gymraeg, Romani Cymreig', in *Taliesin*, Gwanwyn 2015: Cyfrol 154, pp. 24–31.
6 Review of *English Prisons To-Day* in *The British Journal of Nursing*, 1 July 1922, pp. 11–12.
7 Fenner Brockway, *Towards Tomorrow* (London, 1977), p. 61.

8: Gregynog

1 Eveline Holsappel, '"The beauty of simplicity": Arts and Crafts ideals for Wales' in Oliver Fairclough (ed.), *'Things of Beauty': what two sisters did for Wales* (Cardiff, 2007), p. 82.
2 More about this interesting woman can be found in Peter Lord, *Winifred Coombe Tennant: a life through art* (Aberystwyth, 2007).
3 Biographical note by Eirene White MP, to *Whitehall Diary*, Volume One, p. xxiii.
4 Service Civil International Archives, La Chaux-de-Fonds, Switzerland.

9: Ireland

1. Jack White, *Misfit: A Revolutionary Life* (first published 1930; reprinted Dublin, 2005).
2. Ian Kenneally, *The Paper Wall: Newspapers and Propaganda in Ireland 1919–1921* (Cork, 2008).
3. Michael Collins, *A Path to Freedom* (2005), p. 21. First published in Dublin in 1922.
4. J. Anthony Gaughan (ed.), *Memoirs of Senator James G. Douglas: Concerned Citizen* (Dublin, 1998).
5. Dorothy Macardle, *The Irish Republic*, p. 474.
6. Helen Litton, *The Irish Civil War: An Illustrated History* (Dublin, 1995), p. 20.

10: Westminster

1. John Maynard Keynes, *The Economical Consequences of Peace* (Cambridge, 1971), p. 142. First published 1919.
2. *South Wales Daily News*, 15 January 1912; Cyril Parry, 'The Independent Labour Party and Gwynedd Politics 1900–20', *Welsh History Review*, 4, No. 1 (June 1968), p. 53, quoted in David Pretty, *The Rural Revolt that Failed: Farm Workers' Trade Unions in Wales, 1889–1950* (Cardiff, 1989), p. 45.
3. Hilary A. Marquand, 'The Labour Movement in the University of Wales', in *The Welsh Outlook*, September 1922, pp. 217–18.
4. Kenneth O. Morgan, *Rebirth of a Nation* (Oxford, 1981), p. 183.
5. Kenneth O. Morgan, *Wales in British Politics 1868–1922* (Cardiff, 1963), p. 297.
6. D. Densil Morgan, *The Span of the Cross: Christian religion and society in Wales 1914–2000* (Cardiff, 1999), p. 65.

12: Tywyn

1. David Jenkins, *The Agricultural Community in South-West Wales at the turn of the Twentieth Century* (Cardiff, 1971), p. 188.
2. David Jenkins, Emrys Jones, T. Jones Hughes, Trefor M. Owen, *Welsh Rural Communities* (Cardiff, 1960), p. 221.
3. Richard Taylor, *Film Propaganda: Soviet Russia and Nazi Germany* (London, 1998), p. 16.

13: George, Gandhi, and the 'Social Gospel'

1. *Llain y delyn: Fellowship House, Y Tymbl, and its relation to the Quakers in Britain* (unpublished MPhil thesis, University of Birmingham, 2001) by Owain Gethin Evans, a Welsh-speaking Quaker from Aberystwyth.

2   D. Densil Morgan, *The Span of the Cross: Christian Religion and Society in Wales 1914–2000* (Cardiff, 1999), p. 128.

3   Hywel Francis, 'South Wales' in Julian Skelley, *General Strike 1926* (London, 1976), pp. 232–59.

4   Standish Meacham, *Toynbee Hall and Social Reform 1880–1914: the search for community* (Yale, 1987).

5   Richard Lewis, *Leaders and Teachers: adult education and the challenge of Labour in South Wales, 1906–1940* (Cardiff 1993), p. 193.

6   Roger Smith, 'Utopian Designer: Paul Matt and the Brynmawr Experiment' in *Furniture History*, Vol. 23 (1987); Mary, Eurwyn and Dafydd Wiliam, *The Brynmawr Furniture Makers* (2012).

14: The Rhondda

1   Chris Baggs, 'The Miners' Libraries of South Wales from the 1860s to 1939' (PhD, University of Wales, Aberystwyth, 1995), pp. 230–34, and 'Miners' Institute Libraries' in P. H. Jones and Eiluned Rees (eds), *A Nation and its Books* (Aberystwyth, 1998), pp. 297–305.

2   J. A. Thompson, 'The Peace Ballot of 1935: the Welsh campaign', *Welsh History Review*, 11, 1982/83, pp. 388–99.

3   Letter to the press by Dick Sheppard, 16 October 1934. Quoted in full in Sybil Morrison, *I Renounce War: the story of the Peace Pledge Union* (London, 1962), p. 99.

4   Fenner Brockway in Foreword to Denis Hayes, *Challenge of Conscience: the story of the Conscientious Objectors of 1939–1949* (London, 1949), p. vii.

5   Rhys Evans, *Gwynfor Evans: portrait of a patriot* (Talybont, 2008), pp. 49–50.

6   Dafydd Jenkins (trans. Ann Corkett), *A Nation on Trial: Penyberth 1936* (Cardiff, 1998), p. 28.

7   Iorwerth Peate, *Syniadau* (n.p., 1969), p. 118. (trans.)

8   Rhys Evans, *Gwynfor Evans*, p. 50.

Sources
and Further Reading

Documents and Archives
National Library of Wales: Collections of George M. Ll. Davies;
    J. Glyn Davies; Dr Thomas Jones CH; T. I. Ellis; Bryn Roberts;
    Welsh Town Planning and Housing Trust Records;
University of Sussex: Mass Observation Archive;
Swansea University: Miners' Library and Miners' Archive;
Fellowship of Reconciliation Archive (microfiches);
Service Civil International Archive, Switzerland;
University College, Dublin: Éamon de Valera Papers;
Gwynedd Archive (with permission): medical notes on George
    M. Ll. Davies; documents relating to his death.

Newspapers and Periodicals
Cambrian News; *Daily Post and Mercury*; *Heddwch*; *Irish Times*;
    Manchester Guardian; *No More War*; *Peace News*; *Peace Pledge
    Journal*; *The Welsh Outlook*; *Y Dinesydd Cymreig*; *Crynhoad*;
    Western Mail; *Rhos Herald*; *Wrexham Evening Leader*; *Swansea
    Evening Post*.

George M. Ll. Davies' Books and Pamphlets
Our Responsibility for Europe (pamphlet, August 1923).
Reparations and Industrial Ruin (London, 1932).
Politics of Grace (n.d. but after 1925).
Triniaeth Troseddwyr (1940s).
Joseph Rowntree Gillett: a memoir (London, 1942).
Pererindod Heddwch (London, 1943).

Profiadau Pellach (London, 1946).
Essays Towards Peace (London, 1946).
Pilgrimage of Peace (London, 1950).

Other Major Sources

Gregory Anderson, *The White Blouse Revolution* (Salford, 1988).

Martin Ceadel, *Pacifism in Britain 1914–1945: the defining of a faith* (Oxford, 1980).

J. Glyn Davies, *Nationalism as a Social Phenomenon*.

Gwennant Davies, *The Story of the Urdd 1922–1972* (Aberystwyth, 1973).

Gwynfor Evans, *Welsh Nation Builders* (Llandysul, 1988).

Hywel Francis and Dai Smith, *The Fed: a History of the South Wales Miners in the Twentieth Century* (Cardiff, 1988).

Stephen Hobhouse and Fenner Brockway, *English Prisons Today* (London, 1921).

Stephen Hobhouse, *An English Prison from Within*.

Clive Hughes, *'Arm to Save your Native Land' – Army Recruiting in North-west Wales* (Llanrwst, 2015).

R. Merfyn Jones, *North Wales Quarryman* (Cardiff, 1982).

R. Merfyn Jones and D. Ben Rees, *The Liverpool Welsh and their Religion* (Liverpool, 1984).

Thomas Jones (ed. Keith Midlemas) *Whitehall Diary I, II,* and *III* (London, 1969, 1969, 1971).

Jen Llywelyn, 'The Sun in Splendour': George M. Ll. Davies (1880–1949), Pacifist, Conscientous Objector and Peacemaker, and the Creation of a Non-conformist Saint (unpublished PhD, University of Wales, Aberystwyth, 2010).

Barrie Naylor, *Quakers in the Rhondda 1926–1986* (Chepstow, 1986).

Kate Roberts, *Tywyll Heno* (Denbigh, 1966).

F. M. L. Thompson, *The Rise of Suburbia* (Leicester, 1982).

Index

Pilgrim of Peace is just one of a whole range
of publications from Y Lolfa. For a full list of
books currently in print, send now for your
free copy of our new full-colour catalogue.
Or simply surf into our website

www.ylolfa.com

for secure on-line ordering.

TALYBONT CEREDIGION CYMRU SY24 5HE
e-mail ylolfa@ylolfa.com
website www.ylolfa.com
phone (01970) 832 304
fax 832 782